The Complete Book of

SHOW JUMPING

The Complete Book of

SHOW JUMPING

Edited by **Michael Clayton** and **William Steinkraus**

Crown Publishers, Inc. New York

Library of Congress Catalog Card No: 74-24775
ISBN: 0-517-521253

First published in the U.S.A., 1975, by Crown Publishers, Inc.

Created by Walter Parrish International Limited, London, England
Designed by Judy A. Tuke

Printed and bound in Spain by Roner S.A., Madrid
Dep. Legal: SS . 357-1975

Foreword

by Colonel Sir Michael Ansell, C.B.E., D.S.O.

In being asked to write a Foreword to this new book, *The Complete Book of Show Jumping*, I have been paid a great compliment. For it is only in comparatively recent years that the sport of show jumping has been so appreciated and has given such great pleasure to so very many, not only those who compete and ride, but also those who spectate.

Every sport is becoming more expensive and we who participate or watch should make every effort to learn in order that we get more pleasure.

Much can be learned from this book—how the rider has trained his or her horse, how the horse has been systematically encouraged in order that the rider will derive the greater pleasure and I am delighted to read in what detail Mrs Crago has treated this subject. Without this patient work on the 'flat' and the introduction to the show, the rider will not only fail to succeed, but waste much precious time and money.

Raymond Brooks-Ward gives a brief but important chapter on organising a show. This must be the work of an unpaid professional—for the standard of production means success or failure.

Mrs Carruthers tells us how courses are planned and she, with her vast experience, could not be bettered to give this advice, which should help not only the course builder but also the spectator who wishes to get more pleasure by understanding.

Obviously, the later chapters, the glossary and list of results are a valuable record.

To conclude, I feel sure no two better Editors could have been chosen to edit this book. In Bill Steinkraus of the U.S.A., the publishers could not have selected a greater horseman and perfection-ist in this field and I am confident that when editing this book, he will, with his immaculate thoroughness, allow no detail to slip through which is not correct; and again in selecting Michael Clayton, the publishers have been equally wise. Michael Clayton enjoys fox-hunting and this surely has been the basis in both Britain and America for our success. But to really enjoy fox-hunting today with the work and difficulties provided, we must ensure that we get our money's value; consequently Michael Clayton realises the importance of training as amplified in this book, which I feel sure will be read by many.

Mike Ansell

Contents

Colour Illustrations

opposite: Douglas Bunn on Beethoven

Editor's Introduction

by Michael Clayton

No other equestrian sport has won so many new areas of support and interest in the post-war world as show jumping.

In Britain particularly, television has brought millions of fans to the world of show jumping. Most remain spectators on the fringe of the sport, but the fortunate accident that show jumping is particularly suited to TV keeps its appeal strong for many people who have no other interest in horses. This has encouraged growing commercial sponsorship.

There has been a parallel expansion from within the sport. For every one of the well-known names at the top, there are hundreds of thousands of active show jumpers throughout the world.

Is everything perfect? Of course not, but it must be conceded that most of show jumping's problems over the last two decades have been growing pains.

With economic ills now affecting the West on such a broad front, show jumping must share the pressures likely to hit all other international sports. Its broad appeal gives plenty of grounds for optimism that it will survive an economic blitz to experience still more growth in the future.

There is no need here to tread the well-worn path which charts show jumping's changed face since pre-war days, when it was so much a military preserve, and its far wider appeal today. Its history is told in fascinating detail elsewhere in this book.

Looking ahead, it is worth pointing out several urgent problems which need solving in the near future:

1. The anomalous position in international show jumping as between 'professionals' and 'amateurs'.
2. The need for more vigilance in ensuring the banning of prohibited drugs—stimulants, depressants or local anaesthetics. (This, of course, is by no means a problem confined to show jumping, nor does show jumping appear to be the worst offender among equestrian sports.)
3. Strict action by national federations to ensure that public suspicions about training methods employed by show jumpers are never justified.

The first of these problems has an important bearing on the Olympic Games. Britain and the United States have been active in putting their houses in order in line with the directives of the International Equestrian Federation, the F.E.I. At the time of writing, Britain has 43 professional show jumpers who have taken out licences under F.E.I. rules. They are not eligible to represent Britain in the Olympic Games.

So far, virtually no other nationalities have turned professional. There are taxation laws in some European countries which would impose particularly heavy financial burdens on newly declared professionals, and on the sport itself.

The effect at the Olympic Games would be to see Britain and the United States fielding amateur teams, excluding some of their top riders from selection, whilst most other countries are able to select teams from their best international riders all of whom retain their 'amateur' status.

The second and third problems listed above have undoubtedly become the subject of more rigorous attention from the authorities in recent years, and it was encouraging that the F.E.I.'s Assembly in December, 1974 paid special attention to the problems of doping horses which have become so much more acute with the development of sophisticated modern drugs.

The price of freedom from this unsporting, and even cruel, scourge is undoubtedly eternal vigilance.

Whilst the costs of show jumping continue to soar, no-one can deny that the richness of enjoyment from a vast variety of competitions has similarly increased in recent years.

Who will forget the great 1974 Men's World Championship, so brilliantly staged at Hickstead by Douglas Bunn? Pamela Carruthers' courses in the superb international arena were brilliant constructions, designed to test horse and rider to the utmost; never merely trappy, always demanding skill and boldness.

It was disappointing for home supporters that the world title holder David Broome so narrowly failed to qualify for the final, after three fabulous earlier rounds which had culminated with a superb Nations' Cup-type course.

The capacity crowd was thrilled by the needle-sharp final contest between Germany's Hartwig Steenken, Ireland's Eddie Macken, Hugo Simon of Austria and Frank Chapot from the U.S.A. The principle of riding each other's horses which is exercised in this international contest had been criticised, but it certainly added an extra dimension of interest and thrills.

Watching Steenken's extraordinary mare, Simona, testing the skill of her 'guest' riders with her fantastic powers of elevation is indeed one of show jumping's most spectacular memories.

No-one could be surprised by, nor fail to applaud, the achievement of the elegant French rider Janou Tissot in winning the Ladies' World Championship, held in the same year at La Baule. It was scheduled to be the last world championship for the ladies, since the F.E.I.'s plan thereafter was to hold world professional championships in the Olympic year, and an open world championship in the even year between each Olympic Games.

David Broome, robbed of his former world title, nevertheless went on to win the first professional championships, held at Cardiff later in the season. He had further successes on the North American circuit, and finished the year remarkably well at the Dunhill show at Olympia, in London.

America's exciting professional rider, Rodney Jenkins, was runner-up to Broome in the professional championship. He took some time to settle down to conditions in European show jumping in his 1974 tour, but showed greatly improved form to gain some notable successes before the end of his visit.

The other young American visitors were impressive, and promised tough competition in the Olympics and other major international contests in the future. Britain won the President's Trophy for the best performances in 1974's Nations' Cup series, maintaining victory for the third year running.

Whether it was Harvey Smith winning the British Jumping Derby at Hickstead with Salvador, the flair and skill of West Germany's Alwin Schockemöhle carrying off the first amateur championship at Cardiff, or the sheer brilliance of Malcolm Pyrah and the ebullient April Love capturing the record indoor prize for the Courvoisier Supreme Championship at Wembley, there has been much to savour and enjoy recently.

Inevitably, the leading riders get most of the fame, and the applause. Their skill and dedication is essential if show jumping is to continue to hold the attention of so many millions of enthusiasts.

Yet one must never forget the officials who perform the sometimes thankless task of running an increasingly demanding sport.

And most of all, those who take the financial risks of buying and keeping potential show jumping horses, are deserving of the warmest gratitude of all who enjoy this great international sport. The financial burden of owners and riders will certainly not become lighter in the immediate future; even if the price of horses eases somewhat, the costs of keeping them and transporting them long distances are escalating rapidly.

Some of the most distinguished participants and observers of international show jumping have contributed to this anatomy of the sport. I hope their efforts will greatly enhance your enjoyment and understanding of show jumping at all levels in the exciting seasons yet to come . . .

Michael Clayton
London.

Show Jumping in Europe

by Dorian Williams

It is usually assumed that show jumping proper was practised in Europe for the first time in Paris in 1866. At a harness show there, a jumping competition was organised, but as after parading in the arena the competitors were sent out into the country to do their jumping it aroused no great interest.

Although it is likely that show jumping of some sort or another was practised in various European countries during the remainder of the nineteenth century, chiefly as an exercise or sport for cavalry regiments, it was not until the years before World War I, at the beginning of the twentieth century, that show jumping was seriously recognised in Europe as a competitive sport. It was at the first International Horse Show held in Olympia in 1907, organised for the most part and almost entirely financed by Americans as a harness show, that serious competitions were first organised in Britain. In fact it was in Holland that this first major horse show was planned, two years earlier. As a result of discussions held there, attended by such people as Walter Winans, the Jurgens brothers (until recently still an eminent name in show jumping), R.G. Heaton, and Frank Euren (Secretary of the Hackney Horse Society of England), a show was planned for London in June 1907; the Earl of Lonsdale was invited to be President. For the first time the programme was to include one jumping competition in each of the twelve sessions of the show.

Although the main interest of the show, which became at once one of the highlights of London's 'season', was the harness classes, nevertheless the jumping produced a good entry. According to *Horse and Hound* of 15 June 1907, no fewer than seventy-two horses were entered for the first competition for which prize money of £300 was offered, £100 going to the winner. This was twice as much as had ever before been offered for show jumping.

'The numerous jumps', it was stated, 'are closer together than is usual at British Shows, and a judge at each jump jots down the points earned by each horse, the highest total number of points obtained by any horse constituting the winner. This is the Continental system.'

British riders apparently did well despite lack of experience in continental methods, but on the Saturday afternoon 'riding Vendeen, the Duke of Andria first rode to the front of the Royalty and saluted, then rode slowly back to the starting point of jumping'.

Over 7 ft was achieved in one of the high jump competitions. In another the legendary Tommy Glencross, making his first appearance

opposite: A contemporary view of the arena at the first International Horse Show, held at Olympia, London, in June 1907.

in an international show, shared the first prize of £40 with Lt. Daufresne of Belgium. Other international riders came from France, Spain, Holland and Ireland.

According to the *Evening News* of that time 'the first entrant stumbled badly over the bank and splashed into the water with a resounding crash', while a French horse, Duc, refused the second hurdle, dashing into a bank of flowers at the end of the arena. 'He then started to climb into the seats, rearing violently. Finally, however, he decided to give up the task and as a consolation backed into the arena and lashed out at everything within reach.' In the end he was led out having tried to throw his rider into the water!

Although in a four-column account, appearing in *Horse and Hound*, of the first International Show at Olympia in 1907 only a few lines are given to jumping, nevertheless considerable interest was aroused and jumping events were included in most of the big county shows in England that were held during the rest of that year.

A significant visitor to Britain in those years before World War I was Col. Paul Rodzianko, who accompanied the Russian team in 1911; he achieved the remarkable success of winning with his team the King Edward VII Cup in 1912, 1913 and 1914.

Major horse shows were at this time being held all over the world, especially in those countries where the cavalry were of traditional importance: but there is no doubt that in those pre-war years the International Show in London eclipsed them all.

The last show before World War I was held at Olympia at the beginning of June in 1914, and the tremendous display of wealth, affluence, pageantry, suggests a general unawareness of the holocaust less than two months ahead. When the great Olympia doors closed, that 16 June 1914, it was the end of an era of splendour and ostentatiousness. Many thought it was the end of the horse, certainly of show jumping.

But six years later, in a breathless attempt to bring back the past as quickly as possible, the great International Horse Show at Olympia was staged again.

Inevitably, however, with cars now going at more than 60 m.p.h., with the tank replacing the horse in the cavalry, there was less interest in the harness classes than hitherto. As few horses had been bred for showing the standard in the show classes was low: there was an emphasis, therefore, on displays, while show jumping events obviously needed to be better organised if they were to take the pride of place hitherto accorded to the harness.

Unfortunately, although show jumping had been carried on for more than fifty years there were still no proper rules or regulations. Accordingly a group of cavalry officers got together at Aldershot in the autumn of 1921 to form an association which became known as the British Show Jumping Association. Leading lights in the group were Col. V.D.S. Williams and Col. 'Taffy' Walwyn, then Majors. They drew up a set of simple rules that could be easily understood by riders, judges and spectators alike. Immediately there was an improvement in the standard of jumping; people like Tommy Glencross, Sam Marsh, Tom Taylor, Fred Foster, Frank Alison, Phil

opposite: Askan, ridden by Gerd Wiltfang of West Germany, jumping at Aachen.

Blackmore and the Misses Bullows were able to hold their own in any company and draw a big crowd to the ringside at any agricultural show where they were competing.

Strongest competition to these civilian riders came from cavalry officers such as Joe Dudgeon, Malise Graham, Jack Talbot-Ponsonby, Dick Friedberger, Edward Howard Vyse, Mike Ansell, 'Dolly' de Fonblanque and J.H. Gibbon.

left to right: Fred Ahern, Limerick Lace, and Dan Corry; all three were major contributors to Irish show-jumping prestige before World War II.

Between the wars, however, it was the Irish team that dominated the British scene with riders such as Col. Dan Corry, Cmdt. Fred Ahern, Major Jed O'Dwyer, Col. Jack Lewis. With superb Irish-bred hunter type horses such as Red Hugh, Tramore Bay, Duhallow, Limerick Lace, Ireland's Own (a nice bit of salesmanship in their names!) they were successful wherever they went, despite strong international competition from world-famous riders such as Col. Alessandro Bettoni and Capt. Gerardo Conforti from Italy, Capt. Xavier Bizard and Capt. Jean Chevalier from France and Cmdt. George Van Derton from Belgium.

As yet, the Americans had not crossed the Atlantic in force so little was known in Europe of their form. The major international events were in Nice, Rome, Lucerne, Dublin and London. One of the occasions on which the United States were, however, seen in Europe was in 1926 when an American won the King George V Gold Cup in London. The United States were represented at the Olympic Games in 1924, and sent three riders to Amsterdam in 1928; they were naturally represented at Los Angeles in 1932, where only three other nations competed and no full team completed the course. In 1936, in Berlin, they just missed a medal, coming fourth.

Gradually, however, during the thirties the popularity of show jumping in Britain waned. On the Continent show jumping, which was almost entirely confined to military riders, was thriving, the British alone making little progress. All the great names in show

opposite: Port Royal, ridden by Hubert Parot of France, jumping the water at Hickstead.

jumping in the late twenties and early and middle thirties are those of continental riders: Count Alessandro Bettoni, Capt. X. Bizard, Capt. M. Fresson, Cmdt. Menten de Horne, Capt. Chevalier, Capt. Gerardo Conforti, Capt. Antonio Gutierrez, Lt. Paul Mondron: all household names at that time. In addition, there were the Irish. The reason for the sport's decline in Britain was probably the failure of British riders in international events. International success is a great stimulus. The public is prepared to support a successful team: they prefer to forget failures. And except in purely military circles British riders were not successful in the international field, despite the fact that they were obviously of great ability and were mounted on the best of English- and Irish-bred horses.

This failure was almost certainly due to the fact that the B.S.J.A. rules, drawn up originally in 1921, differed slightly, but in a very vital respect, from the continental rules. Whereas by the rules in Britain one could virtually take as long as one liked to go round the course, on the Continent it was appreciated that jumping with no time element was not only too easy, but also boring for spectators; time was therefore introduced on the Continent and was to play an important part.

Each course was measured and a time allowance for the course was worked out. A rider taking longer than the time allowed was penalised. If riders had an equal number of faults then there was a jump-off in which the fastest, with equal number of faults, was the winner.

To be able to jump big fences at speed was, therefore, essential. This was where British riders failed. They had never learnt to jump at speed. Consequently although the best riders frequently qualified for the jump-off, invariably they failed in the jump-off itself. The civilian riders regrettably so disapproved of the continental rules that they virtually boycotted all international classes, even insisting that at Olympia there must be national competitions, open only to British riders, as well as international competitions.

Not altogether surprisingly, the British public lost interest in show jumping, except at the one big international horse show in London where they knew they could see top class international jumping. Towards the end of the thirties many shows at county level did not even bother to include a show jumping competition. At the great Royal Show, held for the last time before the war at Lincoln, there was no show jumping event.

As far as Britain was concerned, 1939 could well have seen the end of show jumping as a major national or international sport. That this was not so is very largely due to the efforts of a small group of enthusiastic cavalry officers who spent the greater part of the war in a Prisoner of War camp in Germany. As, at Spanenburg, Offlag IX A/H, many of the most famous old cavalry regiments were represented, there was not surprisingly a great deal of equestrian knowledge emanating from people who had been connected with horses all their lives, as jockeys, in training establishments, in hunt service, at riding schools or just as people who had ridden since they were old enough to walk.

Together these Prisoners of War amassed a great deal of straight-forward, essentially practical information about horses, particularly about horses jumping fences. Unifying it all was an idea of what show jumping should be in the future. Colonel, now Sir Michael Ansell, had been very much impressed by the type of courses that were being built on the Continent before the war. At Colchester in 1934 his regiment, the 5th Royal Inniskilling Dragoon guards, had mounted a show incorporating into the courses for show jumping events many of the features that had impressed him overseas. These included doubles and trebles in the same competition—unknown in Britain in those days, flowers at the bases of fences (window boxes from the Officers' Mess!) and coloured poles.

Though the new courses had produced many raised eyebrows and considerable criticisms, yet many riders had had to admit that their horses jumped the fences well. Appropriately the major competition was won by Mike Ansell himself. He was convinced, when war broke out, that this was the way that show jumping should go. During his years in a Prisoner of War camp he, with other prisoners, notably Col. 'Bede' Cameron and Col. 'Nat' Kindersley, dreamed of the possibilities of the show jumping in a post-war world, organised along lines that had only tentatively been tried out before the war.

On their repatriation at the end of the war little time was lost in contacting the Offices of the British Show Jumping Association. All, however—and not altogether surprisingly—seemed to have closed down. The Secretary, living in retirement in the West Country, was persuaded to call a meeting in London and to put the B.S.J.A. in order again.

Col. 'Taffy' Walwyn and Col. V.D.S. Williams, the two principal pioneers in 1921, gave their full support, the former agreeing to act as President. Col. Mike Ansell was elected Chairman and immediately showed his resourcefulness. He was determined to improve the standard of jumping which understandably had, except for performances by people such as Ted Williams, Wilf White and 'Curly' Beard, sunk very low; and to stimulate the interest of the general public.

With considerable daring they announced a 'Victory' Championship to be held at the White City Stadium in London, thanks to Mr Frank Gentle, the Chairman of the Greyhound Racing Association who had been impressed with the drive and the determination of these repatriated Prisoners of War. The first prize was to be £100: no bigger, oddly enough, than the pre-World War I prizes, but greatly in excess of any prize in the thirties.

The course was designed with great care, based on the research that had resulted from all the discussion in Spanenburg. For the first time in England a course was being built on scientific lines. The gorse hurdles and white poles, dumped down more or less anywhere in a figure of eight, were replaced by brightly coloured fences, the poles gaily painted, and, to ensure that the horses really saw them, were packed with flowering shrubs, pot plants, and even oil drums: horses will never bother to jump flimsy fences that hardly merit a glance.

Distances between fences were carefully measured to coincide with the average length of a horse's stride. There were subtle 'changes of direction' to make sure that the skill of the rider was properly tested and that a horse could not just gallop round, virtually uncontrolled. The result was that the course was not only more impressive from the rider's and horse's points of view, but also far more attractive to the spectators.

Many of the riders however were somewhat sceptical. One or two diehards went so far as to withdraw their entries: they believed the fences to be unjumpable. They knew nothing, of course, of the deliberations of Offlag IX A/H, nor of those held later at the B.S.J.A. They were merely of the opinion—and some of them were frank enough to admit it—that the course designers had taken leave of their senses.

Most of the better known names in British show jumping, however—Tom Taylor, Ted Williams, Curly Beard, Wilf White, Phil Blackmore—were all keen to have a crack at this new-style course; and before long most of the more sceptical were prepared to admit that they had never known horses to jump better, more boldly or with greater ease.

The gamble had paid off. Theory in a Prisoner of War camp in Germany in 1942 had been justified by practice at the White City in 1945; but an ending as romantic as a fairy tale caught the imagination of the crowd, in particular of the directors of the G.R.A. This was to affect profoundly the whole story of show jumping. In a final jump-off between three horses one rider, Ted Williams, rode two of them, Umbo and Huntsman: the third, Maguire, was ridden by Col. 'Nat' Kindersley one of the original 'schemers' in Offlag IX A/H. It was Maguire who won.

The only sad element of the fairy tale—and fairy tales usually do have a sad element—was the fact that Col. Mike Ansell who had inspired it all would never himself be able to participate, having been blinded at the time of his capture in 1940.

However, what Mike Ansell lacked in physical sight, he more than made up for with his mental vision and he wasted little time in putting the sport on the map.

It was now that the Americans made their first appearance on the international scene since the 1930s. Based in Germany, they acquired a few good horses to supplement those they had originally prepared for the 1940 Games, and they were to make a very considerable impact when first they appeared in England in 1948. Coming initially for the Olympic Games they stayed on for the second International Horse Show to be held at the White City. Their performance was impressive. Led by Col. Wing, who himself won an individual fourth place at Wembley, they won several individual classes as well as the Nations' Cup at the White City. Col. Wing finished third in the main event of the show, the King George V Gold Cup, behind Col. Harry Llewellyn on Foxhunter and Jean d'Orgeix, from France, on Sucre de Pomme.

This was the first time that Foxhunter had made his mark. He was to play a tremendous role in popularising show jumping. It can truthfully be said that he was the first horse to have the sort of star quality that gets through to and grips a lay public, without which no sport can be wholly successful. The gallant Colonel quickly assumed the mantle only held previously by Tommy Glencross. Anywhere in the world where they appeared they were feted, and what was much more important, they continued to succeed, reaching their peak in 1952 when, led by Llewellyn and Foxhunter, Britain won the Olympic Gold medal at Helsinki. The other team members were Col. Duggie Stewart with Aherlow and Wilf White with Nizefela.

Harry Llewellyn and the legendary Foxhunter jumping in the Prince of Wales Cup at White City, London, in 1951.

The individual gold medal went, appropriately in view of the history of show jumping and France's contribution, to Pierre J. d'Oriola who remarkably, was to win again twelve years later in Tokyo.

By now Piero and Raimondo d'Inzeo had begun to attract notice, and represented Italy in the Olympics of 1948 and 1952. In 1956 Piero won the individual bronze medal, while his younger brother Raimondo won the silver. Their team won the team silver medal. Also in 1952 the German team made its first post-war appearance, finishing fifth behind Great Britain, Chile, the United States and Brazil.

Representing Britain internationally in 1952 were (left to right), Harry Llewellyn with Foxhunter, Wilf White with Nizefela, Duggie Stewart with Aherlow, and Peter Robeson with Craven A.

The first lady to ride in an Olympic show-jumping event was Pat Smythe, in 1956. Here she is shown (second from left) on Flanagan, accompanied by Wilf White on Nizefela, Alan Oliver on Red Admiral, and Ted Williams on Pegasus.

But 1956 had greater significance for two reasons: the first was that for the first time a lady rider was permitted by the rules to ride in the Olympic show jumping event. This was Pat Smythe. She had first appeared at the age of seventeen at the International Horse Show at the White City, and had immediately achieved astonishing success, representing her country for the first time at the end of her first year in adult jumping and winning most of the major events, including the Ladies' European Championship on four separate occasions.

Her particular contribution to show jumping was something rather different. By her success she proved that it was possible for a rider who had the talent, determination, dedication, to reach the top without being fortunate enough to be born wealthy. Her first horse, the little mare Finality, was bred from a mare that pulled the milk-float in the village to which she had been during the war evacuated from London, where she had learned to ride on Barnes Common. There can be little doubt that it was the inspiration of Pat Smythe that encouraged thousands of young people to take up riding, and, of course, show jumping. The metamorphosis was emphasised in Rome in 1960, when the British team included two farmer's sons, David Broome and David Barker, the former winning the individual bronze in the fabulous Piazza di Siena. Both Davids had reached their positions by skill and ability. Having reached it they naturally had the opportunity to ride good horses belonging to others. And this is the pattern today. Riders of proven ability, whatever their background, will always find mounts, because fortunately show jumping attracts generous patrons of the calibre of the late Mr Robert Hanson, the late Mr Cawthraw who mounted Alan Oliver, Mr Fred Hartill who mounts Paddy McMahon, and many others. The situation is identical in most other major show jumping countries.

Curiously this broadening of the basis in show jumping is not in such evidence in other European countries, though it is probably true to say that there are in most countries many more people now riding professionally; though it is alleged that in some cases riders are reluctant to admit to their professional status, lest it debar them from the Olympic Games.

The second very significant feature of the 1956 Olympics was the performance of the Germans. In 1956, led by Hans Winkler, riding a Hanoverian mare Halla, the German team immediately established its dominance of the international scene. Since winning the gold in 1956 they have won Olympic Gold Medals in Rome, Tokyo and Munich and a bronze medal in Mexico, a masterpiece of consistency. This modern progress has been helped not a little by the genius of their team trainer since 1968, Hans Heinrich Brinckmann, the outstanding show jumping course-builder since the war.

Until recently it did appear that a handful of nations, Germany, Italy, Britain and U.S.A., so dominated the international scene that it might well be necessary for the International Federation (F.E.I.) to devise two entirely separate competitions, one for the leading nations, which appeared to farm all international competitions, and one for the lesser nations.

In the last year or two, however, there has been a most encouraging revival in the form shown by some of the lesser nations. France is now going to great lengths to produce good teams, hoping to maintain the standard that won them the silver medals in Tokyo and Mexico. Hugo Simon, fourth at Munich, has inspired Austria:

both Switzerland and Holland have been winning major events again. Spain proved conclusively both at their own show in 1974 and in Rome that they have both the horses and riders to carry them back to the position that they held in international jumping at the time when Goyoaga was World Champion in the fifties. Ireland, somewhat in the eclipse (except for Seamus Hayes in the late fifties and early sixties) since the days of Rodzianko's great team of the thirties, has suddenly become a force to be reckoned with, spear-headed by the outstanding Eddie Macken riding horses owned by Iris Kellett who twice won the Queen Elizabeth II Cup in 1949, the first year of the competition, and 1951, and then in 1969 won the Ladies' European Championship.

Undoubtedly South American riders would always provide severe competition in Europe if they were able to come over more regularly. The Brazilian rider, Nelson Pessoa, settled in Europe because of the increased opportunities it gave him to compete in top-class competitions. He won the Brazilian Championship five times, but since he came to Europe he has won more than 100 Grand Prix, four Hamburg Derbies and two Hickstead Derbies, winning the European Championship in 1966.

The Australians are in a similar position; they are handicapped by their distance from Europe and their own quarantine regulations, but have always given a good account of themselves when they have come to Europe.

Twenty-five years ago there was almost a garden-party atmosphere about show jumping. Today it is very different with a far more commercial approach, which has led inevitably to professionalism. The next few years will certainly produce problems. One can but hope that a sport with such firm foundations, with such dedication and enthusiasm at all levels, will survive all the pressures and remain basically free from corruption and malpractices, a sport that can be enjoyed equally by performers and spectators, because it is straight-forward, a test of ability and courage, and involves the skill not only of the rider but of man's favourite animal, the horse.

Certainly it is not easy to imagine the day when show jumping will not be taking place at Ballsbridge, at the Piazza di Siena, at Wembley, at Hickstead, in the Club de Campo in Madrid, at Aachen in Germany, at Madison Square Garden in New York and at the Toronto Winter Fair.

These names are synonymous with show jumping. At some, such as Ballsbridge, and Belmoral in Belfast, there has been jumping for nearly 100 years. Other arenas, such as Club de Campo, have been specially designed for show jumping. In addition shows now are held in the winter months at magnificent exhibition buildings which attract huge audiences for jumping indoors, which, because of its proximity to the audience, the confinement and the atmosphere, lends itself ideally to so exciting and colourful a sport.

Show jumping started indoors. With Ballsbridge as the example, jumping was developed out of doors until such spacious arenas as Aachen and Hickstead evolved, while showgrounds where the accent

was on beauty as well as efficacy such as Lucerne, Rotterdam, the Piazza di Siena, enabled the site to enhance the jumping.

Now jumping has returned indoors and every year, all over the world, countless hundreds of new indoor schools are arising, enabling the sport to be continued the year round.

So full-time a sport is it, that no-one can hope to attain top, international recognition unless they can devote their lives to it full time. Inevitably many, indeed the majority of top class riders, have felt obliged to turn professional. Fortunately there appears to be no shortage of sponsors, national and international, prepared to put up money either to provide big prize money or to pay professional riders a fee to ride for them, or, perhaps most important of all, to buy for riders with proven or potential ability horses to match their skills.

It has all moved a very long way since the early days of the century when the show jumping events had to take second place to the harness classes, when there were only military teams and civilians rode in mufti, often with soft hats. Compared with today courses were unbelievably simple, though it should be remembered that fifty years ago and more horses were still able to jump over 7 ft.

Obviously some will regret the direction in which show jumping has gone. Others, looking at other sports will realise that if a sport is going to attract the attention of the paying public in large numbers, then it must inevitably become commercially viable; this inevitably means always looking and going forward. No sport that looks backwards can survive.

Show jumping will survive because it is keenly, internationally competitive, and so no-one with any influence in the sport can be other than forward looking.

One of the most attractive settings for international show jumping—the Piazza di Siena in Rome.

THE DAILY GRAPHIC

AN ILLUSTRATED EVENING NEWSPAPER.

39 & 41 PARK PLACE

| VOL. XXXIV | All the News. Five Editions Daily. | NEW YORK, WEDNESDAY, MAY 28, 1884. | $12 Per Year in Advance. Single Copies, Five Cents. | NO. 3470. |

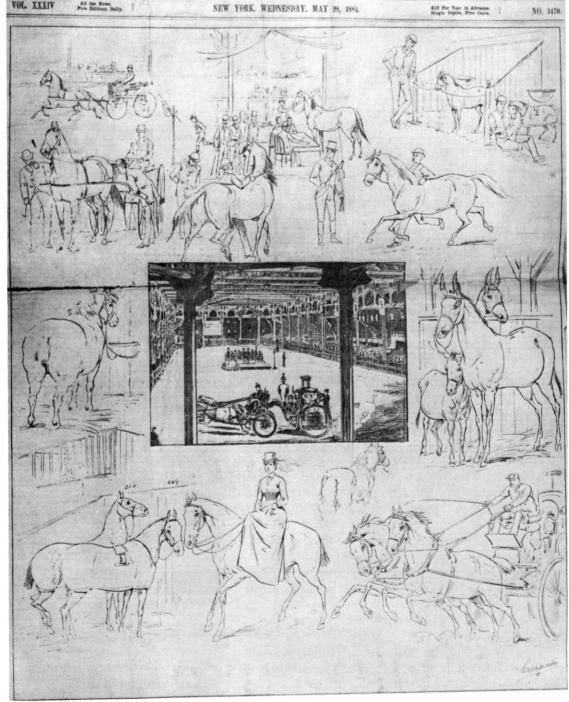

Show Jumping in North America

by Ann Martin

Today, the Jumper Division can argue persuasively that it is the strongest sector of the horse show world in the United States, for during the past decade the number and average value of horses in the division, the aggregate of prize money offered, and the attendance at competitions devoted exclusively to show jumping have all shown spectacular growth. In addition, it can claim that it is the most truly national division, for while western horses, saddle horses, walking horses, and hunters all have their prime areas of activity, jumpers seem to have invaded all states and all regions. No statistics exist on the subject, but it seems likely that the total of jumper classes conducted in the course of the year comfortably exceeds the classes offered in any other division, and thus jumpers may be considered the most 'popular' show horse in America. In England, of course, this is incontestably true.

In the absence of established historical facts, it is interesting to speculate on the origin of American show jumping. We can trace it back for over a hundred years, but it is undoubtedly older than that; most likely an evolution from point-to-point to hunter trial to jumping trial is involved, for the first American jumpers were surely foxhunters.

The development of foxhunting in America runs parallel to its development in Great Britain, though it never spread quite as far because of geographical factors, nor became so much a part of the fabric of society. George Washington was a foxhunter, and no oddity for being one; quite the contrary, in fact. The first American public pack was probably the Gloucester Fox-Hunting Club near Philadelphia which was founded in 1766; but there were already many private ones and a few exist even today. Nothing is more natural than for ardent foxhunters to dispute sometimes the relative merits of individual hounds and horses, and the writings of 'Nimrod' (C.J. Apperley) in the early 1800s are replete with accounts of various 'sporting propositions' that were contested by members of the field to prove a point.

Virginia may be considered as America's Leicestershire, and it seems implausible that there would not have been, among all the horse-race, cock-fight and bird-dog wagerers of the nineteenth century, enough contentious foxhunters to have made up a 'leaping contest'. Upperville, Virginia claims that its horse show, inaugurated in 1853, is the oldest one in America. The claim is disputed by Lakefield, Connecticut, and Springfield, Massachusetts, and we do

opposite: One of the very earliest National Horse Shows at Madison Square Gardens, New York, featured on the front page of The Daily Graphic.

Several horse shows claim to be the oldest—that at Springfield, Mass., is one of the contenders; this is how 'Gleason's Pictorial Drawing Room Companion' of November 12, 1853, pictured the scene of the first Springfield Horse Show held in October of that year.

not know if jumping contests were included in the initial programme along with the brood mares and foals, harness and riding horses. We do know, however, that by the time New York's National Horse Show arrived on the scene in 1883, show jumping was well established and hotly contested.

The National, still the most prestigious U.S. horse show, started big and has stayed big. The very first National was conducted in a Madison Square Garden that was physically located on Madison Square. It occupied the block between Madison and Fourth Avenues and 26th and 27th Streets. It ran for five successive days in October for thirteen hours a day and attracted 352 assorted quadrupeds, including donkeys and mules, in 105 classes. There was a heavy emphasis on harness classes, but there were also riding horses and ponies, hunters and high jumpers, and, as exhibitions, mounted police and fire company competitions. The mounted police had to chase and catch simulated runaways, and the fireman had to harness their horses and hook them to the fire engines against the clock, starting with the alarm bell. The harness was suspended above the pole of the engine, just as was done in the firehouses of the period, and the record time for the show was a dazzling 1¾ seconds!

The National was a great success right from the beginning. Over 80,000 attended the initial show, paying 25 cents for general admission and $1.50 for reserved seats, which was considered extortionate. The 1884 renewal saw the date moved up to May, which proved a mistake, but since 1885 the show has either started or ended on the first Tuesday in November, and thus been something of a social fixture as well as a sporting one.

It took a jump of only six feet to win the high jump in 1883, but the next year a horse called Leo, ridden by a whip from the Rockaway Hunting Club, cleared the bars at 6 ft 6 in in the class for qualified hunters on closing night. Four years later, Leo had tied with William Durland's Filemaker at 6 ft 9⅞ in when the ring committee stopped the competition as too dangerous. Maud, a 14.2½ hands high bay mare belonging to George Pepper scaled 6 ft 10 in in 1888, and three years later S.S. Howland's Ontario set yet another record at 7 ft 1 in. At this point the committee's concern about safety led to a new rule, and in 1892 the fences were not raised beyond 6 ft 6 in, the judges being instructed to separate the horses on the basis of form and manners at that point.

Though high-jumping competitions were unquestionably the glamour event in the early days, the hunting-field origin of the jumper is reflected in the fact that for many years it was a common practice to cross-enter between the hunter and jumper classes if these were not, in fact, already combined. A typical prize list from around the turn of the century offered classes for qualified hunters in each of the three weight divisions (conformation and quality to count 50%, performance over fences, 50%); a Corinthian Class for members of a recognized hunt; a Jumping Class (for the best performance of hunter or jumper over four successive fences five feet high), and a High Jump, Open to All. Hunter and Jumper courses usually called for eight successive fences, 4 ft 6 in high, and at a good show it was necessary to jump seven feet or better to win the high jump.

Heatherbloom, Howard Willet's great high-jump champion from the early 1900s, was customarily shown as a qualified middleweight hunter, a thoroughbred hunter, and an open jumper. His official high-jump mark was 7 ft 10½ in, set at Richmond in 1902, but the same year he jumped 8 ft 2 in and 8 ft 3 in at home for photographers, with Dick Donnelly in the irons. These latter marks, not having been set in competitions, were unofficial although well authenticated.

Course requirements and judging conditions were casual and variable for a great many years. The National Horse Show's *Rules and Regulations* in 1900 stated, 'The fences for the jumping classes will be such as the directors shall select,' and the *Rules on Judging* consisted only of the following: 'Every horse shall be ridden at the fences in his turn, according to the number in the catalogue. In the case of a horse refusing his fences, he shall be allowed two further trials, and no more; if then unsuccessful he shall cease to compete. In the case of a horse going through and breaking down a fence, the fence shall be made up again, and if the judges think fit, one more trial shall be allowed; if the horse fails to jump it at the next attempt, the horse shall cease to compete.'

High-jump rules usually permitted three trials at each height, but there was little uniformity and shows were free to concoct their own variations as they desired. Actually, the popularity of high-jump competitions tended to wax and wane, just as puissance competitions have in more modern times, and for the same reason: big fences being attempted by horses who can cope with them is tremendously exciting, but big fences being knocked down by horses who cannot is dreadful to watch.

The eras that were lucky enough to have a number of top-class high-jump performers thought the competition a marvellous one, but at other times it was almost ignored. In recent years there has been great interest in the U.S. in puissance competitions conducted under F.E.I. rules or A.H.S.A.'s Table 2. The current puissance record set at the National in 1973, is 7 ft 4 in and is held by Tony d'Ambrosio and Sympatico. However, the general trend of the 1970s has been to reduce the emphasis on this type of competition.

Although high-jump competitions attracted the most attention in 'the old days', there were other jumper classes as well, and in retrospect the standard prior to World War I seems surprisingly high, even in the absence of elaborate courses and the variety of types of fences that exists today. A very common class was the Five-Foot Class, and at some of the larger shows, a class was offered in which the course for the first round consisted of two rail fences at five feet, two at five feet six inches, and two at six feet! So, high fences were commonplace in the show ring well back into the nineteenth century, which is to say well before Caprilli 'invented' the forward seat. Photographs from the era show a variety of positions from quite backward to quite forward, and one is tempted to conclude that the most natural horsemen of most times have stubbornly done what came naturally to them, no matter what the book said.

Until now this discussion has been concerned exclusively with 'civilian' jumping that developed entirely from indigenous roots. Shortly after the turn of the century, however, an international form

below and opposite: Tony d'Ambrosio on Sympatico sets a new puissance record of 7 ft 4 in at the National Horse Show in New York in 1973.

of the sport also appeared on American shores, carried by officers from abroad, and hence designated for many years to come as 'military' jumping.

Indirectly, international jumping came to the U.S. as a result of the death of two key officers of the New York show, President Cornelius Fellowes and Secretary John G. Heckscher. Fellowes was the only President the National had ever had, having been at the helm for more than a quarter-century. The 1908 show had incurred a deficit, and since continuing the show might have jeopardized the assets of the two estates, the stockholders of the N.H.S.A. unexpectedly voted to liquidate the corporation and to distribute its assets, which exceeded a quarter of a million dollars. As the wealthiest of those exhibitors who had come to regard the National as a public institution of some importance, Alfred G. Vanderbilt led a move to acquire control of the association, and found himself promptly elected president.

Vanderbilt was an outstanding amateur whip who travelled extensively abroad and had competed at Olympia. While competing there he had not failed to notice the great public interest and enthusiasm that was generated by the international jumping competitions that were inaugurated in 1907, and this was one of the innovations he was anxious to try in New York.

The general tenor of the National had been conspicuously Anglophile from the beginning, so it is not surprising that the first contingent to be invited was a group of five British officers led by Major J.G. Beresford, D.S.O., of the Seventh Hussars. They divided honours with the American officers, against whom they competed and made a fine impression, moving the *New York Commercial* to observe, 'The invasion of the British officers has done much to make the Garden a lively place and the show a success . . . and the pluck of the British officers in charging at the jumps brought out as hearty applause as any vouchsafed the Americans.'

The following year the British returned, along with teams from France and the Netherlands, and the year after that, the first proper Nations' Cup was offered and promptly won by the Dutch. By 1913 international jumping at the National was firmly established as a Military Team Competition Division, and apart from subsequent wartime hiatuses. Since then it has remained a key complement to the 'civilian' jumper division at the National.

Scoring rules had become more sophisticated by this time, and the National's rules, which were widely followed by other shows, since there was then no national governing body, had been elaborated by 1912:

'In the officer's jumping competitions and the classes for jumpers, the following is the scale of points on which horses will be judged in going over the course and taking the jumps: First refusal or bolting, 1 fault; second, 2 faults; 3rd, debarred; horse or rider falling, 4 faults; horse knocking down fence with front legs, 3 faults; hind legs, 2 faults; touch with front legs, 1 fault; hind legs, ½ fault; clearing fence without touching, 0 fault.

In due course, thin pieces of wood called slip fillets (laths, in the British terminology) were placed freely on the top element of fences to indicate more positively whether or not they had been touched, just as was done under B.S.J.A. rules in England. After the creation of the F.E.I. in 1921 the continental practice of scoring knockdowns only was adopted as the standard for the international classes (4 faults for a front knockdown, 2 for a hind; 5 faults for the first refusal, or fall of horse and rider, 10 faults for the second refusal). However, the international riders also competed against national competitors under 'civilian' rules at many shows, and it was not until the post-World War II era that they were compelled to compete only against each other in their own division.

Jumping under touch rules tended to require a different style of riding, and even a different type of horse, than did jumping under the continental, knockdown-only rules. Accordingly, both the United States and England found themselves subject to two rather contrary influences during the twenty-odd years that separated the two World Wars. On the one hand was the influence of their Olympic riders, who were drawn exclusively from the cavalry schools at Fort Riley and Weedon, plus that of the famous foreign teachers who had learned their equitation on the continent, especially in Italy. This influence was primarily forward-seat, which is to say, 'Caprillist', so called after Federico Caprilli, who was the first to promulgate a

opposite: Rodney Jenkins of the United States on Idle Dice at Hickstead.

rational theory of forward riding over fences. Conspicuous among the teachers who were exposed to Caprilli's theories in their country of origin and who brought them back into the United States and England were Piero Santini, a friend and disciple of Caprilli, who taught extensively in both countries, and whose books were best sellers in both; Lt.-Col. Harry Chamberlin, one of the principal architects of the *U.S. Cavalry School Manual*, which shows the strong influence of Saumur in its dressage, and the equally strong influence of Pinerolo in its jumping methods; and Paul Rodzianko, Russian-born trainer of the Irish international team in the 1930s, whose riders brilliantly demonstrated *il systema* and whose book, *Modern Horsemanship*, was powerfully influential on both sides of the Atlantic.

The other strong influence during the 1920s and 1930s was that of the outstanding professional show jumpers, many of them of Irish extraction, who had learned their craft in the 'school of hard knocks' and learned it well indeed. They were perhaps more acrobats than stylists, and they placed their faith in pragmatism rather than theory, but they produced remarkable results, especially when the competitions required the super accuracy that touch rules demand.

Among the outstanding show-jumpers of the era were Fred Vesey, who in 1923 at Chicago piloted Mrs Stuyvesant Peabody's Great Heart over a fence that was measured under A.H.S.A. rules at 8 ft $\frac{13}{16}$ in, still the North American high jump record; Freddie Wettach, whose unofficial high-jump record on Kings Own was 8 ft 3 in and whose By Request was the leading jumper in the early 1930s; Danny Shea, the famous rider of Squire and his fantastic successor, Little Squire; Mickey Walsh, who purchased the great 13.2 hands high Little Squire from Shea for Mrs Audrey Kennedy and piloted him to the Open Jumper Championship at the National; Morton W. 'Cappy' Smith, whose victory with Bartender at the National in 1936 was only the first of many championships there; the outstanding amateur, Arthur McCashin, who beat the cream of the internationals with the trio of jumpers he rode for Julius Bliss, performing as a one-man team; Pete Drever, Jack Prestage, Jim Maloney, Paddy Farrell, and a score of others.

This was the situation that prevailed at the beginning of World War II, when the draft militarised most of the outstanding civilian horsemen; the cavalry dismantled and mechanised its officers, and fuel rationing virtually ended all horse show activity in North America for the duration.

At the war's end, American show jumping started to pick up right where it had left off. Within a few years a whole new generation of riders had emerged to supplement pre-war stars like Mickey Walsh, 'Cappy' Smith and Joe Green who came back stronger than ever, and some truly memorable combinations were formed—Pat Dixon with All Afire and Injun Joe, later to win international fame as Hugh Wiley's Nautical; Joe Green with Circus Rose, who as Miss Budweiser became Arthur McCashin's Olympic mount in Helsinki; Barbara Worth (now Oakford) and Jimmie Williams on the West Coast, Chet Bonham and Bob Egan with the great Sun Beau, Bill Steinkraus with

Harry Chamberlin, one of the leading American figures in show-jumping between the wars, shown here with Nigra, a horse with several Olympic appearances to its credit.

opposite above: The setting for the Pennsylvania National Horse Show at Harrisburg, Pennsylvania.

opposite below: Mary Chapot jumping on Sharrar at the Lake Placid Horse Show.

Displaying an informality not normally seen in international show jumping—'Cappy' Smith.

Trader Bedford and Ping Pong, Raymond Burr with Black Watch and Dave Kelley with Andante, to name only a few. However, the job of furnishing representation for the 1948 Olympics fell again, as it always had in the past, to the military riders rather than the civilians.

Putting together a team for the London Games was not easy, for both the Fort Riley, Kansas Cavalry and the Fort Sill, Oklahoma horse-drawn Artillery had been completely mechanised during the war, and neither horses nor riders existed in any quantity. It was necessary to piece together a team from the remnants of the ill-fated 1940 Olympic squad, supplemented by a few German-trained horses that had been hidden away during the war and quickly acquired by the old cavalrymen in the occupation forces. The hastily improvised 1948 squad produced a fine performance in the Games, winning the gold team medal in the three-day event and the silver in dressage; the best showing in the jumping event was an individual fourth place won by Col. F.F. Wing and Democrat, but the team went on to win the Nations' Cups at White City and Dublin, and went out in a blaze of glory. For go out it did. After the Games the Army riders were officially, completely and irrevocably dismounted, and in 1949 there was no official team to represent the U.S. either abroad or at home at the National.

Into this breach stepped a new civilian organisation which called itself the U.S. Equestrian Team, Inc. Created by a group of retired cavalry officers and horse-minded civilian sportsmen, the U.S.E.T. undertook to select, train and finance teams to carry the U.S. flag in international competition in all three equestrian disciplines, both on the domestic circuit and in the Pan American and Olympic Games.

The first order of business for the new U.S.E.T. was to provide a team for the 1950 fall circuit to compete against a strong field which included Humberto Mariles, the 1948 Olympic champion. The first team consisted of Arthur McCashin from New Jersey, the noted pre-war rider, plus the first two women ever to represent the U.S. in equestrian competition, Mrs Carol Durand from Kansas and Norma Matthews (later Mrs Albert Lauer) from California. The team did well that year and again the next, when Bill Steinkraus and John

Russell (who rode at London as an officer) were added to the squad. When the F.E.I. still refused to permit women to ride in the Prix des Nations at Helsinki in 1952, the trio of McCashin, Steinkraus and Russell rode to a bronze medal behind Great Britain and Chile. This was the first team medal the U.S. had ever won in jumping at the Olympics, and the U.S.E.T. was on its way.

The way was not always easy, for as the European post-war recovery got into full swing, it soon became apparent that the system of improvising teams to go abroad from horses trained primarily under touch rules over courses that bore no resemblance to those in the Games would be doomed to failure. Accordingly, in 1955 the U.S.E.T. hired a former Hungarian Cavalry officer, Capt. Bertalan de Nemethy, as a full-time jumping coach, and instituted a policy of sending a team abroad in some non-Olympic years for competitive seasoning. The U.S.E.T.'s 1955 European tour was only moderately successful, and the team slipped two notches to fifth at the Stockholm Olympics. However, the turning point was past, and the U.S. squad that returned to Europe in 1958, 1959 and 1960 was a powerhouse. The Nations' Cup quartet of Steinkraus, Hugh Wiley, Frank Chapot and George Morris, mounted on horses like Ksar d'Esprit, Nautical, Diamant, Sinjon, Trail Guide, Master William and Riviera Wonder proved itself a top contender for Games honours by winning Nations' Cups at London, Rome, and Lucerne, and verified this form by winning the silver medal behind Germany at the Rome Olympics.

The U.S.E.T.'s coach, Bertalan de Nemethy (left) with the veteran rider Arthur McCashin.

The U.S.E.T. has remained a leading force in world show jumping and a major influence in the domestic show jumping world ever since. There is now a permanent training centre at Gladstone, New Jersey and an elaborate system of regional 'screening trials' through which riders can become eligible to work at Gladstone under de Nemethy. The team has twice won the F.E.I.'s President's Cup, emblematic of international supremacy in cup competitions. Although the team gold medal in the Games remained elusive (in 1972 at Munich, by the paper-thin margin of a quarter-fault), Bill

'Buddy' Brown on Sandsablaze, jumping at Madison Square Garden in 1974.

Steinkraus and Snowbound accounted for the individual gold medal at Mexico in 1968 and Neal Shapiro the individual bronze at Munich on Sloopy.

The example the team provides at home and its efforts to encourage more European-type competitions in the United States has also had a profound influence on show jumping in America generally. Considerable assistance came from the Jumper Rules Committee of the A.H.S.A. (which has been chaired, at various times, by Bill Steinkraus and Frank Chapot) and gradually legislated a very substantial change in U.S. course conditions and rules. Though a touch table still exists under A.H.S.A. Rules (Table 1) most major competitions either use F.E.I. Rules, or A.H.S.A. Table II which is practically indistinguishable therefrom except for the lack of a weight requirement and of a prohibition against standing martingales, which are very dear to many U.S. competitors.

The old rivalry between the international riders and the national ones is at last largely a thing of the past, as reflected in the selection of Rodney Jenkins, the leading U.S. professional since 1970, to represent the U.S. in the 1974 World Championships along with Frank Chapot. Several of America's leading professionals were trained as amateurs by de Nemethy, notably George Morris, Bernie Traurig and Jimmy Kohn, and there is no difference whatsoever, at the big shows, between the courses, horses and style of riding used in the National Classes and those that prevail internationally. (Of course, at the smaller shows, especially in remote or rural areas, much more modest and old fashioned conditions still survive, just as they do in Britain.)

Indeed, the distinction between international and national, team and non-team, and even professional and amateur have tended to become blurred in the United States in recent years, just as they have in Britain and Europe. America's leading national competitors have also often ridden on the team. Riders like Kathy Kusner, Frank and Mary Chapot, Carol Hofmann Thompson and now Rodney Jenkins have switched back and forth between team and non-team horses and shows from week to week, and have become as much a part of one scene as the other. With the F.E.I. having removed all restrictions on the participation of professionals, except in the Olympic Games, it is unlikely that the old divisions will ever return.

In many ways a highly significant figure in this change was Brooklyn-born Benny O'Meara, who died tragically at the controls of his converted World War II fighter plane in 1966 at the age of only 30. O'Meara first attracted attention with Jacks or Better, the brilliant but unorthodox brown gelding with whom Neal Shapiro later won the Grand Prix of Aachen. He also developed Untouchable, Kathy Kusner's mount in the Tokyo and Mexico Olympics, and generally worked enthusiastically to help promote the U.S.E.T. and to welcome the advent of European jumping conditions in the United States. A self-taught rider whose style became more and more classical as he matured, O'Meara was a dynamic and notably progressive figure who helped to forge strong links between the world of the professional rider-dealers and the U.S.E.T.

American horse shows are fundamentally different from many British and continental shows in that the vast majority of them do not offer show jumping exclusively, but only include it on the programme along with many other divisions.

The American Horse Shows Association currently licenses over 1250 shows; there are also unrecognised shows, pony club rallies, local shows, and gymkhanas. Some are uniquely regionalised, like the Kentucky State Fair in Louisville, Kentucky, which features a $10,000 World Championship Five-Gaited Stake. People spend thousands of dollars trying to breed the winner in search of local prestige, because this is the centre of saddle-horse breeding. In California, Western enthusiasm is high with many stock and quarter-horse classes. At the San Francisco Cow Palace fall fixture these feature strongly, including cutting horse displays, and western pleasure-horse performing classes. Barrel racing is a regular fixture. There are also Morgan, Arab, and Three- and Five-Gaited Saddle Classes. The Kansas City Royal is one of the biggest gaited shows, while in Kentucky and Tennessee, Walking-Horse Classes are a speciality.

There is, of course, a certain year-to-year variation in the show schedule, but the following annual fixtures rank high among the leading shows from the jumpers' point of view.

February	Riverside County National—Indio, California.
	Jacksonville Classic—Jacksonville, Florida.
	A to Z—Phoenix, Arizona.
March	Tampa Charity—Tampa, Florida.
	American Invitational—Tampa, Florida.
May	Devon Horse Show—Devon, Pennsylvania.
June	Pin Oak Charity—Houston, Texas.
	Ox Ridge Hunt Club—Darien, Connecticut.
	Southern Californian Exposition—Del Mar, California.
July	Lake Placid—Lake Placid, New York State.
	Chagrin Valley P.H.A.—Chagrin Falls, Ohio
August	Virginia State—Richmond, Virginia.
September	American Gold Cup—Philadelphia, Pennsylvania.
October	Forum International—Los Angeles, California.
	Pennsylvania National—Harrisburg, Pennsylvania.
	Washington International—Washington D.C. (C.S.I.O.)
November	National—New York, New York State. (C.S.I.O.)
	Royal Agricultural Winter Fair—Toronto. (C.S.I.O.)

Originally all U.S. shows built their own courses. Now there are an increasing number of independent fence rental agencies in the major areas. They were set up in the 1960s, have prospered and ship their courses from show to show. Many shows now rent their fences and the hire companies often supply timing equipment and judges if required.

At a C.S.I.O. such as New York, foreign experts who are familiar with the international standard are invited to course-build and judge. Pamela Carruthers from Wiltshire, England, frequently designs courses. Past judges include Belgian Menten de Horne and J.H.A. Jurgens of Holland.

Basically, A.H.S.A. rules give the show organizers a wide latitude in their choice of competitions. Table I touch rules are often used at small shows and for green horses, but most large shows prefer A.H.S.A. rules, under which virtually all of the F.E.I. jumper classes can be conducted, or F.E.I. rules themselves, which are equally permissable.

The A.H.S.A. Jumper Division is composed of four sections—Open, Intermediate, Preliminary and Amateur-Owner. Unless a show restricts horses to a particular section, horses may also often cross-enter in higher levels. The 1975 A.H.S.A. rule book categorises the four jumper sections according to money won as follows:

a A Preliminary Jumper is a horse having won less than $1,000 in jumper classes at any show since March 1969.

b An Intermediate Jumper is a horse having won less than $3,000.

c An Open Jumper is a horse that has won $3,000 or more in jumper classes. Any horse regardless of money is eligible to compete in this section.

d An Amateur-Owner jumper is a horse irrespective of cash winnings that is ridden by an Amateur owner or an Amateur member of the owner's immediate family.

The Amateur-Owner section is probably the fastest growing sector of the show jumping world in the United States at present, for it has created a place for the horse and rider of solid but modest ability who have been virtually forced out of the Open and Intermediate sections, where courses at the big shows may get very large indeed. It is also true, however, that all the jumper sections are slowly growing in strength at the expense of the various other performance and breeding divisions, thanks to the undeniable fact that show jumping possesses the greatest appeal for the lay public.

Reflecting this at the other end of the scale, and perhaps foreshadowing the trend of things to come, has been the emergence in recent years of the one-class-only, Grand Prix jumping Show. The Grand Prix as it now exists in the United States was originally the brain child of D. Gerry Baker, an Ohio professional who returned from a European vacation with a burning ambition to present a really important class over a typically European type of Jumping Derby/ Grand Prix course. His first (and in many ways still the most successful of all the Grand Prix promotions) was the Cleveland Grand Prix, inaugurated in 1965. This one is, in fact, connected to a horse show, in that it is staged on the Sunday following the Chagrin Valley P.H.A. Horse Show on adjacent grounds; however, the Grand Prix course is not used for the regular jumper sections at the show, and the whole event is staged quite separately. Before long the A.H.S.A. set up a Grand Prix committee, which drew up specific course and condition requirements, and established a $5000 minimum for the prize money.

In the decade since 1965 more than thirty official Grands Prix have been run, from New York to California, and there is every indication that the trend will continue. Prize money now often exceeds the minimum, sometimes by a substantial amount. The San Diego (California) Country Estates International Grand Prix Classic in 1974 offered a total of $100,000 for three classes, and the Grand Prix final was worth $25,000 to winner Rodney Jenkins and Number One Spy. A number of foreign competitors have been invited to compete various of the Grands Prix, though often riding borrowed horses, and it is becoming increasingly common for them to enjoy C.S.I. status.

Today, all sports are still gaining ground in the United States, as leisure activities assume greater importance for larger and larger segments of the total population; and show jumping is participating fully in this growth. Indeed, if one could consider that show jumping was a toy of the aristocracy before World War I, and that it became a military pursuit between the two World Wars, then it would be fair to say that it has become truly popular and veritably a proletarian activity in the three decades since V-J Day.

There is still not the mass market for show jumping in the United States that there is in Britain, because the country is still too vast for that, and the market that was more or less artificially created by the B.B.C.'s support of show jumping in the 1950s and 1960s in Britain could hardly have been created within the framework of American commercial television. Nevertheless, CBS-TV and ABC-TV have both paid more than passing attention to show jumping in recent years, and C.B.S.'s telecast of the Grand Prix of Rome and the World Championships in Hickstead in 1974 were among the first such events to be carried by the entire nationwide network. With participation at an all-time high, enthusiasts for the sport hope and believe that such exposure is merely the beginning and that it is only a matter of time until show jumping acquires a degree of national prominence similar to the position it enjoys currently in Europe and Great Britain.

It is more than forty years since North American show jumping enthusiasts had the opportunity to stay at home and have the world's best performers come to them for the Olympic Games. On fact, they were somewhat short-changed by the 1932 Games in Los Angeles, for the world economic depression at that time held the starting field for the Prix des Nations to eleven competitors; only five riders and no teams completed the course, and there were no clear rounds in the competition. Baron Nishi won with seven faults. Even so, the presence of the Games on the west coast proved a considerable stimulus to interest in all three Olympic disciplines. Since modern air transportation has removed an enormous barrier to participation, the boost Canadian and U.S. equestrian activities will undoubtedly receive from the 1976 Olympics in Montreal seems destined to put and keep the North American continent in show jumping's big league.

Selection, Training and Care

by Judy Crago

1 Selection

Unfortunately there are no hard and fast rules about how to select a potential top-class show jumper as they come in all shapes and sizes. However you will need at the very least some basic knowledge, a certain amount of cash, and a great deal of luck. If twenty of the world's leading show jumpers were turned out in a field with twenty hacks and hunters it would be impossible for any outsider to pick the superior jumpers out. Jumping ability is a gift in a horse just as athletic prowess is in a human being. Furthermore though there have been several stallions who produced a large proportion of good jumpers among their progeny, the particular gifts the show jumper requires are not necessarily hereditary. Pat Smythe produced a great many foals from her brilliant mare Tosca, as did Hans Winkler with Halla, but not one of them achieved anywhere near the success of their dam. There are several good horses whose full brothers or sisters have been sold for large sums only to disappoint their ambitious purchasers.

There is, however, one quality which nearly all the top horses will have in common and that is a good temperament. This is an essential part of a show jumper's make-up, as all the physical ability in the world is useless if the horse is mentally unstable. (There are exceptions even to this rule—the great Sunsalve for example was very erratic and wayward but he was the kind of freak one occasionally comes across which seems to violate all the rules.) Bearing this in mind, together with the fact that jumping ability is *more likely* to be found in a well-made sound type of animal with good conformation, what then are the basic points to look for when choosing your potential show jumper?

First impressions are important and there are some horses which immediately catch the eye. 'Personality' is always a difficult thing to define, even more so in a horse than a human, but there is no denying that most of the top show jumpers possess a distinct individual character. It is partly what is commonly known as 'presence'. In dressage competitions a horse's presence counts for a lot, and when an animal such as Merely-a-Monarch enters the arena he seems to be saying, 'Here I am, look at me,' and he makes an instant impression on the judges. For a horse to keep winning consistently in top-class show jumping these days with the standard ever increasing, it is essential for him to have this extra strength of character we call personality.

This foal should be a promising jumper, as it is out of Judy Crago's international mare Spring Fever. But only time will tell.

opposite: Judy Crago on Brevitt Bouncer, jumping at Lucerne in 1974.

above: A good example of a typical Irish head—honest but not aristocratic.

The first thing to look at, then, is the head, as this will tell us a great deal about the horse's personality, temperament and intelligence. The eyes should be bold and large with plenty of width between them, and the ears active and alert, showing interest and intelligence. The head should be in proportion to the rest of the animal. There is nothing wrong with a large, head on a heavier type of horse, but on a thoroughbred the head should have quality with a fine bone structure. It should be well set on to the neck, which in turn should be in proportion—neither too long and narrow, nor too short and thick.

A horse is said to have its head on 'upside down' if the lower side of the neck is longer than the top. A horse put together in this way finds it very hard to bend at the poll when asked to flex, and will therefore raise its head so bending its neck further back and upside down. This will result in 'jamming' the breathing apparatus in the gullet which very often causes a defect in the wind. In addition it tends to make the horse jump with a hollow back. The neck, then, should be arched and the throat fine.

The shoulders must be sloping, not upright, and neither too thick nor too narrow. A horse with a thick shoulder is usually a 'stuffy' mover and therefore will not have the liberty to cope with big spreads. Nor can it move freely if it is 'tied in at the elbow'—the elbows should stand away from the ribs. Behind the shoulder we look for a deep girth line. The back should be strong and not hollow. Short-backed horses are always said to make good jumpers, but there have been a great many top international jumpers with long backs—just think of Ksar d'Esprit. The loins too should be strong and broad as it is this area, together with the quarters and hocks, which produces the necessary propulsion. Sloping quarters or a 'goose rump' are also said to signify jumping ability and the quarters should be strong with a good second thigh.

Make sure that the horse stands up square. Looking from the front, the forelegs should not be set on too close together as often happens in a narrow-chested horse. From the side, the forelegs should come straight down in a line from the shoulders through the forearm to the ground. The joints should be flat and not round, and the tendons and ligaments clearly defined and not puffy. If the leg is 'back at the knee' or the pasterns too straight this creates extra strain on the legs and therefore frequently causes unsoundness. Pasterns which are too sloping are also a weakness, but horses which are 'over at the knee' seldom have tendon trouble.

In the hind legs, strong, well developed hocks are very important and these should be 'well let down', and neither 'over-straight' nor 'sickle hocked'. The hind legs should come straight down beneath the horse so that his hocks do not 'stand away'. To be able to jump big heights a horse must have his hocks underneath him, and he will find this difficult if his hind legs are naturally strung out behind him.

Finally, we come to the most important part of a show jumper's anatomy. It was Jorrocks who first remarked, 'No foot no 'oss' and he has been quoted frequently ever since! No matter how brilliant a horse's potential, he is no good to anyone if his feet are unsound.

below: A typical thoroughbred head.

First and foremost be sure that the feet are all the same size, as it is an ominous sign if one foot is smaller than the others. Large feet are not a bad thing, but beware of 'boxy' ones, or flat soles, or feet with contracted heels. If you are paying a lot of money for a horse it is a good idea to have the feet X-rayed. It is surprising and alarming how many young horses, even those which have done little or no work, have already some abnormality in their feet such as navicular disease which cannot be detected in the early stages by the naked eye. There are several different theories as to the cause of this but little is known as yet. It seems though that foot trouble is either hereditary to some extent, or, more likely I think, due to some deficiency in diet as a foal.

These then are the basic points to look for in the conformation of our potential show jumper, but bear in mind that a horse can possess all these qualities, be perfect in conformation, and indeed in temperament, but still will not necessarily make the grade as a show jumper. By the same token, some few star performers, like Nautical and Earlsrath Rambler, appear to have made the grade with little to recommend them but an outstanding desire to jump fences clean. The number of horses who actually get to the top compared to the number which are brought out each year as potential 'world-beaters' is infinitesimal. However, if you take pains to buy a sound well-made animal of good temperament, should it turn out not to be a Mr Softee, Simona or Idle Dice you will still be able to sell it for a good price as a hunter or eventer. It is not only show jumpers that command tremendous prices these days.

So much for conformation, then. The above rules apply to whatever type, build or breed of horse one buys, and the selection of the particular type is very much a matter of individual and personal taste. The most popular type of show jumper in Britain over the last few years has probably been the Irish half-bred, by a thoroughbred out of an Irish draught mare. These horses have the bone, substance and calm temperament of the common horse combined with some of the quality and scope of the thoroughbred. Currently, however, with the standard getting higher, the courses bigger, and the spreads wider, the horses jumping today require still more quality than most of those jumping ten or fifteen years ago. Thus, a more popular type of horse nowadays is a three-quarter or seven-eighths bred, by a thoroughbred out of a 'hunter' mare, who is herself half-bred or better.

Many people, especially in the U.S., favour a pure thoroughbred supporting the theory that 'anything a common horse can do the thoroughbred will do better'. Certainly the U.S. Equestrian Team have had outstanding successes with their thoroughbreds, most of which came from the race course. On the other hand, there is no denying that most thoroughbreds are temperamental and inclined to be hot-headed, and thus much depends on the style and the temperament of the rider. Peter Robeson prefers thoroughbreds (for example Firecrest and Grebe) but schools them to be ultra-obedient. David Broome likes his horses to be quick and active, and with more fire and initiative. Even the West Germans, who historically preferred

Forelegs set on too close together.

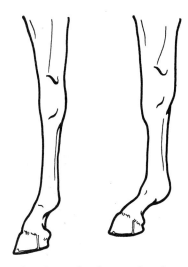

left: Leg 'back at the knee' and straight pastern.

right: Round joint and sloping pastern.

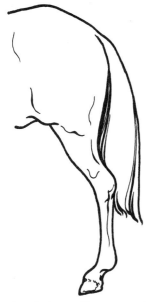

Sickle hock 'standing away'.

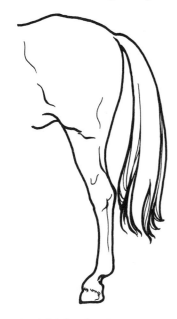

Over-straight hock.

left: Boxy foot. right: Flat foot.

stronger horses such as their own Hanoverians, are now introducing more thoroughbred blood. Indeed, Hans Winkler has always preferred lighter-framed horses such as the immortal Halla.

Colour and sex, too, are matters of personal preference. Some people definitely dislike a black or a chestnut. Others will never have a mare in the stable, particularly a chestnut mare! While mares can certainly be more difficult and temperamental than geldings, there is no denying that a really good mare takes a lot of beating. They are usually naturally careful and dislike hitting fences, but they are rarely consistent until the age of eight or nine. After this a few, with sympathetic handling, will go on to be consistently brilliant and courageous. Several mares figure among the bravest and best show jumpers in the world, but there are definitely fewer mares jumping internationally than there are geldings. If anything goes wrong with a mare and she turns sour it is very seldom that she comes back to be as genuine and reliable as before. Top-class stallions are even rarer than great jumping mares, but the Russian team has shown a distinct preference for them. Frank Chapot's brilliant Good Twist and Hugo Simon's Lavendel are probably the best known 'entire horses' competing today.

With height too there can be no hard and fast rule. A big horse must theoretically have an advantage over a small one and they say 'a good big 'un will always beat a good little 'un', but the exceptions which immediately spring to mind are Stroller and Dundrum. With courses as big as they are today however, there are very few horses under 16 hands which are capable of winning consistently in top company.

Having studied the horse from head to tail you will then want to see him in action so have him led up, first at the walk and then at the trot. When walking he should move straight and 'clean off the ground'. A horse which 'daisy cuts' does not bend his knees and a good knee action is important in a jumper. At the trot he should move freely with an easy stride using his shoulder and following through with his hocks. A long stride at the canter is an advantage over big spready courses, with long distances in combinations, but he must be able to shorten his stride at the command of his rider. It is much easier to see a stride on a 'bouncy' type of horse with a short stride, and these horses are usually more active and able to get themselves out of trouble.

The greatest asset any horse can have, particularly a jumper, is natural balance. This is largely determined by his conformation, and a well-made horse with the qualities we have mentioned should be naturally well balanced. Good balance is essential in any equestrian activity, and although it can be acquired to a certain degree with long, arduous and patient schooling, a horse which has a good natural balance obviously has a tremendous advantage. Unless you are buying an unbroken horse you will want to have a ride on him and from this you will best be able to judge his balance. But first it is a good idea to see him ridden. By watching the rider closely you will be able to decide whether he is getting the best out of the horse and covering up its shortcomings, or whether perhaps he is not doing it

The horse is jumping freely and happily down a lane, but would do better to fold his front legs a little more.

justice. Assuming, as is probably the case, that the horse is fairly green, try to get an idea of how much you can improve him with schooling. If at all possible you should see the horse jump even if it has not yet been backed. To see a horse jumping loose down a lane, or even over a single pole, will probably give you more idea of its capabilities than seeing it ridden, but bear in mind that they usually look more impressive without a rider!

Of course it is impossible at this stage to tell whether a horse will be capable of jumping a Nations' Cup-type course, but we can at least get an idea of whether the potential is there to work on. A young horse jumping loose should come in quietly to a fence with his ears pricked really looking where he is going. If he 'spooks' and 'backs off' a bit, it is not necessarily a bad thing as a spooky horse is usually a careful jumper. When jumping he should really use his neck and back, and 'round' himself over the fence. Some horses naturally fold their knees and get their legs well out of the way from the start, which is a great advantage, though this is a thing which usually comes with more practice and experience.

Finally, unless you are buying a very inexpensive horse (in which case there is probably something wrong with it!) always get your horse vetted by a reputable vet and take his advice. There are quite enough things which can go wrong with a horse without buying trouble to start with.

We have dealt only with selecting a young horse with a view to bringing him on to be a top show jumper. Remember that the odds against him ever reaching the top are stacked heavily against you. For a jumper to win in world-class competition today he must be both bold and careful, calm and courageous, obedient and quick thinking. He must have the athletic ability of a cat and the jumping ability of a stag. Small wonder that out of the hundreds of novices which are brought out each year only a fraction ever become consistent winners at home, and a fraction of these go on to compete successfully at international level. Because of this, some young riders (with well-off parents!) buy ready-made show jumpers to help the difficult transition from ponies to horses. But even with money no object it is becoming increasingly difficult to find a good, genuine 'made' horse which can be bought at all. And remember that the top riders are very hard to follow and have probably got the best out of the horse.

So my advice is, stick to the young horse and if it makes the grade think of the satisfaction you will have in having made it yourself.

2 Breaking

Preliminary work with the young jumper is no different from handling any other young horse. Before starting any work on your new acquisition make sure he is in good physical condition and has been 'done' well. Get a vet to have a look at his teeth—they may need filing or he might have some 'wolf' teeth which will give trouble unless removed. He must be comfortable in his mouth before he can respond to the bit. He may also need worming, so ask your vet to take a worm count. If he is in poor condition at first he must be worked accordingly.

Remember never to work a young three- or four-year-old hard for too long at a time. Some, particularly big horses, do not finish growing or reach maturity until five or six years old. They tire very easily if asked to perform an arduous exercise for any length of time, and can easily develop unsoundness when physically immature.

Make sure that you are always clear, definite and firm in your commands. This is of the utmost importance because the horse is a very willing pupil as long as he understands what he is being asked to do. What is more, once he has learned a lesson he will never forget it. This good memory is a two-edged sword, as horses will also remember any nasty experience which causes either pain or fear. It is thus desirable to avoid any misunderstandings right from the start, so always be patient in the extreme. A horse responds best to kindness, and although it is possible to use force, it should never be necessary and it is certainly undesirable. Once you win his trust and confidence you will find that he is eager to please and quick to learn.

Obviously things will go wrong from time to time—you will make a mistake, or he will succumb to an outburst of youthful high spirits—but each setback will be a lot easier to put right if he has learnt to trust you. Correct him firmly if he shows disobedience and reward him when he acknowledges your authority. He must accept that you are always the boss, and discipline is the basis of all training. An undisciplined horse is never a happy one. Always plan ahead. Before starting any new lesson go through all the stages in your mind, and be prepared for the unexpected, so that in the event of something going wrong you are not caught unawares.

We will assume that your horse has been handled from a foal both in and out of the stable, and that he is halter-broken. If handled quietly and regularly from birth the youngster will have come to accept with confidence that man is his friend. Having been treated in this way with a sound primary education behind him he should be no trouble to break and back. 'Breaking in' is an unfortunate phrase, since it gives the impression of breaking a horse's spirit, and conjures up pictures of 'broncho-busters' and the Wild West. In fact it is only another stage in his training, but remember that it is the most important stage as it lays the foundations for his whole future.

Many horses are ruined at the start of their careers by bad mouthing. You cannot take too much time and care over this all-important operation. It is the easiest thing in the world to spoil a horse's mouth and the hardest thing to re-make it. There are various theories about the best way to mouth a horse, and probably most of them are effective, since basically the same principles apply. I will deal with the method I personally have always found most successful.

For the first lessons some people use a comfortable plain snaffle, but the most popular is the breaking or mouthing bit. This consists of a straight bar from the centre of which hang three metal keys. The horse will play with these keys with his tongue causing the saliva to froth at the mouth, and making him sensitive to the feel of the bit. Make sure he cannot get the keys between his teeth—this will be impossible if the bit is fitted correctly. When first putting the bit in a youngster's mouth, undo the buckle on one side of the bridle. Slip the bridle over the horse's head and place two fingers in the corner of the lips to open his mouth. You will then be able to slide the bit gently through the mouth without hitting him in the teeth, which would frighten him. You can then do up the buckle and the bridle

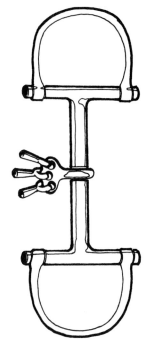

A breaking, or mouthing bit.

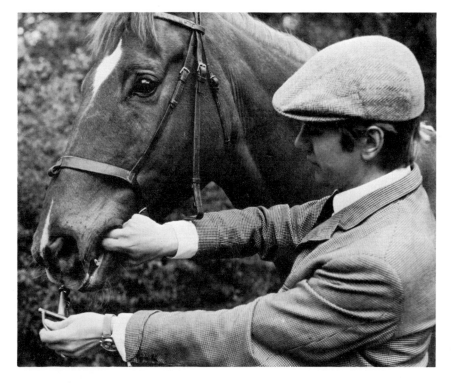

Putting the bit in for the first time.

opposite above: Monsieur Pernod, a French horse being ridden here by Nelson Pessoa of Brazil at Hickstead.

opposite below: Edgar Cuepper of Belgium in trouble with Le Champion.

will be in place. It is a good idea to do this daily in the stable for short periods at a time, before you start to long-rein him. In fact you can leave the bit in his mouth while he is being lunged. Equal care must be taken when undoing the bridle. Make sure that the mouth is wide open so that the bit will slide out easily. He has only to receive one knock on the teeth to remember next time, and he will clench his teeth and grab at the bit to stop it hurting. This can quickly become a bad habit.

At the same time you can introduce him to a roller or surcingle in the stable, and he will become accustomed to the feel of a strap round his belly prior to having a saddle on.

The next step, lungeing and long reining, is the start of the education proper, and the pupil is first introduced to the 'aids' as he learns to respond to the voice and hands. By working in a circle he will learn to relax and at the same time this will supple him and make him flex, improve his balance, and develop his muscles and ligaments. He will learn to carry his head correctly, and to obey simple words of command. In fact you are preparing him both physically and mentally for the next stage, which is riding him.

For lungeing you will need a cavesson nose-band, a lunge-rein and a lungeing whip. The lunge-rein should be attached to the ring on the cavesson, never to the bit. The ideal is to have a covered school (indoor ring) for this work, but as this is out of the question for most people it is as well to start the lungeing lessons in the corner of a quiet field. In this way you are at least partially enclosed with the fence on two sides, and there should not be too many distractions. Do not attempt to take your pupil out of a walk until he has been going quietly and obediently on both circles. In fact it is advisable always to start a lesson at the walk to prevent him dashing off with anticipation. Keep him well out to the end of the line so that he makes full use of the circle. A young undeveloped horse will find it hard to move in a tight circle and it will also be a strain on his legs. Use your whip as a guiding pole to keep him out, and a light flick of the whip should be enough to keep him going forward.

First lungeing lessons.

52

Most horses are stiff primarily on one side, usually the right. I think this is probably because they are always handled from the left side, but there is a theory that it is due to the way they lie in the dam before birth. For later work it is essential that the horse be equally supple on both reins, so you will need to work him more on the stiff side.

Most of the early work will be done at the trot, but it is important to vary the work as much as possible, making frequent changes of pace and direction, to keep the young horse interested and obedient. Use your voice, and always use the same words of command—'walk', 'trot', 'canter', 'halt'—so that he knows quite well what you want him to do. Cantering on the lunge will be difficult and tiring for him at this stage, so do not attempt it until his trotting on both reins is

Cantering on the lunge—do not attempt it until his trotting on both reins is quiet and well balanced.

opposite: Garrai Eoin, being ridden by Ned Campion of Ireland at Hickstead.

From lungeing to long-reining. Note the long-rein through the iron and the iron tied to the girth for more control.

Change of direction (on long reins).

quiet and well balanced. Make sure he is leading on the right leg, and is not disunited (in which case you must start again), and never canter him for too long at a time.

After three or four days he should be lungeing quietly on both reins, and it is time to start long reining. This can be done with either a roller fitted with 'Ds' or a saddle with the stirrups tied to the girth. The long reins should run from the bit through the Ds or stirrups, the inside rein coming back to the hand, while the outside one runs behind the horse just above his hocks. You will now lunge him as before, but with two reins. Gradually you can start to vary his paces with reins and voice as opposed to voice only. Then you can change

Enjoying a walk in the country-side.

direction, but this requires a great deal of tact and concentration to start with. Standing inside the horse, and never directly behind him, shorten the long outside rein, and at the same time let the short inside rein slide through your fingers as he turns. This should be done in one movement so that neither rein drags on the horse's mouth. Great care must be taken to keep an even feel on the reins, and you must be constantly on the alert to avoid a loose rein getting entangled in the horse's legs or round the saddle. Having gained full control, plus the confidence of the horse, you can take him around the fields or down a quiet lane and let him enjoy the sights and sounds of the countryside. Remember that the more driving you do with him the more control you will have when you first ride him.

You will have to decide for yourself when the time has come to back your horse as this will depend on his rate of progress. If everything has gone smoothly and you have had no problems, this final stage in your breaking programme should be quite simple and straightforward. Throughout this whole period it is advisable always to have an assistant at hand, and it is especially necessary when you actually mount for the first time. This you will do at the end of your normal day's work, when you are satisfied that he is quiet and settled. Choose a suitably quiet spot, preferably semi-enclosed. (Many people prefer to back a horse in his stable.) Make sure that your assistant holds him by the cavesson nose band and never the bit. Holding the horse's head with his left hand he can then give you a leg up with his right hand. Do not sit astride him yet but just lie across the saddle. If he should move make sure it is only in a circle and not straight ahead. Slide off quietly and repeat the exercise several times,

First step of backing—lie across the horse, and if all goes well throw your leg over and ease your weight down on the horse's back.

The rider gradually takes control with the reins.

and then if all is going well you can throw your leg over and sit astride him. Pat him and speak to him constantly. After you have mounted and dismounted a few more times your assistant can lead him quietly forward in a circle, and slowly let him out on the lunge rein which will be attached to the cavesson. From here on the rider gradually takes over control with the reins. For the next few days it is a good idea to take the horse out twice a day, giving him his usual work before riding him. This you should only do for short periods at a time so as not to tire him with the unaccustomed weight on his back.

I must stress how important it is not to hurry this stage. Prevention is better than cure, and any sort of disaster now such as the rider getting bucked off, or the horse getting away, should be avoided at all costs.

We will deal with feeding in a later chapter, but at this point one must take extra care with a youngster's diet. It is not a good idea to get him too fit at this stage in his training with a lot of 'hot' feed. Many people make this mistake, reasoning that now that the horse is in regular work for the first time in his life he will need feeding up. From past experience we have always found it safer to play it by ear and see how he is reacting. It is easy to step up his feed once you are sure that it is not going to his head. Until then keep it plentiful, but cool and plain.

3 Early Schooling on the Flat

The horse is leaning on the bit, and the rider is making the mistake of trying to correct it with the hands only

Many riders shy away from the word 'dressage'. 'Not for me all that high school stuff,' they say. But dressage covers a vast field ranging from high school to the very elementary early schooling on the flat. This flat work is invaluable to every horse no matter which branch of equestrianism he is to specialise in later on, whether it be show jumping, eventing, hunting, polo or even racing. It will improve his balance and performance making him supple, obedient and comfortable to ride. It also helps considerably in the physical and mental development of the young horse. Remember that a young horse which has been schooled in this way will be a lot easier to handle when first asked to jump. He will also be physically fitter and there will be less strain on his muscles and ligaments. If you watch the top international riders while they are warming up their horses, you will notice that most of them are very familiar with basic dressage and apply it constantly. This should be sufficient proof of its value to the show jumper.

From the moment you first mount your youngster he must be taught complete obedience at all times. His first lesson, then, is to learn to stand quite still while you mount him. There is nothing more annoying than a horse which fidgets around when you are trying to get on him. If possible, it is best to stand him up against a wall, or better still, in a corner, so that he cannot move away from you. You should be able to stop him moving forwards with the reins. Make quite sure that he stands perfectly still until you give him the signal to move off. If he does not, start again from the beginning, and take your time about it. Do not let him get away with even the smallest disobedience, thinking that 'just this once won't matter'. You must never compromise at any stage of your horse's training and this is what I mean by 'complete obedience'. In the same way he must be taught to stand quite still when you come to dismount.

When you are ready to move off—and not when he is—give a clear signal with the legs and hands. (Here we come again to the coordination of the aids.) He should move smoothly forward into a walk. Do not allow him to throw his head up and come off the bit.

Begin with the very simplest of exercises, and for the first few weeks do not attempt to do any collected work. At this stage the horse must learn to *go forward*—avoid getting him behind the bit at all costs. To start with he may tend to lean on the bit. Do not try to rectify this with hands only. The more you try to pull his head up with hands alone the heavier he will become. Remember that the three aids—hands, weight and legs—should always be coordinated. It is much harder to deal with the horse which comes off the bit, but the same principles apply. Legs and weight must be used to push him forward onto the bit.

When you first start to ride him his muscles will become stiff under the unaccustomed weight, so there must be a period of suppling exercises to build up the muscles and strengthen the back and loins. You may find that he will work well one day and resist you the next. This will always happen if you do too much work with him at one time, as he will then come out stiff the following day. For the first few weeks you should restrict yourself to slow work. Ride him in different places as much as possible, and vary the work to keep him interested. Do not allow him to become bored. Take him for quiet hacks, and over natural uneven ground to teach him to look where he is going. Walking up and down hills is a wonderful exercise. It builds up his muscles, strengthens the loins and hocks, makes him use his shoulders and bring his hocks underneath him. It is most beneficial to do this at a walk as then all his muscles will come into play, but be sure to let him have plenty of rein so that he can really stretch his head and neck. This exercise will also benefit his respiratory organs. From time to time if you can find a level patch of ground trot him in circles on both reins. Most of the work in circles in the early stages should be done at the trot, as at this gait it is much easier to keep a young horse balanced and going forward with impulsion. If you come across a stretch of good level going let him have a canter, but be sure that he is going forward with plenty of freedom as he will not yet have the balance to canter slowly. This will come later on.

While out on these rides it is a good idea to trot him over any little logs or ditches which you might meet, so that he will come to accept that jumping is a natural part of everyday life.

Once your horse is moving forward and is reasonably obedient at all paces he is ready to advance to slightly more intensive schooling on the flat. There are varying opinions as to the best bit to use for the early collected work, but for as long as you can get the required

Walking up and down hills: although the horse is really using himself and is allowed plenty of rein, the rider is slightly behind the movement.

Most of the work in circles at the early stages should be done at the trot. A good example of the horse on the bit and bent into the direction he is going.

Trotting over small natural obstacles while out on a ride, in preparation for lessons to come.

results from a plain snaffle, this is undoubtedly the most satisfactory. While performing all these exercises it is most important that your horse remains constantly on the bit, with his head in the right position and his hind legs under him. This will enable him to round his back and carry the rider comfortably. If he carries his head too high he will be forced to hollow his back, and this will throw his hind legs out behind him. Make sure that he remains on the bit during each transition from one pace to another. If he does not, then pull up and start again.

Your collected work will start with trotting in circles and simple changes of direction for brief periods at a time. This will supple him and make him lighter in the hand, but take great care not to get him over-bent. Remember to keep pushing from behind, but do not let him get over his pace or he will quicken and shorten his stride and start to 'run'. You will find as he gets fitter and stronger that he will use his shoulders and quarters more, and his stride will become longer. Always remember that this collected work should be interspersed with periods on a loose rein, so that he can relax his muscles and stretch his head and neck.

As I mentioned earlier, every horse is stiffer on one side than the other and you must work hard to get him to bend on the stiff side. Your aim is to get your horse evenly balanced and to be able to bend him round your inside leg on either circle. The simple movements such as the turn on the forehand and haunches, leading up to 'shoulder in' and 'quarters in', are a good exercise for the control of both forehand and quarters. You can then progress to 'half passes' and 'leg yielding'. This work on two tracks should be done first at

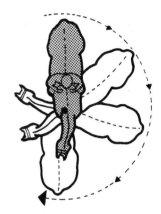

above: Right turn on the fore-hand.

below: Left turn on the haunches.

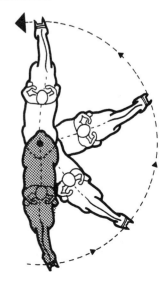

above left: Here the horse is too strong in the hand, and the rider has lost the use of his weight and lower leg: consequently the horse is over-bent and 'running'.

above right: Relaxing on a loose rein.

*far right: 'Right shoulder in'.
right: 'Right quarters in'.*

You should be able to bend the horse round your inside leg on either circle.

the walk and later at the trot. He will be harder to bend on his stiff side, so these movements must be executed correctly until he is equally obedient on both reins. You will then find that your work in circles will be easier, and he will be generally more supple and tractable.

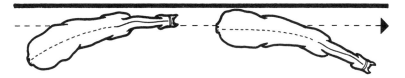

Cantering in circles is the final phase of your early schooling on the flat. It is best to start off from a sitting trot on the turn so that he will automatically strike off on the inside leg. Much later you can progress to simple leg changes, and the counter-canter, which is a good supling exercise and excellent for improving balance. Through-

out these lessons vary your work with continuous changes of direction and transitions from one pace to another. One very important point is to be quite sure that your horse is always moving true and straight and on one track. Most horses will tend to drop their shoulders into the circle or push the quarters out. This can quickly become a habit, but once you have gained full control of the forehand and quarters through your work on two tracks this should not be difficult to correct.

A final word of warning. If at any point your horse should become upset or excited stop what you are doing, and walk him quietly about until he has settled down. It is pointless and probably harmful to persevere while he is in this frame of mind as he will not understand what you are trying to do.

Always finish your lesson on a good note, even if it means spending more time than you had intended on that particular lesson. It is never wise to allot a set amount of time to any schooling session, as the length of time will depend entirely on how the horse is going. When you are satisfied that he has done everything you have asked of him to the best of his ability, let him know he has done well, rewarding him with a word and a pat. Loosen your girth and let him walk quietly round on a loose rein to relax and cool off.

4 Early Jumping Lessons

Your horse can be introduced to trotting poles at the very beginning of his education, even as far back as his early lessons on the lunge. In fact the trotting poles, cavallettis and small jumping lanes should be combined with the work on the flat throughout your early training. This work is very good physical and mental exercise, and it breaks the monotony of the schooling on the flat. Your pupil will learn that jumping is part of his normal routine and accept it as such without any fuss or excitement.

Even if your horse is familiar with trotting poles on the lunge, it is advisable to start again from scratch when you first ride him. You will begin by walking him over a single pole on the ground. When he has done this quietly a few times place another pole about three feet away from the first, and then another, until he is walking quietly over about six in a row. You will need to move them to about four feet apart when you first start to trot through them. Keep him at a steady even pace, always at a sitting trot, but on a loose rein so that he can really stretch his neck and look where he is going. At first you will find that he is rather clumsy and lacks coordination. He will pick his front feet up carefully and forget about his back ones, but as his balance improves he will learn to coordinate his limbs and settle into a good steady rhythm.

Remember that this work should be incorporated with your work on the flat, the aim being to vary your programme and so keep your pupil interested and alert. Take him down through the trotting poles and then trot him in a circle before coming back through the trotting poles from the opposite direction. Vary the angle of your approach,

Walking over poles on the ground.

and change the rein frequently. This will supple him on both sides, and prevent him anticipating your next move. At the same time you will be carrying out the various movements on the flat described in the previous section. This will now be your normal routine, but do not become so engrossed in your schooling that you forget the most enjoyable part of the education. Both you and your horse will still benefit enormously from your rides out in the country, and this will be the perfect relaxation from your concentrated work at home.

When the horse is working quietly and well with the trotting poles you can introduce him to cavallettis. First place a single cavalletti at its lowest height at the end of your line of trotting poles. You can gradually replace all the trotting poles with cavallettis, keeping them low so that he will not try to jump them. You may need to place

Introduction to cavallettis.

them slightly further apart than the trotting poles, but the distance will vary from one horse to another. Later on you can use variations of distance as a good exercise to make him use himself physically and keep him mentally alert, but it would be a mistake to set such problems in the early stages. Simplicity is essential just now so that he will understand and enjoy what he is doing.

It is a good idea to place a few single cavallettis around the field so that you can trot over them as you meet them. He might well put in a small jump over them which will take him into a canter. This is fine as long as you bring him back to a trot afterwards and do not let him get excited. Another way to vary the routine is to move your line of cavallettis to a different place each day. This might sound like fussing over minor details, but it is important to bring as much variety as possible to these lessons.

Jumping a small cavalletti at the end of a line of trotting poles.

Until now your work has been just what you would do with any young horse no matter what his intended future. From now on however, you will start to specialise. This does not mean that your work on the flat will cease—far from it. You will need to continue with this basic dressage right through your horse's career, but from now on everything will be directed towards his jumping. The exciting moment has at last arrived for you to give him his first lessons in jumping, but this will only be an extension of the work you have been doing.

Place a raised cavalletti at the end of a line of trotting poles three to four yards from the last pole. Trot your horse through the poles as usual and he will pop over the cavalletti. After he has done this a few times put a second cavalletti, also raised, six to eight yards from the first. (These distances are only approximate as the length of stride varies considerably from one horse to another. You must decide for yourself the best distance to suit your horse.) Later on you can vary the distances to make him shorten or lengthen his stride but at this stage you should make things easy for him. He will now trot quietly through the trotting poles as before, pop the first cavalletti and take one stride to the second. You can progress gradually from here, increasing the number of cavallettis, and then placing a single pole slightly higher, ten to twelve yards from the last cavalletti. This will give him two canter strides to the little jump. Make sure you have a good ground line at the base of this small fence, and leave at least three trotting poles in front of the cavallettis to keep him steady and balanced.

Throughout all this cavalletti work, and indeed later on for jumping, it is advisable to have an assistant to replace any poles which might get knocked over. It is very distracting for a horse to have his rider hopping off him every few minutes to adjust a fence, and it disrupts the continuity of work.

When he is jumping quietly and confidently down the lane, it is time to introduce your pupil to coloured fences. (Horses are supposed to be colour-blind, and to see everything as shades of grey—but they are certainly suspicious of painted obstacles if they have never seen any before, and it is a good idea to introduce these variations early.) At the end of the lane you can put a brightly coloured pole, and then a small brush or wall. He should now be so accustomed to jumping down the lane that a strange fence at the end should come as no great surprise to him. You can then make this last fence into a small spread, keeping the front rail slightly lower than the back one, but bearing in mind that a sloping spread of this nature will make the distance longer.

After jumping the first cavalletti, he is taking one canter stride to the second.

Now you can progress to small single obstacles. Place a cavalletti six to eight yards in front of a small fence. From a sitting trot let him pop in over the cavalletti and take one stride which will put him right to jump the fence. Jumping these in-and-outs from a trot is a good physical exercise, yet not excessively strenuous. It makes him lower his head, round his back, and look where he is putting his feet. It also discourages any tendency he may have to rush his fences. The 'placing pole' in front ensures that he will always meet the fence right and so gain confidence, with the minimum interference from the rider. Any such interference at this stage would be very distracting, and might make him lose concentration and confidence. You should sit as quietly as possible and leave the jumping to him. Most riders will accomplish this better if they use a neck strap. Even the most experienced rider can get 'left behind' and catch a horse in the mouth, and this can lead to his throwing his head up and hollowing his back, or worse still, refusing. If you hook a finger under the neck strap, these unnecessary mishaps can be avoided.

It is even more important to have a placing pole in front of a fence when you first start to jump from a canter. It is much too early to start trying to shorten or lengthen your horse's stride, and he will often meet a fence wrong at a canter and be forced to pick up from a long way back or put in a short one. He will not yet have the experience to get himself out of trouble and this could easily frighten and upset him. The cavalletti in front of the fence should be big enough to make him jump and not trip over it, but small enough to jump from a 'wrong' stride.

When you first start to jump single fences without the cavalletti in front it is a good idea to go back to a trot for the first few times. Your aim at this stage is to make everything as simple as possible. You will find it easier when jumping from a canter to circle round the fence a few times. Then when your horse is correctly balanced, you pop him over the fence. In this way you can vary the angle of your approach slightly gaining or losing ground as you require. This is easier than trying to 'place' him at this stage by shortening or lengthening his stride. A word of warning, though—be very careful not to make your angle of approach too sharp, or he may run out.

Jumping out of a circle like this also has a calming effect on a horse, and will stop him from rushing. Do not jump the fence every time but canter round it a few times. Bring him back to a trot every now and then and take him right away from the jump and do some work on the flat. Build as many new fences as possible. It is too early to attempt to jump a full course yet, but never jump him backwards and forwards over the same fence. Vary your fences, gradually introducing him to different types of jumps, bringing in small walls, gates, planks etc. Always make sure your fences are well built, with plenty of filling and a good ground line. A fence with no ground line is difficult to jump, and an 'airy' fence with too much daylight encourages carelessness.

Jumping a low parallel is an excellent exercise for developing a good style and making your horse bascule, but build it wide enough to make him really stretch and use himself. This will also make him

Progressing to small single obstacles.

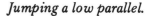

Jumping a low parallel.

look and think what he is doing. In order to clear both the front and back rails he must make the centre of the parallel the highest part of his jump. This is therefore a fence which must be jumped with great accuracy. If you are in any doubt as to your ability to meet such a fence right every time it never does any harm to bring back your placing pole. This is advisable too when first jumping a small double or combination. It is essential that you meet the first part right or you will be in trouble at the second part.

Up until now your horse has been left alone to make his own arrangements in the approach to a fence with the minimum interference from the rider. The approach is the most important phase of a show jumping round, and can in fact be said to commence from landing over the previous fence. It is the last few strides before a fence which determine how that fence will be jumped. The method of non-interference can still be occasionally successful in novice classes, but you are aiming at the top, and in world-class competition

Two related fences, shown here only one stride apart. In the upper photograph the horse is collected and shortening his stride in a seven-yard double; in the lower photograph the horse has jumped further into a nine-yard double and is lengthening his stride with enough impulsion to stand off the second part.

today precision and accuracy are of the utmost importance. A good eye is essential in the rider, and instant obedience in the horse, plus perfect balance throughout.

From now on you must start to control your horse's stride so that you can lengthen or shorten as you wish. You will already have laid the foundation for this with your flat schooling, by your extended and collected work. You can now vary the distances in your lanes and combinations, making them shorter or longer as you require. Before you attempt to jump a full course it is advisable to school over two single fences at related distances. Your approach to the first fence will be dictated by the distance between the two fences. Thus if the distance is three short strides you will need to jump the first fence out of a short collected stride and keep your horse well balanced and collected for the three non-jumping strides so that he will meet the next fence with his hocks well underneath him, having not gained too much ground. Conversely, if the distance is three long strides you must approach the first obstacle with more impulsion, so as to jump further in, and lengthen his stride while still keeping him balanced with hocks under him so that he will not pitch onto his forehand. In this way if he has to stand off from the second fence he will have the impulsion to do so. On no account should you lose contact with his mouth or stand up in your irons—this will tend to 'flatten' him leaving his hocks behind him so that he will jump 'at' his fence rather than over it. Remember that in order to lengthen his stride you must use legs and weight to push him forward, and at the same time keep hold of his head.

When building these 'related' fences do not forget that the distance between them will of course depend on the type of fence and will vary according to the height and spread of the obstacles (see Course Building, page 106).

When your horse is balanced, controlled and obedient over these related fences, he will be ready to start jumping a small course. Although you can vary the type of obstacle, the fences should be kept well within his capabilities at this stage. No matter how much scope and ability your horse may have he is still a novice and should not on any account be overfaced. However, it does no harm to jump one or two well constructed bigger fences in the course, provided you follow up with a few easier ones.

5 First Competitions

From the day you first set out to produce your show jumper your entire training programme should be planned in every detail well in advance. This applies particularly when you start your first small shows. It is often advantageous to start the young horse for the first few times in informal schooling shows designed expressly for that purpose and conducted outside the ordinary horse-show structure.

In Britain through the winter there are held several indoor unaffiliated shows, i.e. shows which are not affiliated to the British Show Jumping Association, and which therefore do not count for grading. Under B.S.J.A. Rules a horse may not jump at an affiliated show until he is four years old, a horse's official birthday being January 1st. Some horses are late foals, having been born in the late summer, and may not be ready to come out as four-year-olds. Then again some horses mature quicker than others, this largely depending upon their general build and conformation. Assuming that he is ready the ideal time to start your youngster in these small shows is in the early winter when he is rising four. He will then be ready in the spring to come out as a novice at the first affiliated shows of the season. Before the advent of the vast number of indoor schools all over the country there could be no such grounding, and the novices came out at the start of the season as real beginners. Now however, most of the 'first-season horses' have already had three or four month's experience through the winter and the standard of novice classes is high. The courses for novices at affiliated shows have for this reason become more difficult, and it is a disadvantage to bring out a complete novice without having had this grounding. It is obviously preferable then to start your horse at these indoor shows if possible, but should he not be ready there are always plenty of small unaffiliated shows through the summer which will serve your purpose.

In the United States, there is no age restriction in the Jumper Division, and horses are classified according to money won in either the Preliminary, Intermediate or Open Jumper Section. Thus your novice is eligible to compete as a Preliminary Jumper whenever he is ready, and to remain in the Preliminary Section until he wins $1000 as a jumper. In practice, however, he is likely to need some unrecognized shows under his belt before he is able to cope with typical Preliminary Jumper courses, since these may include fences up to 4 ft 6 in in height at the larger shows. In the old days when touch rules were prevalent in the United States, many jumpers were started as three-year-olds, and some even won important championships at that tender age. These days, four is probably the earliest a jumper should start in the smaller Preliminary Sections, and for the larger horse or the backward one, his five-year-old year is probably even better.

It is most important, whatever the time of year, to select the shows which have the best facilities. A large arena, good fences, a reputable course-builder and good going are all important factors. Do not be tempted to take your youngster to the little local show down the road unless you are quite satisfied that it will meet your requirements. You have made up your mind to reach the top, and the only way to achieve this is from a serious and professional approach. Selecting the time and the place to produce your horse in public for the first time is the first step in the long, hard road to the top.

Before the day of the show you should make sure that your horse will load without any fuss and travel quietly. It is a good idea to introduce him to a horse-box (horse-van) or trailer earlier in his career if possible, and thus prevent any misunderstanding on the morning of the show. Allow yourself plenty of time to arrive at least one hour before the scheduled start of the competition. This will enable you

opposite: Perfect relaxation—both you and your horse will benefit enormously from your rides out in the country, as a rest from your concentrated work at home.

to check whether or not the show is running to time and if there is a drawn order of jumping. Most unaffiliated shows allow competitors to place their numbers on a blackboard in the collecting ring in the order they choose. In England, a popular type of competition for complete novices is 'clear round' jumping, in which there is no jump-off and each clear round earns a rosette. This provides the ideal start for the beginner, and competitors are usually permitted more than one round if required.

It is up to you to work out your own timetable so that you have plenty of time to get your horse tacked up and ridden in. This timing is very important not only at these early shows but right through your show-jumping career. It can prove disastrous if you have to rush and cut short the warming-up period, and it can be equally detrimental to find yourself hanging around waiting to jump having warmed up too soon. Some horses require more 'riding in' than others, but a novice who has never been to a show will need plenty of time to settle in. From his general behaviour at his first two or three shows you will be able to judge how much work he requires before jumping.

The walking of the course is extremely important whether it be for a novice 'clear round' class or a Nations' Cup. The horse has no way of knowing the problems which may be set, and the rider must make a careful study of the course as a whole and of the individual fences. For a novice competition it is particularly important to give your horse every opportunity to maintain free forward movement. To achieve this you will need to make as much use of the arena as possible, and when walking the course you should walk the line that you intend to ride, the object being to avoid sharp corners which will tend to unbalance and distract him. With the novice, it is well worth risking time faults in order to do so. Most young horses lose concentration when first in the ring and tend to look about them. It is up to the rider to know exactly the line he is to take so that he can concentrate entirely on presenting his horse coordinated and balanced at each obstacle.

A study of the individual fences will enable you to decide whether there is any problem for your particular horse. At this stage, having a fair idea of his likes and dislikes, you should be able to recognise the fences which could create a problem, and so be prepared. There is an old saying 'horses for courses', and this is proved time and again at all levels of show jumping. A really good horse should be able to adapt himself and jump any course, provided that he gets the necessary assistance from his rider, but there are a great many horses which have their limitations and are only capable of jumping a particular type of course. This however hardly applies to novice courses where the fences are relatively small and the distances between them therefore not so important.

Walking the course then is an essential part of the operation and not just an opportunity for a social chat. An inexperienced rider will find it very helpful to walk the course with a seasoned campaigner, so do not hesitate to ask for assistance if you need it. Most of the top riders are only too willing to give advice and a helping hand to the

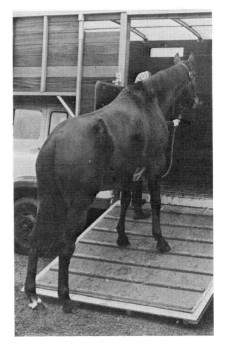

Introducing a young horse to a horse-box.

opposite above: The Maverick, being ridden at Hickstead by Alison Dawes of Great Britain.

opposite below: Dennis Murphy of the United States, on Triple Crown at Lucerne.

novice rider who is keen to learn. It always pays to listen to the experts and to digest every bit of information. Some of the opinions may vary, but you can always learn from listening to other people's comments.

You can also profit a tremendous amount from watching different riders, good and bad alike, for you learn as much by other people's mistakes as by their expertise. For this reason it is an advantage whenever possible to watch a few rounds jumped before your turn comes. This will give you an idea of how the course will ride, whether the distances between fences are true, and which fences are causing the most trouble and why. This usually applies particularly at an indoor show, as the fences indoors are, through necessity, fairly closely related in distance.

Allow yourself plenty of time to unload your horse and tack him up so that he will have the chance to look around him and get acclimatised. It is a good idea to spend the first quarter of an hour or so just walking and jogging him about before you start any serious work, and when he is settled and relaxed you can start to 'ride him in'. This 'riding in' or warm-up should be based on the pattern of your general work at home, the aim being to get him supple and obedient. When you have achieved this to your satisfaction you can give him a few small jumps over the practice-fence to loosen him up and get his mind on the job in hand. There is no need to jump anything big, and here again you should work on the same basis as your schooling at home. You will often see riders jumping enormous fences outside but in my opinion this is completely unnecessary, particularly with a novice. Your aim is to go into the ring full of confidence, and this will be unlikely if you have just crashed through a fence in the collecting ring! Before you have a jump outside find out from the collecting ring how many there are to jump before you. The ideal is to time it so that when you have finished warming up there are still three or four competitors to jump, so that you will have time to walk your horse around and get your breath back, check on your girth and so on. You can usually base your calculations on two minutes per round, and this will give you some idea of how much time you have in hand.

Remember that you have brought your young horse to the show purely for a school, and even if it is a jump-off class and he jumps a clear round there is absolutely no necessity to jump him off. If he has performed well and done everything you have asked of him you may be satisfied to call it a day. On the other hand it will do him no harm to jump another round, providing the course has not been raised unduly, but *on no account* should you attempt to take him against the clock. A great many promising young horses are ruined by jumping against the clock before they have gained enough experience. Your aim is to produce a top-class show jumper and he should not be asked to jump at speed until he has at least one season's experience behind him. It will require a great deal of will power and patience not to 'have a cut', and you will undoubtedly have to sacrifice a few wins in novice classes. This is not a bad thing however, as it is a mistake to upgrade a horse too quickly, and so be faced with big courses before he has had the necessary experience. To win consistently at international level nowadays a horse must have the ability and the temperament to keep jumping clear rounds over big courses. At the same time he must be capable of jumping such courses at speed without becoming unbalanced and upset. This however is looking ahead, and the time factor should be ignored until your young horse is jumping consistently well over bigger courses. Only then, when he is obedient, relaxed and well-balanced, should you attempt to jump him against the clock, and then you will generally find it better to save ground in a timed jump-off by taking the shortest line and cutting corners rather than by asking him to go over his pace, and so lose his jump.

If you can arrange to go to one of these small shows every week without too much travelling you will find that your young horse will benefit far more from the experience gained by jumping in strange surroundings than from jumping familiar fences at home. You should try to get your horse out as much as possible, and a trip to a friend's jumping paddock, or even to the local meet, will keep him interested and at the same time broaden his outlook. Many people consider that the hunting field is a wonderful schooling ground for a young horse, but this very much depends on the type of country hunted. Hunting inevitably involves a certain degree of risk through injury and it is debatable whether the experience so gained justifies the risks involved.

In England the outdoor show circuit begins at the end of March, and from then on you can pick and choose your shows. Most shows have a wide selection of classes, and there are generally at least two in the schedule which cater for the novice horse. There are three grades of horses in England, the lowest being Grade C for horses which have not won a total of £150. Grade B is for the bracket between £150 and £300, and those which have won over £300 are Grade A. Classes are usually either for one particular grade of horse, or for combined grades, such as 'B and C' or 'A and B', and the courses in these classes have their own height restrictions. In addition to these many shows have Open classes, which are open to all grades, and 'Popular' open classes for horses which have not won a total of £300 the previous season since being Grade A. There are also several classes confined to Grade C horses whose winnings are considerably less than £150, such as the *Daily Express* Foxhunter Competition, for horses which have not won a total of £50. With the enormous increase in the number of shows throughout the country it should be possible to find a show nearly every week with a suitable schedule for your particular horse at every stage of his career.

If you can find a three- or four-day show where you can stable, it will be an enormous benefit for your young horse. A show like the All England Jumping Course at Hickstead, for example, which has several different rings, with one or two classes each day for the novice horse, is a wonderful education. You will have the opportunity to jump in a different ring every day, over a different set of fences each built by a different course builder. Added to this you have the advantage of stabling on the show ground, which in itself is an

A novice horse competing in a Foxhunter competition. The horse is the one being schooled in the pictures on pages 64-6.

important part of his education. He will become accustomed to the general activity of the showground and will learn to accept it as part of his normal routine.

After a show like Hickstead it will do your youngster no harm to have a bit of a let down at a smaller one-day show the following week. Then, if you are satisfied with his progress, you can give him a short period away from shows and jumping, just hacking about, enjoying life and relaxing. With the young horse this should be your general pattern throughout his first season. After building him up to

Any young horse must become accustomed to the general activity of the show ground. The picture shows stabling arrangements at Hickstead.

a certain pitch you should then let him down to give him a chance to digest what he has learnt. This applies not only to the type of shows but also to the classes you select. For example, when your horse is going well in 'Foxhunter' classes you can start him in a few Grade C classes, and then drop him back to 'Foxhunter' while he is still eligible. You should continue in this vein, each time progressing a little further, while taking care not to overface him, and giving yourself the opportunity to drop back if necessary.

In the United States the situation is very similar, though in the South and Pacific Coast where winters are mild, the young horse can start on the outdoor circuit at any time. Nonetheless, there is still a marked tendency for the show season to peak at the end of the year, and the first quarter is still the best time to start the real novice. Courses tend to be lower and easier then, and the Preliminary jumper is not expected to be as far advanced.

In addition to the A.H.S.A. classifications of Preliminary, Intermediate and Open Jumpers based on money won, many U.S. horse shows also offer an Amateur-Owner section, for jumpers ridden by amateur owners or members of their immediate families. Amateur-Owner jumper courses start at 3 ft 6 in to 4 ft except at A-rated shows, where the maximum height for the first round is 4 ft 6 in. Hence at many shows, the Amateur-Owner Jumper Section is appropriate for the novice who has had some seasoning at unrecognized shows and is dealing satisfactorily with typical Preliminary courses. If you are not familiar with the show in question, however, it is a good idea to check with some fellow competitor who can tell you what to expect. At some of the larger shows, Amateur-Owner courses are very demanding, and it is of critical importance to avoid overfacing the young jumper in his first season.

Throughout this first season your aim should be to avoid any setbacks if at all possible, and this will inevitably require a certain amount of patience and will-power. Whenever you take a novice horse to a show you must always be prepared to come away without jumping should the conditions in any way be unsuitable. You can never do any harm by not jumping, and if you are not completely satisfied with the course, the fences or the going do not hesitate to withdraw. This can be a very hard decision to make, especially if you have come a long way at some expense, but it is so easy to jar a young horse on hard ground, or frighten him over a bad course, and it can take several weeks to restore his confidence. Indeed, the young horse who is given a fall early in his career may never fully recover his confidence later on.

6 From Novice to International Level

The outdoor show jumping season in Britain and most of the U.S. comes to an end in late September. Indoor show jumping is increasing in popularity, and now many riders keep their horses up and jump them through the winter. Horses will inevitably get tired and stale after a hard season's jumping and travelling, and before the development of the indoor show jumping circuit most horses used to get an enforced rest of three or four months. There is no doubt that most of the top horses used to last longer as a result. At the end of his first season your young horse should be turned out for a complete physical and mental rest, and this is best achieved by letting him down and allowing him as much freedom as possible. If you have the facilities, i.e. a large field with plenty of natural shelter, and the weather is not too severe, it is best to leave him out day and night. As the weather deteriorates you will find it necessary to feed him, and this good hard feed should keep him in good condition so that when he comes up from grass he will already be reasonably fit.

Eight to ten weeks before the outdoor season begins, you will need to get him in and start him off with some slow work. Many people believe that a couple of weeks' walking and jogging on the roads will help to harden a horse's legs. However, with the constant jar inflicted on a show jumper's feet and legs, today's hard road surfaces are perhaps liable to prove just another added stress. Instead, if you can find some hilly country with good going (not always easy at this time of the year), this is very hard to beat when it comes to strengthening his back and leg muscles, and getting him generally fit. The time and place to bring your horse out at the start of his second season will largely depend on how he finished the previous season. If you were satisfied with his progress and he finished on a good note you should be able to carry on from where you left off, perhaps giving him one or two preliminary outings at small shows as a pipe-opener.

Your second season is a continuation of the first, and should follow the same general pattern, progressing step by step while being careful not to overface the horse. Jumping at shows will now be a regular routine, and as long as things are going well it should not be necessary to jump in the periods between shows. Regular jumping puts a great strain on a horse's legs and feet, and he should now get all the experience he needs in the ring without the added wear and tear of jumping at home. Obviously before the first show of the season you will need to do a little bit of jumping to loosen him up and get him back on the job, but once the season is under way you will get plenty of jumping at shows. If anything goes wrong, as is likely from time to time, you will probably have to put in a little schooling at home to restore his confidence, but do not jump him unnecessarily.

A season's show jumping entails countless miles of travelling, and this can prove very exhausting for both horse and rider. Bearing this in mind it is well worth planning your itinerary to include a few three- or four-day shows where you can stable. This cuts out many hours of travelling and hanging about waiting to jump, and perhaps arriving home late at night. If you are already on the showground you will know whether or not the show is running late and therefore exactly what time you are jumping, and you will be able to plan accordingly. As soon as your class is over you can cool him off and put him back in his stable to rest and relax. When you are staying away at a show you should take every step to ensure his well being at all times, and try to keep as closely as possible to his home routine, with feeding times, grooming and exercise. A walk and a jog out in the morning is advisable if you are jumping late in the day, and he may need a little work on the flat.

In between shows it will do him good to have an hour's freedom in the paddock every day, weather permitting. Indeed, if he has a temperament problem and the weather is mild, he may even benefit from being left out all night. This is especially true in the southern United States where it is often too hot to turn horses out during the day. However, this depends largely on your horse, and on the type of pasture. Some horses tend to over-eat on rich grass and become gross and unfit; and it is obviously a mistake to leave them out for too long at a time. A contented horse is an easy one to work with, and from now on, as your show jumping becomes more intensive, you should seize every opportunity to let him relax and enjoy himself. Take him out for quiet rides in the country to keep him fresh and interested and to relieve the pressure which builds up as your season progresses. Do not however lose sight of the importance of your flat work. From now on your jumping courses will become more difficult and will require more balance and control. The various movements such as shoulder and quarters in, half passes, turns on the forehand and haunches, and leg yielding all help to keep your horse fit, supple and obedient. A few hours schooling on the flat each week will prove time well spent throughout your career.

In your second season you will have a wider selection of classes from which to choose, and your choice will largely depend on how well your horse is going. As the entries usually have to be made well in advance of the show it is not always easy to decide which classes will suit you, so you may have to enter for more than one class on the same day. This can obviously become rather expensive, but at this stage it is advisable to leave yourself with a choice of classes on the day of the show. Although most novice classes have their own height restrictions, as you graduate to small open classes your best guide when entering will be the amount of prize money offered in the schedule. Much too depends on who is building the courses. After a season's jumping at shows up and down the country you will come to know the different course-builders and their various methods of designing courses, some tending to build big, formidable courses, and others small trappy ones. A good course-builder is one who goes to neither extreme, and your choice of course-builder will play an important part in the selection of shows for your novice jumper.

The American rules still include a scoring table in which touches are scored (A.H.S.A. Table I) for the express benefit of the novice horse who should not be asked to jump either too high or too fast. Because straight Table I classes can become unwieldy at the large shows, however, the new Table IV Touches and Time classes have become increasingly popular in recent years. Under this table, touches are scored in the first round and no timings are taken; the jump-off, however, is against the clock with only knockdowns to count. This mixed table has proven very popular with riders and owners of Preliminary jumpers, and may also be used in amateur-owner and junior sections and at local shows.

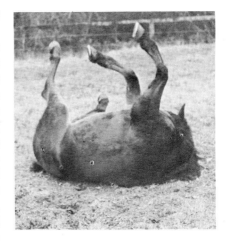

A contented horse enjoying a roll in the paddock.

A chance to relax between classes at the La Baule international show on the French coast.

The hazards of the puissance class.

Apart from the straight jump-off classes, there are a variety of good competitions suitable for the inexperienced horse who is graduating from novice classes. One such is the Accumulator competition, in which the course consists of seven single fences increasing in value and severity. This gives you the opportunity to jump a few bigger fences without the risk of getting into trouble with combinations. The test, or puissance, serves the same purpose provided you are prepared to withdraw after one or possibly two rounds, but in my opinion the puissance is a bad class in principle, at least for any horse which is naturally careful. To keep raising the fences each time a horse goes clear until they prove beyond his capabilities is contrary to all the principles you have applied to his training so far.

The Bareme C classes (A.H.S.A. Table III), in which seconds are added to the total time taken over the course for each fence knocked down, are also bad classes for a young horse. Though the courses are seldom very big, these classes usually develop into a flat-out gallop, and at best will serve no purpose in furthering his education. On the other hand the Bareme A classes (A.H.S.A. Table II, Sec.1), in which time, in the event of equality of faults, decides the winner, are a good introduction to jumping against the clock. The courses are usually bigger than those under Bareme C and a steady clear round will beat one with a fence down (providing there are no time faults) so time is less of a deciding factor. These classes provide a valuable opportunity to introduce the novice horse to the main ring at the big shows, as the courses are generally smaller than in the jump-off classes.

Another type of competition which I personally think is of great value in educating the young horse is the Six Bar competition. In this competition six upright obstacles are placed in a straight line with a distance of about 11 metres (2 strides) between them. As in your work down your jumping lanes at home this is a very good exercise both physically and mentally for your young horse, as he must use great concentration and physical effort in order to clear the six bars in a row. This is therefore quite a strain on a youngster, and you should be prepared to withdraw him after two or three rounds should the fences get too big.

In England there are now several of the 'permanent' courses which have materialised up and down the country since Hickstead first introduced the 'continental-type' fences in 1960. The natural hedges, ditches, banks and waters have for long been a feature of the continental European shows, but until recently most of the British shows were strictly confined to the national-type fences. As a result a horse jumping with the British team on his first trip to the Continent would be confronted with these strange permanent fences for the first time in his life at international level. Now however, novice

The Aachen show ground in West Germany showing the natural obstacles which were a feature of continental European show jumping before they were widely used in Britain and America.

If he is not used to permanent obstacles, the novice horse can often find these a problem.

horses have ample opportunity to get accustomed to these natural obstacles in miniature, and learn to accept them as normal fences, so that by the time they graduate to the international arenas they hold no terrors for them.

The trend towards continental-type obstacles and more permanent courses has also been apparent in the United States in recent years, though the trend appeared later and has been slower to establish itself. Development of Grand Prix jumping or international participation over European types of obstacles as the show jumper's ultimate goal has started working back to lower levels, and many shows now ask the young horse to jump a small water or perhaps a small bank.

Even though the natural obstacles the green horse will face in the show ring are not likely to be very difficult, it is nonetheless important to have prepared for them in advance, for the show ring is the wrong place to introduce the horse to a wholly new fence. Water-jumps in particular require very careful preparation, and you would be well advised to create or improvise a series of small ditches and water-jumps at home so that the young horse can become thoroughly familiar with the technique of negotiating this type of obstacle. At the beginning, these should be narrow enough for the horse to trot over—three or four feet is quite enough—and no more should be required until the horse can negotiate these miniature obstacles without the slightest confusion or awkwardness. Both waters and dry ditches should be deep enough and steep enough to surprise the horse if he should put a foot down short, however, for while you want him to be confident, you certainly do not want to teach him to be careless.

It is essential for a horse to be a good water-jumper, as you will meet this obstacle in every big class at international level, and a foot in the water will almost certainly cost you many a good win. Most novices jump well at the start of their careers as they tend to 'spook' and jump high over it. Any horse jumping enough height will have no difficulty in getting the spread, as even jumping a height of four feet he will cover up to sixteen feet in width with no effort. However, after meeting a few bad waters, a horse will quickly lose his respect for the obstacle, and start to jump low and flat, and to land on the tape or in the water. The lower photograph shows how a bad water jump encourages this. The water is a mere puddle with the tape

Two contrasting water-jumps. The upper photograph shows how a well-built jump encourages good jumping.

several inches beyond the edge of the water. The mare has not jumped any height at all, and is diving at the tape. A few years ago these badly built water jumps were all too common at the County Shows in England, and the British horses were notoriously bad water jumpers. There was also a tendency for riders to gallop their horses at water in sheer desperation to try and get them to jump the width. In fact this has exactly the opposite effect, as with too much pace a horse has not time to get in the air and has to jump flat. A quiet collected approach allows the horse to jump balanced with his hocks under him so that he can get the required height. Once a horse starts going in the water it is very difficult to correct it, but jumping water with a pole over it will get him in the air. The upper photograph shows the same mare jumping a beautifully built water jump in Rome, and illustrates how a well constructed and clearly defined obstacle will be treated with respect.

If you are lucky enough to have a really good horse it is easy to become over-ambitious with him in his second season, particularly with the glamour of the international circuit perhaps just around the corner. When he is going well the novice courses will seem all too simple, and you are likely to be tempted to start him in a big competition before he is ready. Remember your horse is not a machine and will have his off days, and even the best riders make mistakes, so it is asking for trouble to risk frightening him over bigger fences until he has had a thorough grounding over courses well within his scope.

If anything should go wrong and he loses his confidence you must always be prepared to drop him back to a few smaller classes, or perhaps miss a show or two and concentrate on repairing damage at home. Try to decide exactly when things started to go wrong, and if you can determine the source of the trouble it will give you some idea of how to rectify it. Sometimes it is obviously the result of one bad mistake or perhaps even a fall. Frequently though the loss of confidence is gradual, and accumulative, and the cause more difficult to define. The origin in this case could be a series of smaller mistakes, such as the horse dropping short on the back rail of spread fences, or not being able to make the distance in doubles and trebles. These errors are usually caused through lack of impulsion, or through jumping too high and not covering enough ground. Once a horse starts to lose confidence he will tend to 'back off' his fences and so lose impulsion, thus getting into yet more trouble, and if not corrected he may lose his nerve altogether. This is particularly likely to happen with a naturally careful horse which dislikes hitting fences, or a short mover. In this case the only thing to do is to go right back

The horse lacks confidence in his approach to the fence, and in 'backing off' has lost the impulsion to jump it.

to the early stages of his training over small fences, and here your jumping-lanes can be put to good use. Keep the distances accurate to start with, and as he gains confidence you can gradually extend the distances and so encourage him to lengthen his stride and cover more ground. A well built spread fence at the end of the lane, as long as it is not too big, will help to restore his confidence over spreads.

At the other extreme there is the over-bold horse who is inclined to be careless. Very often he is too much on his forehand with his hocks behind him, which forces him to jump long and flat and so cover too much ground without getting enough height. Here again a jumping lane will prove invaluable, but this time you should keep the distances short, so that he will have to use his back and jump off his hocks. Jumping in and out of a short double of uprights is also a good exercise to make him shorten his stride and round himself. There has always been a good deal of controversy about schooling over fixed fences and iron bars, and such training methods as rapping. Due to the laths on the fences when show jumping was in its infancy, an ultra-careful horse was more successful than a bold one. Dislodging one of the laths cost half a fault; the courses were much smaller than is general today, and rapping was an accepted form of schooling. There is no doubt that it is still used at home by many people, although any such form of schooling at shows is strictly forbidden by the B.S.J.A. Throughout this section of the book I have emphasised the need to build up a horse's confidence with firm but gentle handling; to resort to such methods as rapping is surely to destroy this confidence. Furthermore, with courses as big as they are today it is essential that a horse has time to use himself fully over each fence, and that he should not be panicked into snatching his feet out of the way. A horse which is continually careless is unlikely to win consistently at international level, but it is possible to give him a reminder simply by building a fence in such a way that he will have it down either in front or behind. However, with a good horse this should not be necessary.

If you are in any doubt as to the cause of your particular trouble, or how best to deal with it, do not hesitate to seek expert advice. Even the most experienced riders need somebody 'on the ground' to correct their faults from time to time, and an onlooker can very often *see* what a rider cannot always feel from the saddle. It is very important to correct these mistakes, however small, in the early stages before they develop into a habit.

After a good winter's rest your preparation for your young horse's third season will be the same as for the previous year, probably starting off with one or two small classes to warm up. This third season is the most crucial in your show jumper's career, as he should now graduate to the big classes and it is only now that you will be able to tell whether or not he has the capabilities of jumping big courses consistently. For this reason it is vital to take every precaution against any possible setback at this stage, and to plan your itinerary with the utmost care and consideration. From now on you should start to reap the reward of your previous years' patient training and planning, but even now winning should be of secondary importance. Education should still take precedence over the chances of honour and glory in your selection of shows and classes.

The size of the courses you are likely to meet now will leave very little room for error, and will therefore require a great deal more accuracy and precision than the novice courses. In show jumping, unlike many other sports, a single mistake is usually enough to cost you the competition and there is no second chance. I have already emphasised the importance of walking the course, and in top class competition today with the standard so high the courses require the maximum concentration from the rider. Every detail must be carefully studied, and the rider must decide in advance how to ride each fence individually and the course as a whole, while at the same time allowing for any unforeseen circumstances. The rider must always be prepared to change his mind in case of any emergency, as he cannot always predict accurately the reactions of his horse. This applies particularly to combination fences, and to single fences with related distances, as much will depend on how your horse jumps the first element. For example, should your horse 'back off' the first element of a double or a treble he will require more 'pushing' in the middle to regain impulsion. Conversely, if he jumps in too far you will need to 'take a pull'.

When you pace out the distances between related fences you should be able to decide how many strides your horse will take and whether to shorten or lengthen. A few of the top riders rely entirely on their sense of stride and do not bother to walk distances beyond about 16 yards, but unless you have an exceptional eye, it is safer to plan in advance. It is, however, a very dangerous practice to commit yourself irrevocably to a certain plan. For example if you have decided to take four strides between the fences and your horse does not jump the first one as well as you anticipated you may find you are forced to take five short strides. Here your reactions will have to be very quick and you must make your decision and act upon it in a split second. If you wait a couple of strides and then decide to shorten, it will be too late. Such immediate reactions and quick thinking, together with instant obedience from the horse, are essential ingredients for successful show jumping.

When planning how to ride your course you must obviously take into consideration the different types of fences, the size and shape of the arena, the position of the collecting ring, the rise and fall of the ground, and the going. All these factors will have a bearing on how you should ride the course as a whole. When jumping against the clock you should pay particular attention to the relative positions of the fences and map out the shortest route between them. Remember that the fastest times are usually put up by the riders who take the shortest line, and not by those who gallop. There may be somewhere on the course where you can save time by cutting inside another fence, but always make a careful study of the plan of the course beforehand to see whether or not there is a line you must follow. It is obviously a big advantage to be drawn last in a speed class or a timed jump off so that you know exactly what you have to beat and how many risks you have to take. If you are drawn first you will

Pacing the distance between related fences (see p. 118).

have to rely on your own judgement as to how fast you can ride the course without losing your accuracy. It is then left to the opposition to try and better your time.

Obviously the rate of progress from novice to international level or from preliminary to open will vary enormously from one horse to another, sometimes by as much as two or three years. The show jumper which has been brought on slowly will very often last longer than the one who has come up quickly and is an overnight sensation. When your horse has proved himself by performing consistently in big classes he should be ready for the international circuit, and here again your choice of shows is important. If you can get an invitation to compete at some of the smaller international shows, with permission from your own federation, you will find them a good introduction to international competition, and a stepping stone to the bigger C.S.I.O.s. The moment for which you have been waiting,

This makes it all worthwhile: British Nations' Cup team, Aga Khan trophy, Dublin.

opposite: Gato Montez, being jumped at Hickstead by Alvarez Cervera of Spain.

working and planning since the day you selected your young horse as a potential international has at last arrived when you are selected by your federation to represent your country in an official team. This is the highest honour which can be bestowed upon a rider, and when you have selected, produced and made your own horse there is no greater satisfaction. It is now that all the long hours of patient schooling, the careful planning and the personal sacrifices will prove worthwhile.

7 Travel, Care and Protection

Travelling efficiently with horses is born of experience, and only from travelling with your own horse will you gain the necessary experience required to organise and plan a long trip, and to cope with the endless problems which seem to arise. The most important factor in travelling is the comfort of your horse, particularly on a long trip. After two or three seasons' jumping both you and your horse should be well accustomed to the long hours spent on the roads journeying from one show to another. This is especially true in the United States, where distances are vast by British standards, and it is relatively commonplace to transport your horse 800 or 1000 miles to a circuit of shows. In England, the equivalent of this is the trip over the channel to the Continent, though of course, showing abroad is still quite a different thing from competing in your own country, even though the physical distance from home may be shorter. Although travel today has been greatly improved what with air transport and ultra-modern horse-boxes, there are always seemingly unavoidable delays en route, particularly at the national borders, and it pays dividends to plan accordingly and be prepared. It is seldom possible to get your horse out of the box during these hold ups, but you must leave yourself enough room to be able to check on his well-being and change his rugs when necessary. Bandages should always be put on with an even pressure; make sure the tapes are not too tight. Bandage from the knee or hock right down to the coronet, with plenty of gamgee or cotton wool beneath. This should supply the necessary protection. It is a good idea when travelling to take all the bandages off every six to eight hours and to give the legs a brisk rub with the hands before replacing them. Of course, this is not always possible.

There is a variety of travelling equipment available from most saddlers, such as knee boots and hock boots, which give additional protection, but in using these one has to be very careful that the straps do not chafe and rub the skin. If you use padding to prevent this be sure that the straps are not too tight or they will stop the circulation. There is also a kind of gaiter boot designed to take the place of bandages. These are conveniently quick to put on, but are usually lined with foam rubber or sheepskin and tend to be too hot. A lightweight tailguard over a tail bandage is a good idea as long as it is not too thick and bulky, but do not forget to remove the tail guard and bandage when you change the leg bandages.

The correct way to bandage— make sure the tapes are not too tight.

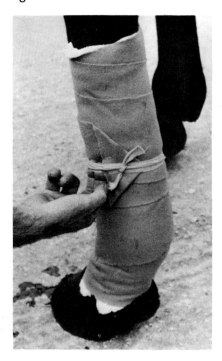

In Britain a roller is used to keep the rug from slipping, and since this again must not be too tight, it should be fitted with a breastplate to stop it slipping back. The practice in the United States is not as different as the terminology. The American jumper's clothing consists of a thin stable sheet under a wool blanket, held in place by a surcingle or body roller if the blanket does not have surcingles attached, as is usually the case. It is uncommon to see a breastplate used in conjunction with the roller, however. After a long day's travel a quick dressing over will freshen your horse up, and a walk out in a halter will help take the stiffness out of him. After watering and feeding him leave him alone to rest and relax, as the continual motion of travelling is very tiring for a horse. Feeding on these long trips should be light and plain. A good motto is little and often, and the same applies to the water—just a few pints at a time should be sufficient. This not only lessens the chance of colic but also breaks the monotony of the journey. Hay can be fed in small amounts, but it is a mistake to let a horse stuff himself from an unlimited supply.

When packing for these trips you must take everything you ordinarily use at home, plus a few extra things you might need such as additional tack, a spare set of horse shoes, and extra rugs for all weathers. You will probably need only a fraction of what you take, but it is better to be prepared for any event. It is essential to have some form of veterinary chest with the basic medicines and first aid equipment. It is more convenient to use small packing cases rather than one large trunk, particularly if you are travelling alone. Small containers are handier to move around and easier to unpack if you need something in a hurry. Much depends on how much room you have in your box and how long you are going to be away, but when possible you should take enough feed to last until you get

opposite: Mister Softee and David Broome, of Great Britain, at Hickstead.

Ready to travel.

home. If this is not possible you should at least take enough to last you a few days after your arrival, and then you can mix the strange food with your own and so make the changeover gradual. When you can take only a limited amount give preference to your own prepared feeds, bran, chaff, sugar beet or other concentrates which you feed at home. Oats and hay are always more readily available away from home, and are approximately the same the world over.

A sound knowledge of feeding and stable management, and of basic veterinary care, is essential not only when travelling but in the general care of your horse throughout his career. Feeding is obviously of the utmost importance and you will have no trouble in getting advice on how to feed your horse. Most people have their own particular ideas on feeding, and consider their own methods and their special brand of feed the very best. However you will have to discover what is best for *your* horse, and what is most suitable to his type and his temperament and to the amount of work he is doing. Temperament is a major factor to be taken into consideration when feeding. While one horse may take any amount of 'hot' feed without it going to his head, just a few pounds of oats will render another unmanageable. To feed such a horse too hard will only necessitate additional work, resulting in further strain on his legs and feet. Your feed then will depend on your horse's work and behaviour, so never be afraid to adjust it accordingly.

In order to get the maximum benefit from your different types of feed it is a good guide to remember that the ratio between phosphorus and calcium is 4 to 1. Bearing this in mind you should be able to work out a correctly balanced diet to suit your particular horse. Basically the good plain feeds, chaff, bran and oats, are the best, as with these you know exactly what your horse is getting. You should always aim to buy only the highest quality. Horse feed is expensive, but it is false economy to buy second rate feed as there will only be a large proportion of waste. Horse cubes (pelletized food) are a convenient way of feeding but fed on their own must become very boring. You can add a little maize or sugar beet (soaked) to make a change, and give at least one damp feed a day. The most satisfactory way to give the night feed is to crumble the bran with hot water and then mix it into the rest of the feed. A good salt lick is a must, and from time to time you may need to feed minerals as a supplement. In this case you should find out through your vet exactly what your horse is lacking and so feed that particular mineral in concentrate rather than one of the multi-mineral tonics.

Before you tip a feed into the manger make sure he has finished up the last one. Never feed on top of leftovers. If you have a shy feeder it is a good idea to take his feed away from him if he hasn't finished up after an hour or so, and give him a fresh one at the next feed time. To have the same feed left in the manger day and night will only discourage him further. If a horse is off his feed temporarily plain feed will be more likely to tempt him than a manger full of rich additives. A pick of grass or a pound or two of carrots each day may act as an appetiser.

Regular feeding times are advisable, but when away at a show you may have to adjust these according to when you are jumping. The main meals, breakfast and the night feeds, will probably be the same, but it may be necessary to split the lunch feed into two small ones, one a couple of hours before you jump and the other just after. The number of feeds per day is a matter of personal choice. Some stables feed only two meals a day, and some three or four. There are varying opinions about feeding hay too, some giving it with the morning and evening feeds, while others leave a permanent supply in the stable day and night. We always give three feeds a day at approximately 8 o'clock, 1 o'clock and 6 o'clock, feed hay only with the evening meal, and then leave the horses to rest through the night. Feeding a horse is basically a matter of common sense, and you will not go far wrong if you always feed plenty of good quality plain food.

The general care of your horse is obviously of the utmost importance right from the start of his career, and when he is travelling and jumping at international level it is even more so. You should try to plan each day in advance, allowing yourself plenty of time for travelling, exercising, grooming and feeding without having to short-cut. When going to a show it is advisable to allow extra time in case of any emergency such as a breakdown. It is better to arrive early even if it means waiting for a while before your class starts than to find you have not enough time to ride your horse in and warm him up properly. You should know roughly how long you will need to work him, either at a show or at home on a normal day, and allow yourself plenty of time in case you find he needs a little extra work.

Riding-in to ensure that your horse is supple and obedient.

Grooming your horse is important and has a twofold purpose—to clean him and to inspect him. If you groom your horse thoroughly every day you will immediately recognise any strange lumps, bumps or swellings should they materialise—and they possibly will. It can take you anything up to an hour to groom a horse really thoroughly, and do not forget to oil his feet. This is the most important part of your grooming routine and should be done every day without fail. Clean the foot right out, making quite sure he has not picked up anything hard or sharp, and then oil the foot both on the sole and the frog and around the outside of the hoof. A good quality animal fat is the best for this as it replaces the natural oil taken out of the hoof when shoeing and keeps the hoof and frog soft and pliable. Check the shoes, making sure that they have not sprung or twisted and that there are no clenches up. If the shoes are drilled for studs, which is a good idea, be sure to check the stud holes too, particularly before a show, making sure that there are no small stones lodged in them.

Last but not least is the care of your tack. This again is for two reasons, as not only should you clean your tack but you should check it over for any weaknesses in the leather or the stitching, or in the buckles, bits and stirrups. It is of the utmost importance to maintain your tack in sound condition, and this side of the stable routine is all too often neglected.

When looking after your own horse it is essential that you should be able to see at a glance if he is off colour, and to be able to treat the common minor ailments yourself. A great deal of the basic veterinary care is common sense, and you can also learn a tremendous amount from watching and listening to other people more experienced than you. Whenever you have to call a vet never be afraid to ask him how he has diagnosed the trouble, what he is doing to treat it, and why. Whenever possible, ask him if you can give the necessary treatment under his supervision, and you will soon gain the confidence and experience to be able to cope with at least the minor emergencies, such as colic, a chill, or a slight virus infection. At the first sign of discomfort or loss of appetite you should take the horse's temperature which is normal at just under 101°F. If it is up a point or two you know all is not well, and if you are in any doubt whatsoever as to the cause of the trouble or the treatment do not hesitate to call your vet.

A well equipped veterinary chest is essential both for travelling and for use at home, but make absolutely sure that you know the correct use for all the contents. There is absolutely no point in filling it up with a collection of medicines and injections with which you are not familiar, and this can be dangerous. The basic essentials are a colic remedy, a diuretic to induce staling and keep the kidneys working (these are particularly advisable on a long journey), some form of penicillin or antibiotics to combat temperatures, an anti-tetanus injection if your horse has not been immunised, something for a cough or respiratory troubles, and of course a thermometer. For simple first aid you will include the usual sprays, ointments and powders, for minor cuts and bruises, a good eye

Oiling the foot is an essential part of the daily grooming routine.

ointment in case of a bump or something in the eye, poultices for big legs and joints, and a plentiful supply of gamgee, cotton wool, bandages and Elastoplast.

Competitors at U.S. and international shows are cautioned that they must be familiar with A.H.S.A. and F.E.I. drug rules, for jumpers are eligible for drug-testing, and almost any drug that shows up in the urine sample (except for phenylbutazone, which is legal) will render the trainer, owner, and rider liable to disqualification and penalty, just as at the race track. Most colic remedies and 'tonics' include prohibited substances, and even vitamin B-complex supplements and penicillin-procaine may not be administered within twenty-four hours of competition. Be certain that you are familiar both with any pertinent drug rule and the contents of your medicine chest.

Your tack is a matter of personal choice, and you will have to bit your horse according to his mouth and your hands, and how he is going for you. As I said earlier you should try and keep your equipment as simple as possible and a plain snaffle is the ideal. Unfortunately however it is not always possible to gain the instant obedience which is essential in big competitions with such a mild bit. You may therefore find it necessary to ride him in something more severe, but always try the simplest gear first. You will get into far more trouble if your horse is over-bitted and comes off the bridle than if he is too strong, and it will be more difficult to correct. It is a good idea to do your exercising and schooling in a plain snaffle and to keep any extra aids you might need for your competition work. In this way you will have to ride your horse more positively to make him work, and you will find him that much more responsive and obedient in the ring.

Brushing boots and overreach boots (bell boots) are essential on some horses and you will have to decide whether or not your horse needs any such protection. Make sure that the boots are well made to give the protection where necessary, and never put them on too tight. If your horse has to stand around for a while between classes or before a jump off take his boots off or at least loosen the straps to give his legs a rest. Bandages are sometimes used for support, particularly when jumping on hard ground but great care must be taken to ensure an even pressure. If fastened with tapes these should not be tied tightly. The bandages should come right down to the fetlock joint where the support is most needed, and again these should not be left on for any long period. Remember that bandages, even with gamgee or cotton wool, do not give as much protection against a horse brushing or striking himself as well fitting, lined, leather boots.

Studs are considered an essential item in Britain, and are becoming more and more common in the U.S. as well. The size and the type of your studs will depend on the state of the ground. For deep slippery going you will need large square studs, and for ground that is hard you will need small sharp ones. When the going is good the small studs are best in front with larger ones behind. There are various different ideas as to where the studs should be placed in the shoe, some

The horse, through being seriously over-bitted, has come behind the bit.

A good set of brushing boots.

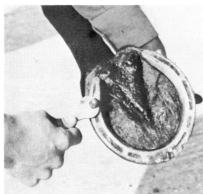

Inserting a stud in the outside quarter of the shoe.

preferring two in each shoe, one at each heel, but here there is always a danger that he might tread on himself with the inside stud. An alternative which I prefer is to put one stud on the outside quarter of each shoe. If you have any hard road surfaces on your way to the ring it is better to leave the studs out until you reach the collecting ring, as it must be difficult for a horse to walk on a hard surface in 'high heels', so to speak.

In between shows, and particularly after a long tiring journey, let him relax in the paddock for an hour or two each day. To keep him fit he will need to be exercised every day, but it should not be necessary to work him hard.

As soon as the season is finished he should be turned out for a complete rest. As I said in an earlier chapter he will benefit most from this rest if you can leave him out day and night so that he has a complete break both physically and mentally. As long as he has some good hard dry feed inside him, and perhaps a New Zealand rug if the weather is bad, he will be able to stand the cold and wet. When it is time to get him in again you should allow yourself a week before you start any serious work. During this week you will need to worm him, get him shod, and have a vet look at his teeth. These will probably need rasping, and you should check at the same time that no wolf teeth have developed. It may also be a good idea to have your vet take a blood count, as with so much artificial fertilising and lack of natural grazing nowadays there is a tendency for horses to become

When the horse is turned out at the end of the season, he may need a New Zealand rug.

anaemic. After this week of preparation, during which you will only need to walk him out, or perhaps put him on the lunge for a jog round, you can then start in earnest your programme to get him fit and ready for the season to come.

Throughout this section of the book I have emphasised that there can be no short cuts to success. I know there will be many disappointments and setbacks on the hard road to the top, but believe me, your patience will be rewarded when you have finally reached your goal.

Show Organisation

by Raymond Brooks-Ward

This short article is not intended as a comprehensive practical guide which will enable any inexperienced horse lover to set up a large horse show—of course there is no substitute for experience, and particularly experience gained working with people who really know what they are doing. There are not that many of them. But some ideas of the general principles involved will assist not only aspiring organisers, but competitors who have to understand some of the practical difficulties, and also spectators, whose pleasure can only be increased by knowing something of what goes on behind the scenes. Many references are made to large shows but the principles apply just as much to small ones, where the organisers can make or break an event. Indeed, they apply in large measure on both sides of the Atlantic, though there are differences in terminology, procedural details, and the extent to which various of the desirable practices are mandatory under the rules.

The great period of expansion for British and American show jumping was after World War II; other writers in this book describe how at this time the English-speaking world started to see the great possibilities of the more imaginative approach to the sport already commonplace on the Continent. But just as, in Britain, it was Sir Michael Ansell who among others realised that show jumping could be almost as big a spectator sport as football, so too it was he and a few other imaginative organisers who realised the dangers of overdoing the jumping. Hundreds of horse show committees had changed their schedules overnight: here was a cheap way of entertaining the horse-loving public—until the spectators were subjected to endless, and therefore boring, jumping events often lasting for four hours without a break.

Sir Michael's maxim was, 'No jumping event should last more than an hour and a quarter'; he understood that a show must provide ever-changing entertainment if it is to succeed, and the Horse of the Year Show in London was to prove that his philosophy was right. It is still a basic formula upon which many other indoor shows are modelled, starting off with a jumping class, often a novel one with riders choosing their own course against the clock; from there to the heavy horses in their musical drive. The final judging of a show class is followed by the rip-roaring Pony Club Mounted Games and then a parade of horse personalities. Finally everyone settles back in their seats for the main event of the night, the big jumping contest. Now one sees the result of months of careful planning to provide the right

opposite: A well-run indoor show —the R.A.I. hall in Amsterdam during the Jumping Amsterdam show.

balance of events just as the old-time managers of music-halls arranged their programmes with changes of scene and tempo, finishing with the 'Top of the Bill'.

Like everything that is well done, running a successful horse show, indoor or outdoor, looks all too easy. But of course it isn't. The essence of the operation is realistic planning. This starts with the schedule, which apart from being submitted to and approved by the governing body, should itself be realistic.

Let us consider first what principles should be followed in choosing what competitions should be included in a show. Your choice of classes will depend partly on where the show is being held—it should be planned bearing in mind the kind of spectators and competitors it is likely to attract. This is particularly important in the United States where there are very considerable regional variations in the way shows are built up, and where distances are so much greater than in individual European countries. If possible there should be a good number of leading horses and riders; on the other hand the sport would probably have no present, and certainly no future, without the many novice owners and horses; so there should be classes to encourage them too. If you are unable to include special competitions for them they should be offered special prizes.

The entry fees should be as low as possible, particularly where young riders are concerned. Similarly, prizes should be as high as can be managed. Entries should be closed as near to the show date as possible, although early enough to allow the preparation of an accurate timetable and catalogue.

It is also worth remembering that competitors like to know who is judging; this will have a bearing on the entries received. So make arrangements for your judges well in advance so that their names can be included in the schedule. Bear in mind that if there are long periods of continuous jumping, there should be at least two judges, so that they are not working for too long without a break. The need for colleagues to act as deputies applies also to time judges.

Born optimists will be convinced they can jump fifty horses in an hour; over a course of moderate length twenty-five or thirty is a more realistic estimate. So, for that number, with one jump-off against the clock, an hour and a quarter should be allowed. There are various points which can be usefully borne in mind when the schedule is being drawn up—classes may be limited in terms of the number of entries; competitors should be limited to no more than three horses. A note can be included in the regulations to the effect that, where a certain standard has been reached, horses making more than a certain number of faults may be retired.

The course-builder can help by placing the start and finish near the collecting ring and by raising the easily manipulated fences in the jump-off. A wall which has to be demolished for a new layer to be put underneath to raise the height can cause a lengthy pause, especially if, as often happens, the vital components are providing seating accomodation for the spectators. Again, a knowledgeable course-builder will produce just the right number of clear rounds— too many competitors in a jump-off can delay matters.

A most valuable asset, for the organiser, is a good collecting ring steward who can rule firmly but politely over the competitors. An order of jumping should always be drawn up in advance and adhered to. The collecting ring steward can make up or lose time, without the audience knowing what is going on. For instance, if you are running late, one horse can be sent in down one side, while the competitor in the ring is jumping the last fence on the other side. The judges can help by ringing the bell promptly at the start of a round and by bringing in a 'standard' when the prize money has been filled up. This should apply in major classes where the horses have, if anything, too much jumping; the competitors will see little point in going on after a horse has hit two fences and there are already eight clear rounds. Standards are never popular in novice classes, and anyway these classes should always be put on in the morning with plenty of time allowed for disasters before the majority of the public arrive.

In Britain shows do not usually finish after 10.30 pm. This does not always apply on the Continent, where many shows go on until the early hours of the morning; certainly audiences in continental Europe seem quite prepared to stay much later than British audiences. An example, and indeed one of the best-run European shows, is Jumping Amsterdam, where the programme starts at 8.00 in the evening with two jumping classes, and the displays take place after that.

Stabling facilities in days gone by — Walter Winans's opulent boxes at the International Horse Show, London 1911.

A timetable of sorts should be included in the schedule, particularly when it is likely that competitors will be travelling to the show on the same day: obviously where longer distances are involved, such as is commonly the case in North America, most competitors will stay overnight at the site of the show. If it happens that the timetable will not accomodate the number of entries received, the show organisers can consider erecting another ring, if the space and the materials are available; or making an earlier start. This obviously requires that the competitors be given adequate warning.

In addition to rings for the competitions themselves, show authorities must of course also provide practice jumps—horses need to be warmed up before a competition just like any athlete. The practice jumps must be on ground that will not cut up; there should be an upright and a spread. There should also be enough space for a number of horses to manoeuvre.

Efficient management of the timetable depends also on effective organisation of all the peripheral matters on any show ground. It is perhaps as well to remember that the commentator can make or break a show. Endless chitter-chatter and in-jokes about the

Covered temporary stabling of the kind found at many British shows.

competitors' antecedents may seem funny to the initiated, but will not mean much to the majority of the spectators. A commentary should not distract the horses and riders during the actual jumping, or anticipate the judges' decisions; it should be factual and concise, exciting when necessary, and above all in a language which everybody can understand.

A show executive must make sufficient arrangements for the safety of both public and competitors. There should always be a vet in attendance; and everyone involved should know what to do if there is an accident to a horse (or rider) in the ring; injuries to horses, and the action often necessary to deal with the situation, can be distressing to spectators, and a canvas screen should be available for use if necessary.

If the show facilities are to be set up on the day before the event there may be a need for security arrangements overnight. In any case, police, fire, and ambulance authorities must be brought in. The police are invaluable, both to ensure trouble-free arrival of competitors and public, and to help organize the public once they are there. Entrance and exit facilities to the show area are important—if several hundred horse-boxes all arrive at one narrow gate at the same time on the morning of a show, chaos will ensue; it will be well on in the day before the competitors are in the show ground, let alone negotiating jumps in the ring. Adequate parking space must be provided, both for horse-boxes and for the public, on ground which will not turn into a quagmire if it rains.

The show authorities also have a duty to discourage the dropping of litter on the show ground—it will be obvious even to the most thoughtless spectator that broken bottles and tin cans, besides being unsightly, can be highly dangerous to people and horses alike. Toilet facilities must be provided for public and competitors; there should be adequate catering facilities, and water near the stabling for the horses.

In Britain sponsorship now plays an important part in any show. Twenty years ago sponsorship was running at something like £20,000 a year. Today, in show jumping, dressage, and horse-trials it is approaching the half-million mark. In fact it is fair to say that the majority of shows could not exist without this kind of financial interest. We have seen all too often that sponsorship can fail, for a number of reasons. Sometimes the sport has accepted everything the sponsor is prepared to give, and has done nothing in return. Perhaps the sponsoring firm has gone into a sport for which it is totally unsuited because of one of the management's interest in a particular event. In the right sort of marriage a sponsor should see a good return on his money and, most important, the sport should benefit from the financial support it receives.

Let us take the Royal Windsor Horse Show as a typical example. It is the last of the British pure horse shows held out of doors; that is to say, its schedule is most comprehensive and contains classes for every single type of horse and pony. There was the possibility that it would be forced to close unless help came from a company. Merck, Sharp and Dohme, one of the largest pharmaceutical companies in the world, sponsored the show in 1973 and 1974. That is to say, they not only presented the prize money, but also provided the very necessary finance to run it as well. This is a happy relationship: the sponsor is able to call classes after certain products and to have facilities for entertaining guests; but at the same time the show authorities are allowed complete and autonomous power in the staging of the event. It is important that the sponsorship should not be too obtrusive, but at the same time the company involved should get a fair return in the press and if possible on television for the efforts involved.

With the sponsorship of individual classes it is more than ever essential to plan the days' efforts, so that if a company is presenting the major money in a show-jumping class, that event should take place at peak audience time. Shows have only themselves to blame if they run so late that the sponsor is the only person left on the ground in the darkness to present the awards. The following year the show will almost certainly find itself without that particular sponsor.

Show Management in the United States

In a general way, the same evolution in jumping competitions that has taken place in England has also occurred in the United States, but its occurrence has been slower, later and less profound. This is due to the fact that the U.S. horse show has typically offered a greater variety of different divisions for different types of horses, and also shown greater regional variation than its British counterpart. Jumpers have usually been included on most programmes, but they share the spotlight with hunters in the East, with saddle horses in the South and with Quarter Horses in the West. And whatever the area, a single show ring is often used for all classes, including many smaller divisions in addition to the area's dominant ones—equitation and pony classes, harness horses, pleasure classes, all the various breed divisions, and so forth.

Thus the U.S. show manager is often limited both by the physical area in which he must work which is often no larger than the typical indoor arena even when the horse show is outdoors, and also by the extremely complex and detailed rules promulgated by his national federation, the American Horse Shows Association. The rules section of the current A.H.S.A. Rule Book runs to more than two hundred pages of fine print and covers no less than twenty-three different divisions, from Appaloosa to Western. The Jumper Division rules stipulate in considerable detail what the show manager must do—how many classes he must offer in order to qualify for a particular classification, how much prize money, even how many fences he must provide in the warm-up area.

This proliferation of rules has been an inevitable consequence of the vast physical distances in the United States, which enormously complicate the business of establishing a single national standard or practice for anything, show jumping included.

For the same reason, much more of U.S. show jumping's evolution has been accomplished through legislation than has been the case in England, where the force of a single personality like Sir Michael Ansell's, or Col. Jack Talbot-Ponsonby's, or a single televised horse show such as the Horse of the Year Show or White City, could readily influence an entire nation. In general, the U.S. West Coast shows operate with little knowledge or regard of what happens on the East Coast, some 2500 miles away, and thus it is only through the imposition of relatively detailed rules by the A.H.S.A. that any degree of national uniformity has been achieved.

The two key bits of legislation that have been most influential in bringing U.S. jumper classes into the modern era have been the requirement for 30% of the fences to be of the 'spread' variety (height plus width), and the imposition of minimum standards for any competition termed a Grand Prix. In the long run, the latter change may prove even more influential in bringing the United States into the European pattern of show jumping, for it has encouraged shows to abandon their little permanent show ring with its short, eight-fence courses, and to develop a larger outside area in which truly European-type courses could be constructed.

Much of the credit for the development of Grand Prix jumping in the United States must go to D. Gerry Baker of Gates Mills, Ohio, who returned from a trip to Europe in 1964 with the determination to obtain financing for and then produce a truly European type of Grand Prix as the feature of the local Cleveland show he managed. This was the origin of the Cleveland Grand Prix, which started in 1965 and since then has drawn almost a dozen imitators willing to meet the stringent requirements that were subsequently drawn up by the A.H.S.A.

Ordinarily, the American Grand Prix Jumping competition is accorded a session or even a day all to itself, and constitutes an entire afternoon of show jumping. Even under these circumstances it has become apparent, from time to time, that there can be such a thing as too much jumping. In consequence, there is now a trend towards qualifying a certain number of horses (fifteen or twenty) for the final competition, reflecting a growing appreciation of the basic soundness of Sir Michael Ansell's feelings about the limitations of the public's attention span. However, his conviction that jumping competitions should never exceed an hour and a quarter is very frequently violated in the United States, especially early in the year when Preliminary jumpers are starting their show careers over relatively low fences. The reason for this is not that American audiences are more long-suffering than their British counterparts, but simply because many American horse shows virtually ignore the spectator altogether, and are run for the exhibitors entirely out of monies provided by the exhibitors in the form of entry fees.

Needless to say, most American jumper owners are anxious eventually to phase out the practice of competing for their own money as it were, and eventually a solution may be found in America as it has in Great Britain in form of sponsorship by commercial firms. This pattern has already been followed by a few major shows, such as the New York National, which has found sponsors for a large proportion of its international and national jumper competitions as well as some important classes in other divisions as well. Pressure from exhibitors for an A.H.S.A. rule establishing a minimum ratio of entry fees to prize money offered has been slowly increasing for a long time, especially at the larger shows. Until such legislation is adopted however—and it may be a long time—shows will simply have to try to keep prize money as high and entry fees as low as is economically possible, and to let the popularity of their show with exhibitors reflect how well they have succeeded.

Looking to the future, there can be no doubt that American show managers will lean more and more in the direction of European-type jumping competitions and show organisation. The success and influence of the U.S. Equestrian Team, the relative proximity of the major European shows through air travel and the example of successful Grand Prix competitions in the United States will all continue to nudge the United States towards fuller acceptance of European patterns, and tend to narrow the gap between Europe, Britain and the North America more and more in years to come.

Course Building

by Pamela Carruthers

Until recently the general public had little idea how much work goes into designing a show-jumping course, and for that matter, until recent years not much did. Before World War II in Britain the sort of course you would usually find at a horse show comprised just two or three fences down each side of the ring, and one up the middle.

In the United States a very similar situation prevailed; twice around the outside for a total of eight fences, or once and a half around and down the middle, perhaps over a combination of three verticals—these were the show jumpers' standard fare. There were exceptions, of course; the late Ned King's courses at the New York National were famous for both their attractiveness and their difficulty, and shows like Devon and Olympia always offered something out of the ordinary for jumpers. On average, however, courses stayed pretty much the same, week after week, until the horses could almost jump them blindfold.

This was rather tedious for everyone, even including the competitors, and it would have been particularly so for the average man-in-the-street—but he never came to the horse shows anyway in those days. Horse shows on the Continent drew sizeable crowds to witness military jumping in the 1930s, and continental European courses compared very favourably in character with those in use today. However, the typical British or U.S. civilian jumper considered that style of course strictly in terms of military or 'trick' jumping, if indeed he was familiar with it at all. And the typical spectator at the average U.S. or British show before World War II was either a competitor, or a member of his family.

A number of developments in the immediate post-war years precipitated a dramatic change in courses in a relatively short period of time. The post-war boom in riding as a recreation, the advent of television coverage that could bring show jumping to the attention of the average sports lover, and especially the inclusion of civilian riders in the international teams all conspired to place a whole new set of demands on the course-designer. In Britain, among Colonel Michael Ansell's many contributions to the development of show jumping was the essential realisation that Britain must change her style and standard of course-building if her riders were to compete on equal terms with those of the leading European nations.

In the old days there was so little variation in courses that the ring crews could virtually improvise them in the absence of the steward whose responsibility the courses often were, and there was usually a

opposite: Neal Shapiro of the United States, riding White Lightning at Lucerne.

106

cavalry officer available to stick up something a little fancier if required.

Now, with virtually no cavalry left, there are few people who can afford to give voluntarily the tremendous amount of time and concentration needed for modern show jumping course-designing.

Yet neither in Britain nor in the U.S. is it yet well enough paid to be a full-time job. Indeed, I question whether making it so would automatically produce better results; almost inevitably one would tend to become mechanical and repeat oneself. Half the thrill of the job is the paperwork beforehand, producing different courses to suit different horses and riders, and deciding what problems to pose. All too often the person who intends to take on the work as a profession, rather than for the pleasure he is going to receive, will have a series of plans which will be produced again and again; this becomes very monotonous for the riders.

The really good course-designer is someone who is in love with the job, and prepared to admit mistakes. The problem is to find people with the skill and aptitude combined with real interest, and in a position to devote to it the time required, while pursuing some other occupation.

The rider who has competed internationally is obviously one person who may have both the time and the inclination to take up this task. Perhaps it is now up to the national federations to give keen, would-be course-designers the opportunity to work with experienced people—first at national level and then if their work merits it, going on to international standards.

What are the aims of the course-designer? First and foremost he must produce a course which is pleasant to ride; it must be a challenge to horse and rider, and he must contribute to a result by presenting fair problems. The faults must be spread round the course so that the public's interest is held throughout. Obviously on each day of a show, the arena must be made to look as different as possible, and the problems varied as much as possible.

The idea is to try and bring all the horses and riders on so that they will be ready to jump a really big course at the end of the show. The skill of the designer is tested to the utmost in achieving this without too many clear rounds which waste time and bore the public.

On the other hand, great care must be taken not to make the problems such that the young horses and riders get into trouble and lose confidence. Ideally, five or six clear rounds in big competitions are about right, and one can hope for a thrilling jump-off with the best horse on the day winning.

If it is a good course even those riders who have not achieved a clear round will have enjoyed their ride. The course-designer should feel at the end of a show that the horses are jumping as well or better than at the beginning, that he has kept the show running to time, and that he has produced some exciting competitions for spectators and television audiences alike.

If you wish to learn the art of course-building, you must of course spend time working on your own, but at the same time try to go to

opposite: Hugo Simon of Austria, jumping on Lavendel at Hickstead.

the bigger shows and watch carefully. If possible ask if you can act as an assistant. Do this with as many different people as possible, as all the top designers have slightly different ideas, and there is something to be learnt from each of them. It was Phil Blackmore who was so helpful to me in my riding days, and roused my interest in course-designing. At that time he was almost alone in his field in Britain. I could do well over his courses at the big shows, whereas I would have no success over much smaller courses at the lesser shows, and I realized then how important good courses were. Jack Talbot-Ponsonby gave me advice once I had started working at small

The International Arena at the All England Jumping Course at Hickstead.

shows. I then had the opportunity to go to Rotterdam where Jan Jurgens was most helpful to me. I also went to Rome and Aachen. And I cannot emphasize enough what an advantage it has been to me to go and see how other people work.

The newcomer will find that many riders will ask for alterations in the course. Some of the requests may be both fair and sensible, but others may be to suit their particular horse.

At first make your courses simple, and try not to do anything that will cause controversy, so that you know it is not necessary to change anything. Later on, when you know the competitors better, you will learn from whom to accept advice.

If you make mistakes—and everyone does sometimes—admit it, and the riders will learn to respect you for doing so.

The first things the course-designer needs to know before setting pencil to paper are the size of the arena and the position of any permanent fence. He also needs to know where the judge will be sitting so that both start and finish are not completely at the other end of the arena, which will mean a lot of cable if an electric timer is used, and a long walk for the timer if timing is done by hand. He should know where the entrance and exit to the arena are, and naturally if there are going to be public stands, he should design the course to give them the best view.

The course-designer also needs to know the timetable so that no time will be wasted in changing from one competition to another. In addition, it is a great help to have a list of the fence material as it is always better to have a short, well built course, even using fences twice, than a long one with airy fences lacking in filling material, particularly for less experienced horses.

What are the means we have to use to obtain a result? First, there is the track you are going to ask the horse to follow. Secondly, the type and position of the fences you are going to use, and thirdly, and possibly most important, the distance between each fence.

I much prefer working outside in a fairly large arena. I think it gives a course-designer much more opportunity for variety in the track, use of fences and the distances you can use. At the same time I think it is good and interesting to work both indoors and outdoors.

I always work on graph paper when doing my course plans. Working outdoors I use one inch to represent ten yards, and working indoors, ten feet. In fact, working outdoors, I always talk of distances other than in combination fences in yards, assuming the arena is 300 feet by 240 feet minimum. If it is less than this I consider you have to use the type of course that you would for an indoor show.

In a very big arena I would use half an inch to represent ten yards, as when working you do not want to have to cope with a very large, unwieldy plan. It is a complete fallacy that you need a small arena to shorten the courses. In a fair-size arena you need fewer complete changes of direction (each time you get to the end of the arena it just about doubles the distance used between fences).

Now having got my graph paper, I draw in the exact size of the arena and mark in any permanent obstacles or trees, the exit and entrance to the arena, the position where the judges will be, and for my own benefit, the main spectator stand. I personally always draw my plans so that they will appear the right way up from where the judges are sitting. I know that at the end of a long day I find it very trying to work from a plan which is upside down, and for the competitor, as long as the entrance is clearly marked, there should be no problem.

I always start planning by using match sticks to represent fences, and I always work out the main competition first. The matches are useful as they are so easy to move around if I don't manage to find a good track for the jump-off. The first fence should not be too near the entrance, especially for novice horses. Therefore, as at a one-day show one does not want to cause the start and finish to be moved too often, the start may have to remain the same all day. In which case no one will start near the entrance.

So I work out a fairly simple plan. When I have found one that will work if used as two or more courses I draw a line of the track so as to be sure the turns are smooth on both courses; for my own purpose I draw the lines for the fences, and number the different courses with different coloured ink as it is useful to have a master plan to work from, both for when I draw out each separate course

An upright fence constructed with poles.

Another upright, known as a ballustrade, typical of the well built fences for which Hickstead is famed.

for competitors and judges, and for when I come to build the course itself.

At an outdoor show where the course need not be dismantled between classes, it is worth trying to have it in position for the whole day as so much time is saved between competitions if fences do not have to be moved. One sometimes has to compromise slightly in that one jump-off and one course will turn out better than the other. But, surprisingly, it is not always the course you expect which is the best. The jump-off should flow just as freely as the first round; really it is more important even than the first round, as it is in the jump-off that the competition is won or lost, provided one has not made the course too stiff and achieved only one clear round; though this I feel is permissible in a 'touch' class (where touching the fence with fore legs means one fault, and with hind legs half a fault).

After a spread fence in a jump-off I do not like to ask a horse to turn back on his tracks as I feel the horse is so often punished for a good jump over a wide fence by being pulled sharply round, especially by the less experienced rider. So if the rider is going to be asked to turn back immediately on landing, or turn through more than ninety degrees, then that fence should be an upright one so that it can be angled.

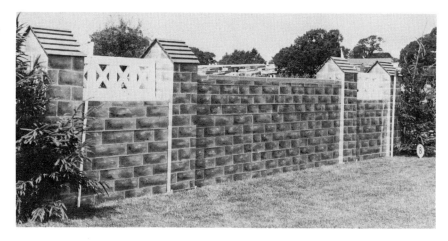

A wall—this type of vertical requires boldness but offers the horse a good ground line.

Another upright, constructed of planks and poles.

113

In theory I do not like touch classes, which are used in the U.S., but in practice they do stop novice horses being asked to jump too big fences too soon. At the same time, I feel the prize money for them should always be small, as I think over-rapping causes a horse to lose his natural arc and if riders want to win, they tend to do this. If a 'touch' class is really more of a schooling class, there is not the same temptation; a young horse will always win the money when he is ready, if he is good enough.

We may now consider the 'tools of the trade': the type of fences available to the course-designer in presenting the competitors with courses which may be challenging, but which should always be fair. Basically there are three types of fences: vertical, parallel and staircase, and they all have their advantages if used in the right way. A vertical or upright fence has an absolutely straight front with no flowers or filling pulled out in front to help the horse. It is hardest jumped going towards home and downhill. Two spread fences followed by an upright will very often be a bit of a problem. A parallel bar, or oxer, is a spread fence, either with the front rail slightly lower than the back, when it is known as an ascending parallel, or with both top rails the same height, in which case it is slightly harder to jump and is called a true parallel.

Oxers should have only one rail on the back as a safety precaution. If the horse misses his stride he is much less likely to fall if there is only one rail to knock down. The front face of the fence should be solid as this encourages a horse to jump. A spread fence is harder to jump going away from home or uphill.

Finally, a staircase or triple-bar-type fence is really the easiest of all to jump, but if used going away from home it may cause a problem; or if it is encountered going towards home and followed by a vertical fence, the triple bar will not fall, whereas the vertical fence may. The staircase fence is the one I would probably use as the first fence, especially for novices.

It is by judicious variation in the placing of the different types of fences that fair problems may be set. The stride of an average horse is twelve feet or four yards. Fences, therefore, need to be placed at multiples of four yards apart. This is a very general rule. The type of fence necessitates a slight variation of this rule, particularly in double and treble combinations.

A combination fence is a group of two or more individual fences that need only one or two strides between them, and here the type of fence used has a great bearing on the distance (see table).

For novice horses the average distance may be used, or a slightly long distance, but I personally do not advocate using short distances at this stage. Novice horses should learn to jump boldly into combinations—later they can be taught to shorten up. Scope is all important in an international horse and this must be encouraged in novice horses.

With more experienced horses the distances between obstacles in combinations can be varied. If the average distance between two uprights in a combination is taken as 26 feet, this could be reduced

A true oxer—a hedge with parallel rails each side, originally designed to keep oxen from damaging natural hedges.

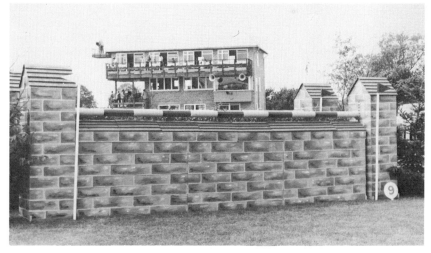

A variation in the oxer theme, using a wall on the take-off side, and (below) a parallel pole beyond the hedge on the landing side.

A formidable oxer using rustic poles.

A natural growing hedge forming part of the permanent oxer at Hickstead.

A parallel using planks on the take-off side.

A low wall and brush filling before a wall topped with coping 'stones' to provide a variation on the staircase formula.

A staircase fence filled with brush.

A treble combination—this requires maximum impulsion between each element.

to 24, which over two big uprights would be very difficult, or it could be extended to 28 feet, which would probably present very few problems.

On the other hand, if you assume a distance of 24 ft 6 in between two ascending oxers, that could not be reduced by more than six inches. You could increase the distance by one foot at the most, but you could not use a wide spread in the second oxer. In short, the distance to an upright is more flexible than the distance to a spread.

After combinations one can base one's calculations on a 12-foot stride, but up to a distance of 72 feet it is wise to take into account the types of fences. At 48 feet, upright to upright works out just right, triple bar to upright would be short, and upright to triple bar very long. It is important to remember that any uphill approach shortens a horse's stride by six to nine inches in a combination, and it also shortens the stride between fences; going downhill can lengthen a horse's stride by up to a foot in combinations. Heavy going also shortens a horse's stride.

Permanent fences consist of growing hedges, water jumps, ditches and banks, and ramps of many varieties. If the arena is big enough, they certainly give it character. They have to be used in moderation so that the take-off and landing do not become too poached. But they do add a different challenge to the horses.

Young horses should be given a careful introduction to them, particularly water jumps and ditches, as these he will certainly meet later on in big competitions, and provided a horse has confidence, they should present no problem. A water jump is one of the easiest obstacles for a horse to negotiate if it is well constructed, and he is

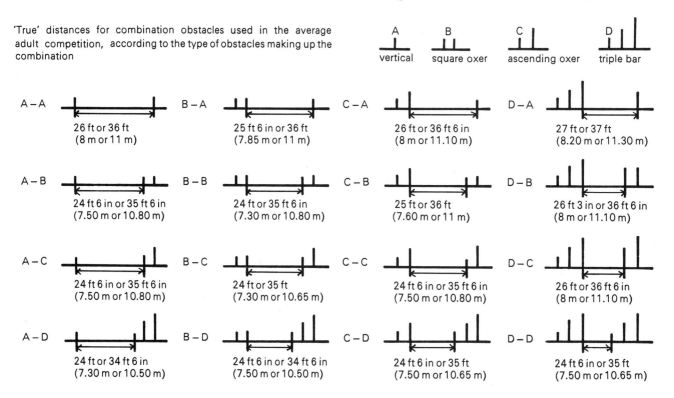

'True' distances for combination obstacles used in the average adult competition, according to the type of obstacles making up the combination

A vertical   B square oxer   C ascending oxer   D triple bar

A – A   26 ft or 36 ft (8 m or 11 m)
B – A   25 ft 6 in or 36 ft (7.85 m or 11 m)
C – A   26 ft or 36 ft 6 in (8 m or 11.10 m)
D – A   27 ft or 37 ft (8.20 m or 11.30 m)

A – B   24 ft 6 in or 35 ft 6 in (7.50 m or 10.80 m)
B – B   24 ft or 35 ft 6 in (7.30 m or 10.80 m)
C – B   25 ft or 36 ft (7.60 m or 11 m)
D – B   26 ft 3 in or 36 ft 6 in (8 m or 11.10 m)

A – C   24 ft 6 in or 35 ft 6 in (7.50 m or 10.80 m)
B – C   24 ft or 35 ft (7.30 m or 10.65 m)
C – C   24 ft 6 in or 35 ft 6 in (7.50 m or 10.80 m)
D – C   26 ft or 36 ft 6 in (8 m or 11.10 m)

A – D   24 ft or 34 ft 6 in (7.30 m or 10.50 m)
B – D   24 ft 6 in or 34 ft 6 in (7.50 m or 10.50 m)
C – D   24 ft 6 in or 35 ft (7.50 m or 10.65 m)
D – D   24 ft 6 in or 35 ft (7.50 m or 10.65 m)

Hickstead's water-jump, built to Olympic dimensions.

well ridden, but if he is rushed into it he will lose his rhythm and concentration; once he starts jumping into the water it is a difficult habit to cure.

A pole over the middle of a small water jump with a take-off hedge is the best introduction, if possible jumped towards home. Ditches, both wet and dry, can be used in many ways, and in my opinion are very useful as tests of courage in combinations in big competitions. Banks and ramps are obstacles more suitable for speed classes, though they are obviously part of a big competition like a Jumping Derby, which uses many permanent fences. Even in a small arena, I do like at least to have a water jump and a water ditch. The other permanent fences are fun, but not a necessity.

I have helped to design the Derby at Hickstead, and have done one in South Africa and one in Canada. These competitions certainly have a crowd appeal all their own. So few clear rounds are jumped, that whenever one occurs the crowd goes crazy with enthusiasm.

Large outdoor shows

These nearly always last over several days. The arenas should be bigger and the course-designer have more material to work with.

The calibre of horse and rider must always be taken into consideration. But certainly now it is possible for the course-designer who has gained experience at smaller shows to put that experience to good use and use his imagination more freely. Again, I always plan the last big competition first, and make sure I have a good testing jump-off for this, as it is very important to give the most experienced riders and horses the opportunity to win the Grand Prix.

A big competition must be won by jumping ability plus the ability to jump big fences at speed. The layout should be planned so that the various different courses employed during a particular day can be changed rapidly. This means they must all be built either in the evening after the show or early the next morning, and the course-designer must make sure that the lesser competitions have as good courses as the big one.

Obviously some turn out better than others, but he must never knowingly compromise with an easy way out. When the arena party is not big enough, the whole layout must be worked out to try and make each day look different with as little moving of the fence material as possible. But this solution should be avoided when circumstances permit.

Ideally, there should be enough material to construct about twenty fences each day plus the permanent fences, and enough labour to move these fences each day. Obviously a complete change makes the competitions more interesting and testing for the horses and riders and keeps the spectators' interest better. Also the ground stands up better if the lines are varied. Each day the way the fences are used should be varied. The many different permutations possible of the different types of fences are used in the combinations, sometimes with long distances and sometimes short.

Personally, I never intentionally use a short distance to a wide spread. I consider this an unfair test, but I often use a short distance to a vertical or upright fence. Closely related fences can be used, but I consider it is the fences that are further apart that are in many ways more of a test to the rider.

A horse's stride varies, so that if a fence is over 72 feet from the last one, the rider can decide whether he will take the obvious number of strides, or whether it is better for his particular horse to add a stride, or perhaps take one less in a jump-off, to save valuable time. It is very interesting, particularly in big courses, how sometimes a distance becomes more difficult than either course-designer or riders foresee. This is often psychological.

There was recently a very interesting case in the 1969 Men's European Championship, on the Nations' Cup day. There was an oxer followed by the combination and then a vertical fence. Most riders were having problems. Alwin Schockemöhle, who fell at the water, got up and proceeded to jump the line as I had intended, flowing freely through. Other riders became over-anxious, trying to put in an extra stride before the combination, and lost their rhythm.

The designer's paper-work is not finished with the planning of the track, type of fences and distances. He still has to work out how he can use the fence material to produce an artistic and visually interesting layout, not mixing colours or types of material too much in combinations, so that the final result will be a pleasing set of testing and varied fences. Finally, when the course is built and flagged, it has to be decorated with trees, shrubs and flowers.

Indoor shows

These can be divided into two categories: the smaller ones, where one layout has to be used in several different ways for one day, as there is not the time or labour to change it and the bigger indoor shows, where probably the course has to be taken out after each competition to allow for other events.

The plans of courses for indoor shows must be very accurately drawn. You look an awful fool if the course just will not fit in and it really is a matter of inches in most indoor arenas. The course designer has to rely much more on related (72 feet or less) distances, so cannot afford to make mistakes, especially when the fences get big. It is much more difficult to vary the tracks, and it can be a great test of imagination to try and produce enough different problems. If your course plan is accurate it should be easy to set up the course itself, but because distances are so much more critical in an indoor arena, if one fence is incorrectly placed then nothing will fit in. Indoor course plans should be simple, it is surprising how much variety can be introduced by varying the start and finish and the type of fences used.

If a fence has to be jumped twice in a round it must be possible to rebuild it quickly. If it is to be jumped both ways it must be either an upright or a hog's back type, except in certain special competitions when oxers are required. In these circumstances an oxer, to be safe, must not have too much filling, otherwise horses may have a nasty fall. Again, if a fence is jumped twice in a round, it should never be used twice in a jump-off.

An indoor course—a general view of one of the jumping classes at the Horse of the Year Show at the Empire Pool, Wembley.

The European Championship

I have designed the Men's European Championship twice, and the Ladies' once. This is a really gruelling event. I think that it is a good idea to have a different formula for the European, World and Olympic competitions, but the European Championship probably puts the biggest strain on the horses who compete in all three rounds.

The first day calls for a Table C timed class over fifteen numbered obstacles with a double or treble combination included. Here is the designer's first problem—is it better to have a reasonable length of track to accommodate this number of obstacles, or to shorten the track, and have the horses jumping frequently with very little distance between fences? In my view the first is really easier for the horse. In this competition the rider can compete with two horses. In fact, it is only on the final day that he is limited to one. The course, though a speed competition, needs to be built to the limit of size and spread permissible, as otherwise the competition on the first day can have too much bearing on the final result.

Naturally turns must be included where the well schooled horse can gain time by smooth, obedient response to the demands of a skilled rider, but the track should present a smooth, flowing line with occasional options that the skilled rider can take. Obviously the riders who are accustomed to the type of course built by a particular

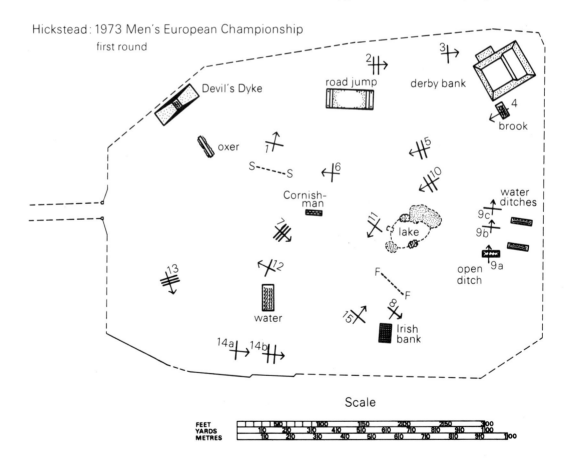

Hickstead: 1973 Men's European Championship
first round

Scale

designer will have a certain advantage over those who have never ridden his courses before. All designers have their individual ideas on how best to obtain a result. It would become very monotonous if they did not; one should always try to pose fair problems, and never intentionally use trick fences or distances. In the 1973 European Championship, on the first day, there were several places where time could be gained. For instance, Fence 6, a vertical, could be slightly angled to shorten the approach to Fence 7, and here the distance could again be shortened if the rider had confidence that his horse had sufficient scope to jump the wide triple bar from a short turn. There was the same option between 9c and 10, and 12 and 13. At the end of this competition the result was much as it should have been, the Grand Prix-type horses coming out better than the speed horses, as surely they ought in any part of a European Championship.

The second competition of the European Championship is conducted over two rounds of a Nations' Cup-type course. This certainly is the easiest part of the competition for which to design a course. Naturally it must be demanding. The double of vertical fences, 1.52 m and 1.56 m, had only 7.60 m between the two. This, going towards home, is a fairly short distance. There were faults all round the course, but the line 10-11-12 proved the really difficult part of the course. The first few horses were not the best, and the

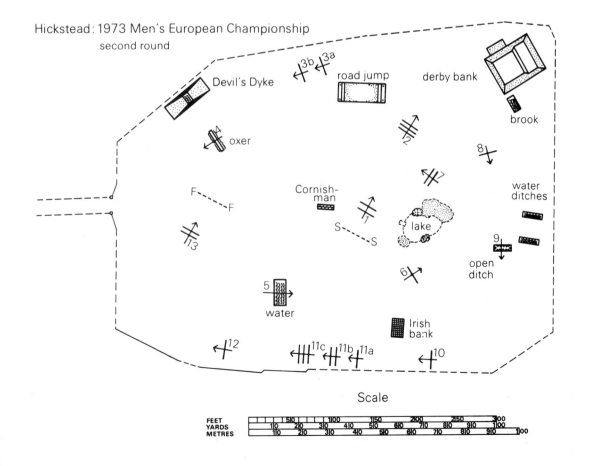

Hickstead: 1973 Men's European Championship
second round

Scale

FEET
YARDS
METRES

123

riders seemed to get over-worried about this line of fences. They mostly put in an extra stride between the vertical at Fence 10 and the first part of the three combination at 11. They then had to ride really hard to produce the impulsion to reach the end of the combination. The distance was 7.50 m from 11a to 11b, and many of the riders had the front rail of 11b down; or alternatively they found the distance from 11b to 11c (7.40 m) long, and had the back rail of 11c down. Again, having lost their rhythm, they found fence 12 a problem. Alwin Schockemöhle, on the other hand, had an unexpected fall on his best horse, Rex The Robber, at the water, and then jumped this line of fences with a beautiful rhythm and met no problems. Up to this point it looked as if the championship lay between Dr Orlandi with his two chestnut horses and Paddy McMahon on Pennwood Forgemill, Schockemöhle having dropped back owing to the fall of The Robber. Meanwhile Hubert Parot of France was jumping very consistently.

So to the last day with everything to play for. It really is important to try to keep up the excitement to the last minute. The course for the last day is a real problem. In any arena it is not easy to fit in eighteen numbered fences, and to work the course out so that the sixth fence and the thirteenth fence will be in a good position to produce a flowing course for the second round when the middle six fences are omitted. It is difficult to calculate exactly how tired the

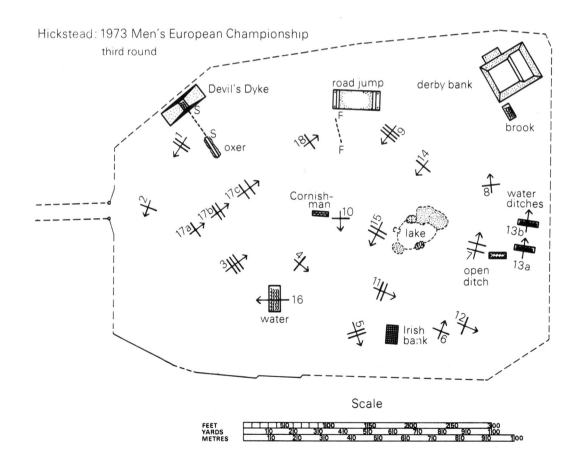

Hickstead: 1973 Men's European Championship
third round

Scale

horses will be after two gruelling days of jumping. If the course is too easy it will be almost a foregone conclusion that the result of the previous day will stand, yet if the course is too demanding it will not be a pleasant spectacle for the public.

Because the course had to have eighteen numbered fences with a double and treble combination in the last six Nations' Cup-type fences I did not include a combination in the first six fences, which are supposed to be a test of handiness. There is a case here for a change in the rules—to reduce the puissance fences to five and insist on at least a double combination in the first six. The limitation on height and speed of the puissance-type fences means that they do not have much bearing on the final result other than to add to the endurance demanded of the horses. Though many people considered the course on the small side, no horse jumped two clear rounds. The faults again were well distributed, most probably occurring at Fence 13, an oxer double combination over water ditches. Certainly the fact that the competitors with the most penalty points go first, and those with least, last, puts great pressure on the well placed riders and this pressure did affect Dr Orlandi who had looked certain of a medal.

The course-designer's aim should be to keep the excitement right up to till the last horse jumps the final fence. And on this occasion, had Paddy McMahon had a fence down in the last round, he would have dropped well down in his placing in this competition, and as a result, would have lost the gold medal. Naturally the odds against this kind of situation are great, but it is very gratifying when it does happen.

The World Championship

The World Championship competition is the most important assignment for any course-designer. The first stage comes well in advance, with the preparation of rough drawings, first of all of the track, and then one has to finalize the type of fences to be used. This is best done on the plans, as it is easier for the designer's assistants and the competitors to see at a glance the type of fences to be used.

For the 1974 World Championship at Hickstead, the entire international arena could be used without restrictions for the first three days of the competition, while on the final day an area had to be left for the competitors to work in. Space also had to be left for the bands to manoeuvre, and for the presentation ceremony. This sort of consideration can be a problem, as course-designers dread moving fences for displays, some of which do not always seem to appreciate the problems that it can involve—but this was not the case at Hickstead; the only requirement was that room should be left at the entrance for the bands to get in and out. Otherwise, with the aid of a course plan, the band display could be planned round the obstacles in the arena. The course plans done, the next stage is to work out the type of material to be used for each fence. At Hickstead there is a wonderful selection of fences to choose from and the aim was to try and use it all to the very best advantage.

opposite above: The decorative use of plants and flowers can create a really attractive jump, as with this parallel, part of Mickey Brinckmann's Nations' Cup course at the Munich Olympics.

opposite below: The parade of the finalists at the Men's World Show Jumping Championships at Hickstead in 1974. Left to right: Frank Chapot (U.S.A.) on Mainspring, Hartwig Steenken (West Germany) on Simona, Eddie Macken (Ireland) on Pele, and Hugo Simon (Austria) on Lavendel.

The new uprights with five-centimetre intervals for the cups were to be invaluable. The ground is fairly undulating at Hickstead and in such conditions it was difficult to construct a square oxer when the uprights with three-inch intervals were used. The oxer was always lower either at the back or at the front. The plans were already drawn up as a guideline; it worked out very well, and on only two occasions were there changes. The intention had been, on the first day, to use the biggest gate at Fence 11. When we tried this it was found that it was too big for the height limit of the class and the next size looked too far off the ground, so we substituted ten foot white rails which required really accurate riding. As they were closely spaced, the visual effect was very attractive.

The other change was the colour of the rails on Fence 4 of the puissance day. The plan was to use green and sand rails on the triple bar of brush, but it was decided that green and white rails showed up much better. The puissance day entailed most thought as there had never been a puissance at Hickstead, though there is a puissance wall. But this seemed completely unsuitable for a vertical fence at 1.70, so it was used for the first fence with a small wall in front. Special blocks were built for the ordinary wall, with a similar wall on either side to give width for the final fence. We had never done this before and were rather apprehensive as to how it would look, but in the end our efforts produced a really attractive fence. The fences used in the World Championships were not used in the two other competitions that were held on each of the first three days. So this entailed a great deal of work every evening, made possible only by the wonderful co-operation of all the team of assistants.

This competition is very different from the European Championship. The riders are limited to one horse throughout. This is a fairly good and new rule, as it prevents the rider who has one very difficult horse from riding his better horse to gain his qualifying points, and then opting for his difficult horse in the final. Again, the first day is a Table C competition. The 1974 course was designed virtually to the limit of height and spread permitted. The rider knows he wants to accumulate enough points to finish in the top four after three competitions, so though it is nice to win, it is really wiser not to take too many chances, but simply to try to finish in the first four. There were points at which corners could be cut, but with big fences most riders played safe, especially into Fence 5, a square oxer. After jumping Fence 8 the original intention was to give the riders the option of going round the bank, or turning left to approach the brook, but the Technical Delegate and the had of the Jury decided that there should be a fixed line on the plan here. I only use a fixed line very occasionally. They felt the option left too much to chance for such an important competition. Fence 11 was narrow and called for accurate riding; perhaps more faults occurred here and at the two double combinations; 3 a b was uphill, and 7 a b, oxers over the water ditches, is never an easy fence. Probably horses are looking at the ditches instead of paying attention to the rider. The three combination proved almost too easy, but at the end of the day, Pele (Ireland), Lavendel (Austria), and Simona (Germany), were all clear.

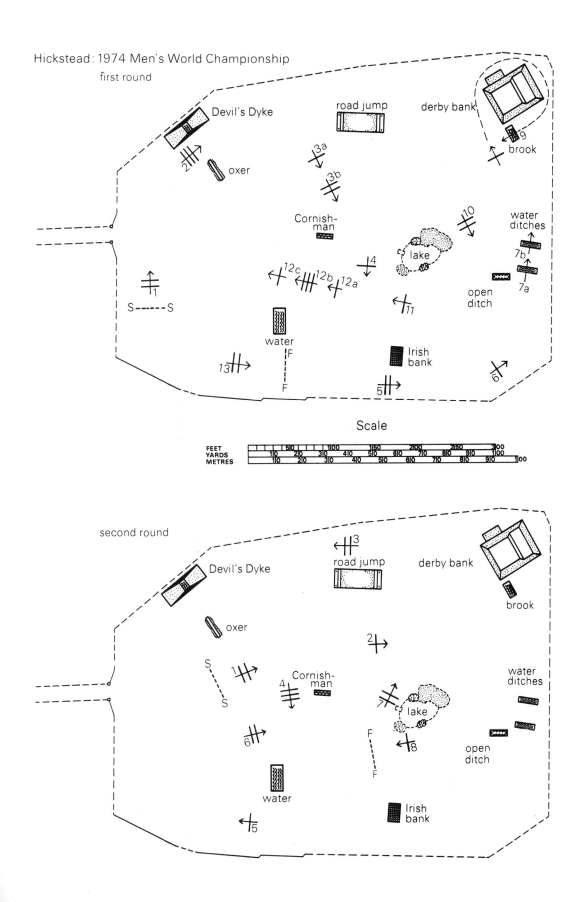

Hickstead: 1974 Men's World Championship
first round

Devil's Dyke
road jump
derby bank
oxer
brook
3a
3b
Cornish-man
10
water ditches
7b
4
lake
12c 12b 12a
11
7a
open ditch
1
S-----S
water
F
Irish bank
13
5
6
F

Scale

FEET   50   100   150   200   250   300
YARDS 10 20 30 40 50 60 70 80 90 100
METRES 10 20 30 40 50 60 70 80 90 100

second round

Devil's Dyke
3
road jump
derby bank
oxer
brook
2
S
1
4
Cornish-man
water ditches
7
lake
6
open ditch
F
8
water
F
Irish bank
5

129

Hartwig Steenken and Simona.

There were two other clear rounds, but too slow to come into the reckoning. Forgemill (Great Britain), with a fence down, lay fourth and Sportsman, ridden by David Broome, sixth. He had the misfortune to have to go first; had he gone later he might well have gone faster, but even so, with a fence down, he would only have had two more points, and this would not have put him in the final.

The second day is a puissance competition with a height limit of 1.70 m in the first round and 1.80 m in the only barrage. Most horses will jump a puissance wall at 1.70 m without any trouble, so one had to depend on the spread fences to get a result. Many people thought these were built too big, but as there were nine clear rounds, and when the fences went up there were still four left equal after some really memorable jumping, this criticism had little foundation. It is interesting that in the end it was the vertical grey and yellow rails at Fence 2 which sorted the competitors out in the barrage.

The third day of the championship had the same four riders in the lead. But on this day, with two rounds over a Nations Cup-type course, those who had not dropped too far back could still come into the reckoning. For a World Championship this course should virtually match up to the course for the team competition of the Olympic Games. The only alteration made by the technical delegate was to lower the first part of the double of verticals to 1.53 m. This did put rather more emphasis on the last line of Fences 12 and 13. It is always considered that the home team have an advantage in that

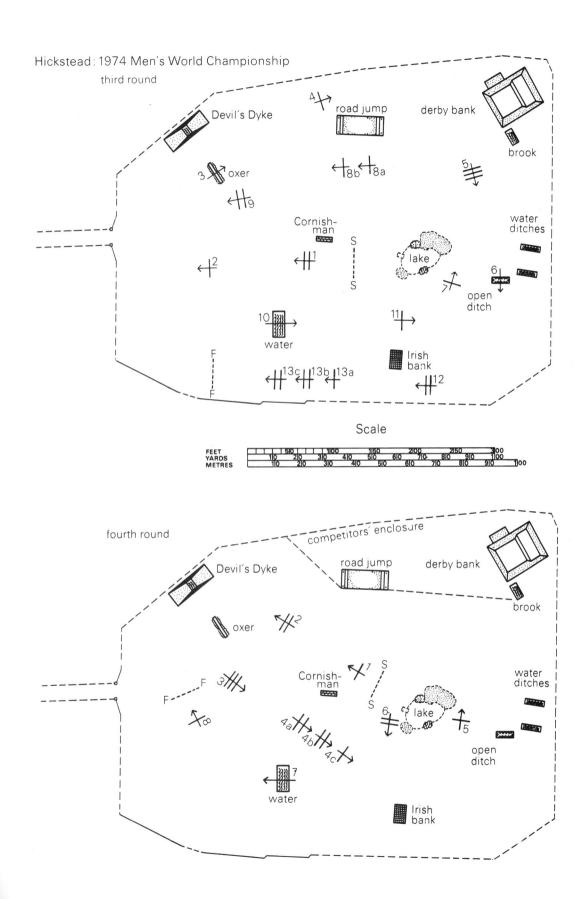

Hickstead: 1974 Men's World Championship
third round

Devil's Dyke

4
road jump
derby bank

brook

3 oxer

8b 8a

5

9

water ditches

Cornish-man
S
lake
1
2
S
6
open ditch

10
11
water

13c 13b 13a
Irish bank
12

Scale

FEET	50	100	150	200	250	300		
YARDS	10 20 30	40	50	60	70	80	90	100
METRES	10 20 30	40	50	60	70	80	90	100

fourth round

competitors' enclosure

Devil's Dyke
road jump
derby bank

brook

oxer
2

1 S
Cornish-man
S
3
6
lake
5
F F
water ditches
8
4a
4b
4c
open ditch

7
water
Irish bank

131

they are accustomed to the permanent fences, but it was interesting that Harvey Smith, who has always had an aversion to the natural hedge which was Fence 3, faulted there, though it was no great problem to other riders and David Broome, who has never liked the water jump at Hickstead, had a costly fault there in the first round when few others were penalised. Undoubtedly the combination at Fence 13 did have a large bearing on the result of this competition, Simona coming through with the only double clear round. Pele (Ireland) and Lavendel (Austria), were both clear in the first round, but had four faults each in the second, to finish equal second in this round. But Forgemill was not jumping with his usual *joie de vivre,* and got into real trouble in the combination which dropped him right out of the reckoning. So, coming to the last round, fourth place for the final rested between Frank Chapot on Mainspring and David Broome on Sportsman and in this case the experience of an older horse, as is Mainspring, won the day. So there were four really great horses and experienced riders for the final day. The question here was how Pele, a really great young horse, would react to different riders, a great ordeal for a horse with so little experience. It seems a little hard that all the points gained up to this point are dropped for the final day.

This course was really a challenge to the designer. How was one to design a course for four great horses and riders which was demanding enough, and yet would not ask too much of the horses who had to negotiate it four times and with strange riders? Fences 6 and 7 were undoubtedly those which produced the result. Fence 6 was a true oxer, slightly downhill, and coming away from the other horses. It has been said this fence was possibly too flimsy. An oxer with rails really close together, and well filled in with Christmas trees, cannot really be considered flimsy. A better criticism would be that the three-combination at Fence 4 was far too solid; though it was rattled on several occasions, no one faulted there. It was built in this way to give a combination which the riders could attack, as if they had to ride carefully they could have trouble on strange horses. It worried all the participants that their horses might get into real trouble with strange riders. That this did not happen was due to the tact and experience of all four riders. It came to a jump off of two. It was certainly unfortunate for Eddie Macken to have to go first, but undoubtedly Steenken and Simona, who had finished first on points up to the final day, were really worthy winners. It was a case of a really experienced horse and rider just beating a young horse and rider who will undoubtedly have many more great wins to come.

Needless to say, there was much talk afterwards as to whether this formula was correct. All agreed that this time it produced a really good outcome. But certainly there are other formulas which might be more sure of producing the right result. If the existing formula is retained, there is a case for omitting the water jump from the final day, as a horse should not be asked to jump a big water five times in one day.

In a competition of this calibre, obviously some horses are going to find the courses more than they are capable of jumping, but the fact that only one pole was broken throughout the whole of the championship shows that there were no really bad falls and certainly many of the really young riders made a very good showing. Young Neessen on Jumping Amsterdam was very impressive in Rotterdam in 1973 and he jumped an impeccable second round on the third day with just a very close call at the water, and no problems with the final line of fences. There were disappointments too. Hubert Parot, who had done so well in the European Championship, just did not seem to find his form till the third day. It does seem that the more that is expected of a rider, the greater the tension. To some riders this makes them even more accurate, but mostly they tighten up and do not achieve their peak performance. It is imponderables of this nature which make it that much more difficult to decide the exact problems which should be set in the different courses.

The Olympic Games

These are divided into two competitions, the Individual and the Team. It is unlikely that any one rider will have two sound horses of Olympic calibre, so in all probability one horse is going to take part in two very big competitions in one week, having to jump probably more testing courses than he has ever jumped before and in each case, if he is to gain a medal, to jump each course twice at least. The

The Olympic course at Munich in 1972.

course-designer has many problems. In all probability the ground has not been used before, so he has not got the feel of it. There are many nations of varying capabilities riding in the event. He has to make the course demanding enough so that the best combinations of horse and rider gain the medals. At the same time he does not want to cause carnage amongst the less experienced. This only gives show jumping a bad name and serves no purpose. But it is a very difficult assignment.

The first round is over twelve to fifteen obstacles, up to 1.60 m high and 2.20 m wide and must include a water jump of at least 4.50 m. The top twenty horses from this round go into the second round over ten fences, with the height now 1.70 m, but the spread limit strangely reduced to 2.00 m. These can be two completely separate courses, or, as at Munich, a different track incorporating many of the same fences. This seems the sensible answer. Obviously there are bound to be some hard luck stories amongst those who fail to get through to the second round; equally among those that do. In the second round in Munich the real test was the rustic double of oxers. In the first round the upright fence before this double was a good distance, and the double consisted of a triple bar to an upright at 7.70 m (25 ft 3 in)—pretty short. In the second round the upright was moved closer to the double so that it was exactly half a stride wrong and the double became two wide oxers with still 7.70 m between so it became very long. The rider with the obedient horse with scope had room to shorten his horse's stride after Fence 2 and get going again before he came to the double. Neal Shapiro with Sloopy achieved this beautifully, but neither Graziano Mancinelli on Ambassador nor Ann Moore on Psalm achieved this. They both had clear first rounds and eight faults in the second, whereas Sloopy had four in each round, so the competition went to a jump-off of three horses. Ambassador won the gold medal, but to Sloopy went a moral victory, in that he came back a week later and showed comparable form in the team event, the only medallist to do so.

The constructing of the individual course was comparative child's play compared with the team course as there was plenty of time to put it up and even more fences if necessary. The team competition had to be erected after the final of a football game the previous night, to be ready for inspection by the technical delegate at about 6 a.m. on the morning of the competition. The water jump and ditch had to be dug, a very tricky operation avoiding underground pipes, drainage and heating. Again, the course has to be jumped by nations with a large range of ability, and at times the arena has been strewn with broken timber, but in Munich it was a very fair and testing course, and under the new rule only the top twelve teams came back. This is excellent as no one wants to see horses struggling to jump a course knowing they have no hope of a medal.

The going in the stadium is likely to be more difficult in that the Games are nearly always held in a new stadium where it may not have been possible really to test the drainage, and anyway old turf is always more springy than new. But again, the going was excellent in Munich, whereas in Mexico it was probably the cause of the course being very much more difficult than it appeared to be.

The fences in Munich had been thought out over many years and were beautifully presented, and as a result, the general standard of jumping was good. It is going to be very difficult for other countries to live up to the standard of these courses and fences in the future. The German shows have always had such a wide variety of fence material, and this, with all Mickey Brinckmann's experience and ideas, culminated in the production of many and varied obstacles beautifully presented and decorated. The year 1972 really produced an equestrian Olympics to remember.

The development of course-building has not been uniform throughout the world, of course, and there are some interesting variations which all help to make up the sport's fascinating international character. The following are some observations I have noted in the thousands of miles I have travelled on my own 'international show-jumping circuit'.

United States

In the U.S., the Florida circuit has done a great deal to give the young riders the opportunity of riding outdoor European-type courses. Since 1970 it has gone from strength to strength. Up until 1972, it culminated with the Gold Cup. This is a competition run with a qualifying round on one day and then two rounds the next day, the scores being cumulative, rather a gruelling formula for horses so early in the season. It has now been moved to Philadelphia in September, where it makes a suitable finale to big-time outdoor jumping for the season, in the eastern United States.

Currently the Florida Circuit consists of three or four shows leading up to the American Invitational. The location of these shows has varied, but every effort is made to use fairly big arenas with dry ditches, Liverpools (water ditches) and water jumps. There are classes for all grades of horses, so that by the end of the circuit even the preliminary horses are jumping the permanent fences with confidence. Undoubtedly, the ideal is to get horses' and riders' confidence in an arena and then start to introduce the permanent fences.

With young horses and riders, it is always wise to use the Liverpool as a water jump to begin with, with the brush in front and a rail approximately 2 ft 6 in over the middle. When the horses have confidence over this, remove the brush so that the horses get used to seeing the water and then the rails can be used as an oxer, over the middle or at the back. When they are jumping this freely, the proper water jump can be used, as small as possible, again with a brush in front. Personally, I like the brush to be fairly high, approximately 1½-2 ft, as I think this teaches the horse to jump up as well as out. Again, use a rail, this time slightly closer to the brush than the centre, as if a horse hesitates it is bad if he lands between the brush and the rail and frightens himself.

I now plan the courses for the entire Florida circuit and there are advantages and disadvantages to this. It does mean that I can make the courses progressively more demanding. But it is also a great test of my ingenuity to keep the courses varied and interesting, so that the open horses come to their peak for the Invitational.

The circuit in 1974 started with Jacksonville and rather unfortunately, the poles here were considerably heavier than on the rest of the circuit. This meant that the fences had to be rather too big for the first show and certainly, some of the preliminary horses became discouraged. This is a big problem for a course-designer as you have to work with the material available and achieve the best results possible. In this case, it was better to use high, vertical fences rather than wide spreads, as a horse will get into less trouble over these. I also consider that all sets of fences should have shallower cups for gates and planks as a safety factor. This is general practice in Europe but not in the U.S.A. and Canada, and safety is important. On the rest of the circuit, the Ammerman Lytle rental fences were used and the poles were certainly much safer. There were no more breakages but there were certainly fewer falls and this really is important.

Owing to the climate and the fact that outdoor jumping is not practical further north in February and March, this probably is the strongest collection of horses and riders of the whole season. Later on there are various choices of circuits. This year there were the top riders from the East with others from all over the United States and Canada, so that the competition really was of international level. The problem for the course-builder was to get a result without too many clear rounds and without asking the ultimate of the horses in every competition. I did try to build up to a really big course for the Grand Prix which finished each show. It shows the strength of the competition, in that each Grand Prix was won by a different horse. Rodney Jenkins was the only rider to win twice but on different horses. This surely indicates a very healthy situation in the United States. Obviously, each Grand Prix posed various problems and though there was a different winner, on the whole it was the same horses who were in the ribbons.

After the Florida circuit the top horses mostly have a slight break, only starting again at Devon at the end of May. Certainly the riders in the United States have to be adaptable as they go from the comparatively small rings of Devon to compete in a big outdoor Grand Prix. In my opinion the average United States riders have an edge over the average Europeans when competing in a small arena. They have all learnt to be very stride-conscious. They tend to decide exactly how many strides they will take to a fence, even in the hunter classes. I like to set one fence straight, and the next one at an angle, as beyond 60 feet this gives the rider an option depending on the arc he decides to take. But this seems to be unpopular as the judges mostly like the hunters to achieve a distance in a given number of strides. European riders are far more accustomed to large arenas, varied going or footing and more slope to the ground, so they do learn to use their eye more to see a distance. I think many riders find it hard to use their eye if they are concentrating on achieving a certain number of strides and in long distances between fences many things can occur to vary a horse's stride. It is the rider using his eye to judge his distance who can most easily adapt the length of his horse's stride. But judging from what is happening in the United States, including the terrific increase in big competitions all over the country, it will not be long before there are as many beautiful spacious arenas as there are in Europe. Gradually television is taking an interest; if this interest becomes established there will be money for sponsorship. Some of this should go to improving the arenas, introducing more variety in the fence material, and reducing the entry fees. In Europe the financial outlay for showing and entering a horse is not too high. In the United States the outlay is so great that many talented riders just never get an opportunity to develop. They cannot afford to risk the money necessary to participate in the big competitions.

The United States still believe in giving their team experience in Europe, and just as I believe it is imperative for a course-designer to travel and get new ideas, so I think it is good for riders. Territorially the western United States has a long way to go to catch up the east, as there is a large land mass as well as an ocean between them and Europe. But they give the impression that they mean to catch up quickly.

The setting for the Devon Horse Show, in the United States.

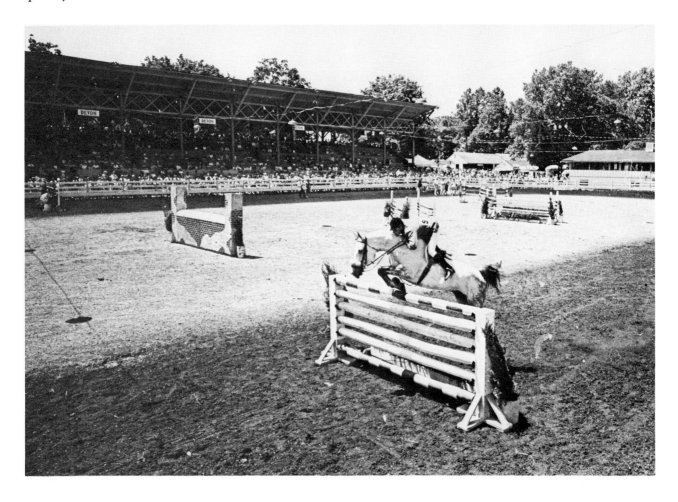

Canada

The Canadians are taking a different line of approach to the Montreal Olympics. With one team gold medal already under their belts, and this achieved without foreign experience in the year of their victory, they are concentrating more on an organised series of Grands Prix through the summer seasons. This worked very well before Mexico when they had a team of seasoned riders, but I wonder whether it is possible to expose young riders to enough pressure without outdoor international competition. Naturally, they have the advantage of being in their own country, but this is not always the advantage it is considered to be—certainly the pressure affected the German team in the individual competition at the Munich Olympics. It was almost a foregone conclusion that they would win a medal, probably the gold, yet somehow many things went wrong for them. Still, Canada can use the Pan American Games to give their riders experience. Moreover, Canada can say that by staying at home, most of their big competitions being designed by the Canadian Olympic designer, they will gain all the experience necessary.

It would be very hard to design the courses for the Games if one were only working with a very small number of top quality horses. There comes a time when those horses and riders must be asked some questions. With very few top riders and horses it is only too easy to lose one's nerve. So many people consider a competition poor if there are not sufficient clear rounds for an exciting jump-off; the specifications are such for the Olympic Games that the competitions will be won by horses with real scope and jumping ability, so that thrilling timed jump-offs are not the best training for the really important event. There are probably enough really experienced Olympic riders, even though they may not compete in 1976, who will realise this and give their course-designer every encouragement to design courses to encourage the big powerful jumpers.

Great Britain

Certainly before World War II the jumping courses on the continent of Western Europe were far superior to those in England, U.S.A. and other countries. After the world war Western Europe still had the advantage of experienced men to carry on the work and teach younger people. Britain, among what one could call the backward countries, was among the first to realize the potential appeal of show jumping as a sport and to the public. Naturally, not all course-designers could come up to the modern demands at once and there were many arguments over distances, types of fences and so on. Hickstead was the first permanent jumping-ground in England and to begin with the permanent fences were viewed with great suspicion. But undoubtedly Hickstead has played a very big part in producing a situation where Britain now has more riders than any other country fit to represent her abroad. Any course-designer who works at the bigger shows in England is really working at international standard, but he suffers from one big disadvantage. Few shows or arenas are entirely devoted to jumping, with the result that the fences may have to be removed and replaced several times during the day As a result of this fence material must not be too heavy, and much of the artistic aspect is lost, as the fences are generally not sufficiently decorated and filled with greenery. The fence material is moved from show to show so that with the best will in the world, the courses tend to look too much alike.

Certainly, more permanent grounds have been started recently. The cost of upkeep of these grounds is enormous. It would seem the ideal in the future is for them to be part of a sports complex. But in this case it is essential for someone with real knowledge of the sport to be in charge of the show jumping side. These grounds may start off with a basic set of the show jumping association fences, but they must then branch out into their own as soon as they can afford it.

Fences that live in one place can be heavier and more varied. They will also last much longer. Variety makes jumping much more interesting for the public and the competitors. Many of the smaller grounds have quite steep gradients to them. This used to be considered a disadvantage. At Hickstead there is both flat and sloping ground and this provides an extra test of the ability of horse and rider.

For many years in Europe the arenas have tended to be flat, but at the Munich Olympics Mickey Brinckmann, probably the most experienced of living course-designers, said that he considered we had reached the limit of what could be asked of horses in height and spread, and that the use of gradients should be introduced so that horses were not being asked to jump to the limit at all times.

In England, a small, densely populated country, there seem to be horses in most areas, and riders can start off at small local shows close to where they live. It is here too that course-designers will start and may hope to find a judge with experience of good courses who can give friendly advice. The more experienced riders and horses can, without too much travelling, attend the bigger shows. As a result of this the standard is very high, higher probably than at any national shows in the world except Germany, with the U.S.A. rapidly catching up.

The number of shows means that many people are needed to design the courses, and realisation is only just dawning on show management how important these people are. In a world where prize money is forever increasing, the people who put up the courses for these valuable horses to jump are expected to work long hours in all kinds of weather for a reward which certainly does not measure up to the dedication and skill that is required to do the job well. For some the pleasure of seeing the horses and riders improving is reward enough, but others simply cannot afford to do the work for so little, however much they enjoy it.

Ireland

The Royal Dublin Show at Balls-bridge has a unique atmosphere and the show-jumping courses include natural Irish banks.

Ireland's Ballsbridge arena in Dublin is among the most beautiful in the world. The courses and the fences have improved steadily under Eddy Taylor's guidance, but the country shows still have a long way to go and riders need to jump good courses consistently to provide a team with real depth.

Germany

Germany has the reputation for having solid, impressive courses. In Mickey Brinckmann they have one of the most knowledgeable and dedicated designers. He is a tireless worker and is always prepared to discuss the problems he is setting, and why, with anyone who wants to learn. Naturally, over the years, he has had many people working with him and they now work at shows all over West Germany having had their basic teaching from a real master. He is able to set courses to bring on young riders and bring out the best in the more experienced ones. And certainly, any young rider going to Aachen is going to gain a great deal of experience, and will come away far more confident of his ability to jump big fences and long distances. Mickey does 'ask questions' with his distances in combinations, but always fair ones.

France

In France, nowadays, there are not nearly so many riders interested in show jumping as in England, so the sport does become more centralized. The prize money is subsidized and very large, so the riders tend to stay and ride in their own country. This is a pity as they definitely lack the incentive of top competitions that can only be achieved by competing at international shows, though I am happy to have seen them competing much more often recently outside France, and with considerable success. The same riders tend to go to all the big shows in France, and this is bad for riders and course-designers alike as there is too much sameness about every show. Nevertheless, their federation is interested in bringing on people who are keen to learn the art of course designing. In England they have to make their own way, but certainly in France they do get more opportunities to work at the big shows with experienced designers. There are many beautiful permanent grounds with good fence material; clubs have taken the place of the old cavalry barracks and have excellent amenities, both for schooling and for shows.

In France there is less emphasis on jumping big fences than in England and Germany. On the whole they have a less powerful type of horse, and naturally the courses tend to favour this type of horse, with more accuracy being demanded.

The parade of teams before the Nations' Cup competition at La Baule, in France.

Italy

The same thing really applies in Italy. The oxers are often built with rails in front and filled in with a fairly low bush or wall so that it almost gives the impression of a false ground line, and certainly in Rome there is often a small fence on the end which seems to catch many people out. The Italians and the French also use fences fairly close to the water jump, so that if the horse's stride does not accommodate to the distance the water jump will give problems. You very rarely see this problem in Britain or Germany.

Switzerland

In Switzerland the federation is very interested in course designing. As this is a small country it is possible for all the people who do the work to get together and discuss the coming season and the courses that are to be built at the various shows, and the work is supervised and approved.

The Netherlands

In the Netherlands for many years J.H.A. Jurgens was the leading designer. No one took more trouble in the way he presented his fences, and horses always jumped them well. He used a lot of closely related fences and sometimes his turns caused consternation among the riders beforehand, but he had a flair for knowing what is possible, and what is not. The disadvantage is that very few people who have tried to copy his style exactly have the same flair for distances and turns and courses which Jan Jurgens designed and built appear very smooth and jumpable, whereas when others try the beauty of rhythm of horse and rider is completely lost.

There remain countries where the sport is not so strong and yet even in these the facilities are often excellent. In 1973 I went to the Balkan Championships and both in Bulgaria and Greece I was impressed with the variety of fence material, and the fact that there were excellent permanent fences, water ditches and banks. In Mexico City, the centre of all show jumping in Mexico, there are many clubs with beautiful permanent arenas and a great variety of permanent fences. They have also got some very good fence material for their international shows. In fact, there has been a great improvement in the standard of horses and riding in Mexico in the last few years and there is a great willingness to learn from others.

In recent years South Africa has been isolated in equestrian terms because of the horse sickness ban, but has some excellent horses and riders, and has gone to great lengths to have courses that will bring riders up to international standards. There are two excellent permanent arenas in the Johannesburg area with all kinds of permanent fences. Their fence material is improving all the time, and so is their standard of jumping. Harold Preston, South Africa's chief

opposite: Bill Steinkraus riding Bold Minstrel over the Derby Bank at Hickstead.

course-designer, has spent a considerable time in Europe studying all the different styles used at the major shows in Europe and has taken the knowledge he gained back to South Africa and is helping the riders by producing consistently good and testing courses. I am sure that when and if the South Africans go to Europe they will be a team to be reckoned with.

Summing up

There is more general interest in show jumping now than there has ever been. Television has certainly brought some comprehension of the fact that the fences are not just placed at random. Some competitors are critical, while others accept any problems with which they are presented. However, more course-designers are getting together to discuss the problems of their work every year, and the general widening of interest will ensure an increasing number of knowledgeable course-designers in the future.

Although by the end of the World Championship I felt worked out, show jumping is a very compelling sport and I am not really ready to drop out of it yet. If I am still learning I feel I must have a contribution to make to the sport. My aim now is to get as many young people interested in the work and give them all the advice and help that I can.

opposite: Alan Oliver of Great Britain, riding Sweep III at the Royal Norfolk Show.

Great Riders and Horses

by Pamela Macgregor-Morris

The riders and horses are each grouped together according to nationality. The countries appear in alphabetical order.

Riders

Arrambide, Dr Hugo   Argentina

Hugo Arrambide is a Doctor of Law from Buenos Aires and a considerable sportsman. In addition to his show-jumping activities, which have taken him all over Europe, he is also the owner of a pack of hounds.

Born in 1930, he rode in the 1964 Olympic Games in Tokyo as a member of the team which finished fifth. His first top international horse, Chimbote, by a thoroughbred stallion out of an Argentine Criollo mare, was then six years old. A year later he embarked on a European tour with considerable success, winning the Rome Grand Prix and finishing equal first in the Grand Prix at Aachen, dividing the spoils with Captain Piero d'Inzeo of Italy on the Irish-bred Ballyblack.

Back again in Europe in 1966, Arrambide and Chimbote finished third in the European championship, from which non-Europeans are now debarred, behind Nelson Pessoa of Brazil on Gran Geste and the present captain of the United States Equestrian Team, Frank Chapot, on San Lucas, in Lucerne.

Arrambide's next good horse was Adagio, who won him the Grand Prix in New York in 1969 after a warm-up at the European shows. At the time of writing he is riding Camalote and Mio-Mio, who like their predecessors are typical of the wiry, athletic Argentine horses bred in their thousands on the *estancias* and deriving their toughness and handiness, which stands them in such good stead on the polo-field as well, from their early training as cattle-herding animals.

Dr Hugo Arrambide, on Mio Mio.

opposite: Pele, ridden by Eddie Macken.

147

Gen. Carlos Delia.

Delia, Gen. Carlos   Argentina

General Delia, who made light of his fifty years in the Men's World Championship at Hickstead in 1974, has been in the Argentine team for nearly a quarter of a century but is still as slim and active as when he first joined it. He is not able to train with it very often, either, for his military duties sometimes take him far from his native land. He has recently concluded a tour of duty in Washington, D.C., as the military attache to the Argentine embassy.

During his career he has produced two outstanding horses—the chestnut Discutido, with whom he won the 1956 Hamburg Derby, and who later went to David Broome and became the leading horse in Great Britain in 1961, and Huipil, a dark bay horse who was the leading horse in the 1960 World Championships at Venice in which Delia himself finished third behind Raimondo d'Inzeo and David Broome. Huipil was subsequently owned and jumped under a Brazilian saddle cloth by Nelson Pessoa.

One of the most charming and courteous international riders in the world, and a consummate horseman, General Delia is a real credit to the sport he serves so well.

Fahey, John   Australia

John Fahey, a farmer from New South Wales, was born in 1943 and became the first Australian show jumper to attain world status when, in 1964, he and Bonvale took Peter Robeson with Firecrest to a jump-off before finally conceding them the Olympic individual bronze medal.

John has been show jumping since he was eight years old, and he rode again in the 1968 Olympic Games in Mexico City, again with Bonvale, and finished twenty first. In the team event, when Australia finished ninth, he had the best score for his country.

In 1969, still on his way home from Mexico, he embarked upon a British tour, but Bonvale broke down early in the season, leaving him only with his second string, Maestro, who was not in the same class. Nothing daunted, he

John Fahey, on Bonvale.

returned with a new pair of horses, Warwick III and The Red Baron, in 1972, and at the end of the season in England he sold them both to the young Devonshire rider, Tony Newbery. Tony made a successful international debut on Warwick III in 1973 and has since come up into the first flight, both as a team rider and as the winner of several prestigious individual competitions.

Simon, Hugo   Austria

Hugo Simon was a second-rank German team rider until 1972. Then, since he was fired with the ambition to ride in the Olympic Games, and had been omitted from the West German short list, he decided to take an unusual course. Having an Austrian grandmother, though living in Germany, he applied for and was granted dual nationality, and he was duly accepted by the Olympic committee as an individual rider for Austria.

It was quite a successful move, for on the grey Hanoverian Lavendel he finished equal fourth, with only .75 of a time fault keeping him out of the final medal shake-up. In 1973 he carried the Austrian flag with considerable ability at most of the top shows in Europe, and finished fifth overall for the Men's European Championship at Hickstead, in addition to winning the Victor Ludorum on Flipper at London's Horse of the Year Show.

The following year he returned to Hickstead for the Men's World Championship, and this time he went one better, finishing among the four finalists who swap horses on the last day. Eventually he wound up sharing third place, again on Lavendel, with Frank Chapot on Mainspring for the United States.

Hugo Simon.

Pessoa, Nelson   Brazil

Nelson Pessoa.

Nelson Pessoa, born in Rio de Janeiro in 1935, was twenty-one when he first travelled to Europe, in 1956, riding a flea-bitten grey called Relincho with the Brazilian team. Not many years later he was back in Europe to stay, settling first in Geneva and later in France, where he now runs a thriving establishment which schools, campaigns and deals in international horses at every level.

Pessoa has won a great number of Grand Prix competitions all over the world, in addition to a European championship, three Hamburg Derbies and two British Derbies at Hickstead, riding the grey Brazilian-bred Gran Geste, who is now retired.

Having planned to turn professional after the last Olympic Games in 1972, Pessoa finally took the plunge in the spring of 1974, when he had found a sponsor in Pernod. He thus became the only self-confessed professional rider on the continent of Europe, a little over a year after Britain's 'shamateurs' had decided with a little prompting from the British Show Jumping Association to relinquish their amateur status.

He has been based in Europe since 1961, finding there more opportunity to compete in top-level international competitions. That year he won the puissance in London on Gran Geste, and in 1962 on another Brazilian horse, Espartaco, he won his first Hamburg Derby after jumping off with Raimondo d'Inzeo of Italy on his Olympic gold medallist, Posillipo, and World Champion Merano. A year later he had the only two clear rounds in the Hamburg classic with Gran Geste and Espartaco, and won the British Derby with the former in a four-horse final.

In 1964 Gran Geste won him the Aachen Grand Prix and the Grand Prix d'Europe, and in the same year on the little Argentine-bred Huipil he just missed the barrage for the Olympic individual bronze medal in Tokyo finishing equal fifth. He won his European title in 1966.

Day, James ('Jim')   Canada

Jim Day, who was born in 1946, was the youngest member of the team which won the Olympic gold medals in Mexico City in 1968. The previous year, also riding Canadian Club, he won the individual gold medal at the Pan American Games in Winnipeg, at the expense of Brazil's Nelson Pessoa with the brilliant grey Derby specialist, Gran Geste.

Jim Day is the son of a famous horseman, Dick Day of Aurora, who has trained and produced many excellent hunters and jumpers; his mother is a well known judge at the Canadian shows. Jimmy himself is married to the former Janet Burns, whose father, Charles Burns, owns the winner of the 1969 Grand National at Aintree, Highland Wedding.

He won the North American Junior Championship in 1964, when he was eighteen, and joined the Canadian team in the same year. He rapidly proved the selectors right, by winning the international championship at Harrisburg, Pennsylvania, the show which then initiated the North American fall circuit.

Jim Day, on Canadian Club.

At the Munich Olympic Games in 1972, riding Steelmaster, on whom Day had won the Canadian championship in 1969, he was well in the running for an individual medal. Steelmaster jumped a clear first round, but the hit both parts of the rustic double in the second round, had three quarters of a time fault to add as well, and ultimately finished in fourth place, equal with the reigning European champion, Hartwig Steenken with Simona, and Hugo Simon, the German-based Austrian rider, with Lavendel.

Elder, James ('Jim')   Canada

Jim Elder, who was born in 1934, is the son of Robert Elder, who for many years was the Master of the Toronto and North York Hunt. His brother Norman was in the Canadian Olympic three-day event team in 1960, and again in 1968.

Jim himself, who is president of a refrigeration company in Toronto, also started his competitive career as a show jumper, riding in the Canadian team on the North American fall circuit for the first time in 1950. However, he turned to eventing to gain a chance at the Olympics (Canada at that time sent no jumping team) and in 1956, at Stockholm, he won an Olympic bronze medal. In 1960 he was tenth individually. Eight years later he was riding show jumpers, and in Mexico City in 1972 he rode The Immigrant to the vital round which clinched the Canadian victory in the Prix des Nations.

One of his first good horses was O'Malley, the wayward chestnut gelding on whom, after two years' training, he won the international puissance at the Royal Winter Fair in Toronto, then selling him on; O'Malley then came to England, as the property of the late Robert Hanson.

Then Jim Elder produced Pieces of Eight and Johnny Canuck. The latter, who like so many other good jumpers was part hackney, part thoroughbred, was top jumper at the Royal Winter Fair in Toronto in 1964—his first international outing.

At the 1972 Olympics, Elder did best of all the members of the defending side in the Prix des Nations. Riding Houdini, he made only one mistake in each round.

Jim Elder, on The Immigrant.

Gayford, Thomas ('Tommy')   Canada

Tommy Gayford and his father, Major Gordon Gayford, have both ridden for Canada at one and the same time. Tom joined the team in 1949, when he was nineteen years of age, and at this time his father was still riding.

He started riding at a very young age on a superannuated polo pony, and kept it up throughout all his time at school and university. Both father and son are in the same firm of stockbrokers in Toronto, and they also share a fifty-acre farm at Gormley, some ten miles to the north of the city, where their horses are kept.

In 1952 Tom was a member, and his father manager, of the Canadian Olympic three-day event team in Helsinki, but he now confines himself entirely to show jumping. He captained the team which won the Olympic gold medals in Mexico in 1968, riding Big Dee, originally destined to become his father's hunter.

Perhaps the horse on which he really made his name was Blue Beau, by the outstanding sire of jumpers, Blue Yank, out of a half-bred mare, foaled in Ontario in 1949. Also destined for the hunting field, he was sent to Tom to be schooled over fences and proved to have so big a jump that he was diverted to the show ring. He jumped with the team for over ten seasons, from 1955, and in 1963 set up the puissance record in New York, clearing 7ft 1in.

In 1972 the Canadian Olympic team for Munich was without Tom Gayford for the first time since 1952.

d'Orgeix, Jean   France

The son of a famous show jumper, Jean d'Orgeix started show jumping with great success internationally just before World War II. He became a frequent and popular visitor to the London shows with Kama and Sucre de Pomme, two of the volatile little French Anglo-Arabs that were so successful at that time.

Jean d'Orgeix.

His greatest success, after winning the Grand Prix in Rome in 1948 and the *Daily Mail* Cup at the Royal International Horse Show at the White City, when it was in its prime, was to take the Olympic individual bronze medal at the Olympic Games in London. The French team was eliminated after one of its members fell, but d'Orgeix made sure of taking a medal back to France when he finished in the middle of a three-way jump-off for the silver and bronze, dividing Ruben Uriza of Mexico on Hatvey and Colonel Franklin Wing of the United States on Democrat.

Early in the 1950's, having married the French rider Michèle Cancre, he left Europe for the Far East, spent several years coaching the Cambodian equestrian team, and later conducted hunting safaris in Africa. Now he is back in France, having succeeded to the title of his father, the late Marquis. In 1973 he started to train the French team—to such effect that they were second to Italy in the Nations' Cup in Rome in 1974. In his native land he is expected to effect a renaissance of French show jumping, and with his ability and enthusiasm he probably will.

In 1949 his controversial book *Horse in the Blood* was published in an English-language edition with a foreword by Colonel Harry Llewellyn, who said: 'It is he, a young man in his twenties, who has perfected the art of retaining precision at speed over show ring obstacles with its technique of cutting corners and jumping fences at angles. If you miss d'Orgeix you miss half the show.'

d'Oriola, Pierre Jonquères   France

The most successful French rider since World War II, 'Pierrot' d'Oriola, who farms a large acreage in the Pyrenees, was born in 1920 and is the only Olympic show jumping double gold-medallist in existence at the time of writing. He won his first gold medal on the chestnut Ali Baba at Helsinki in 1952, and his second in Tokyo twelve years later on Lutteur B, when France also won the team silver medals. He also won the Men's World Championship on Pomone B in Buenos Aires in 1966, having finished second in 1953 and third in 1954.

Pierre Jonquères d'Oriola, on Dark Noe.

d'Oriola, with d'Orgeix, was the first civilian rider to break into the hitherto exclusively military French team after the war. On the little Anglo-Arab mare, l'Historiette, he won the Grand Prix in Zurich in 1946, and the next year at London's White City he won the first post-war King George V Gold Cup at the Royal International Horse Show on Marquis III, another fiery little Anglo-Arab with a temperament and volatility to match his own.

He has achieved success with a remarkable variety of horses, among them l'Historiette, Marquis III, Virtuoso, Ali Baba, Voulette, Arlequin D, Lutteur B, Gingembre, Nagir, Pomone B, and many others. But in recent years he has gone in for bigger horses than the Anglo-Arabs on which he was so brilliant in his youth, horses with more size and scope and able to cope with the bigger fences that have become commonplace with the advancement of the sport.

After the 1970 season Morning Light was bought by the French champagne manufacturers Moet et Chandon, from Iris Kellett, at a price in the region of £35,000 ($80,000). He was renamed Moet et Chandon after the firm, and sent to d'Oriola. Their partnership was not a happy one, and Moet et Chandon later joined the string of Hubert Parot. d'Oriola does not as yet seem to have found a horse to compete with his giants of the past.

Lefebvre, Janou *see* Tissot, Janou

Lefrant, Guy   France

Born in 1923, Guy Lefrant has been an active competitor in one or other of the equestrian disciplines from 1948 until the present day. Although his first military duties after graduating from St. Cyr were in the infantry, he soon transferred into the cavalry, and was posted to the Centre National des Sports Equestres at Fontainebleau, where he started out as a three-day event rider. In the 1952 Olympic three-day event at Helsinki he won the individual silver medal on Verdun. In Rome, eight years later, he won a team bronze medal on Nicias. He switched to show jumping for the 1964 Olympic Games in Tokyo; it was here that he first rode with the French Olympic show-jumping team, which won the silver medals. Accompanied by d'Oriola and by Janou Lefebvre (now Tissot) he rode a horse called Monsieur de Littry, by that legendary French sire of jumpers, Furioso.

Outside the Olympics, he has ridden in show jumping and three-day events with equal virtuosity—he was national show-jumping champion of France in 1951 and 1955, and national three-day event champion in 1958 and 1959. He is unquestionably one of the most successful French military riders to have appeared since World War II. He retired from the army in 1969.

Parot, Hubert   France

Hubert Parot owns and runs an instructional establishment near Fontainebleau, south of Paris, and is the most successful French newcomer for several years. His best horse is probably the Anglo-Normand chestnut Tic, his 1972 Olympic mount. Also on Tic, he won a leg of the Men's European Championship at Hickstead in 1973.

Parot's stock in the international field went up a further notch when he succeeded in forging a successful partnership with Moet et Chandon (formerly Iris Kellett's Morning Light, on which she won her European title at Dublin in 1969) after the double Olympic gold-medallist and 1966 world champion Pierre Jonquères d'Oriola had failed to come to terms with him.

Hubert Parot, on Tic.

Marcel Rozier, on Tournebride Là.

Riding with a finesse which belies his stocky frame, Hubert Parot has proved himself a valuable addition to the French team and his personality endears him to his fellow riders. Always ready to help the young with advice he is equally considerate of the older members of the show-jumping community. Tic's octagenarian owner rides at his stables early every morning, and still competes in three-day events on horses he has bred and sent to Parot to produce.

Born in 1933, Hubert Parot first rode in the French Olympic team in Munich in 1972, when France fielded a team without its mainstay of former Olympic Games, Pierre Jonquères d'Oriola. Parot, riding Tic, put up the best performance of the entire French team, for a total of 18 faults in his two rounds.

His younger brother Michel is also a show jumper, and holder with Tonquerville of the French high-jump record at 2.41 metres, set in 1973.

Rozier, Marcel   France

Marcel Rozier, who was born in 1936, is the secretary of a riding club in the Forest of Fontainebleau, near Paris. He came to show jumping fairly late in life, his first equestrian interest having been race riding. Four years after he started riding in show-jumping events he was a member of the French Olympic team in Mexico City; he retained his place in the team which competed in Munich in 1972.

His first top-class horse was Quo Vadis, a thoroughbred foaled in 1960 by the American racehorse Pot o' Luck, now standing at stud in France. After having sustained a double fracture of the leg in a fall with another horse, Prince Charmant, Rozier made a rapid recovery and was back in the saddle five months later; at Aachen in July 1967 he gained two individual second places riding Quo Vadis, and earned a place in the French Nations' Cup team.

In Mexico in 1968 he won a team Olympic silver medal, also on Quo Vadis, and more recently he has enjoyed considerable success on the thoroughbred stallion Sans Souci, as well as on Tournebride-Là. He rode the former to a joint victory with Neal Shapiro on Sloopy in the Grand Prix at Aachen in 1972.

Marcel Rozier and Hubert Parot are the two most successful riders in the French team at the time of writing, and were selected to represent France in the Men's World Championship at Hickstead in 1974.

Tissot, Janou   France

Janou Lefebvre (as she was known before her marriage), born in 1945, was the youngest rider ever to compete in the Olympic Games when, at the age of nineteen, she rode Kenavo D in Tokyo and came away with a team silver medal.

In Mexico City four years later she won another team silver medal, this time riding the bay thoroughbred Rocket, the horse on which she won the Ladies' World Championship in Copenhagen in 1970, and successfully defended it in 1974.

The daughter of a French father, an engineer who spent many years building roads in the Far East, and a Chinese mother, Janou was French champion in 1961, when she rode in the French junior team which finished fifth in the Junior European Championships at Hickstead. She joined the senior French team two years later, and at Aachen she and Kenavo finished second in the Grand Prix to no less a rider than Captain Raimondo d'Inzeo of Italy on his gold medal horse Posillipo.

At the Mexico Olympics Rocket had the best score of the French team and finished in seventh place overall. The following year he and his rider won the Grand Prix and the championship at the French official international show in Nice, won the *Daily Mail* Cup in London, and the Meisterspringen in Aachen.

It was thus a natural progression to the women's world title in Copenhagen in 1970, especially as Janou had already won the European Championship on Kenavo in 1966 at Gijon in Spain. Janou won from the holder, Marion Mould with Stroller, with Anneli Drummon-Hay on Merely-a-Monarch finishing third.

In 1971 Rocket went to Switzerland to undergo a remedial operation on his back, and he was not fit in time to join in the fight for the European title, won in St Gall, Switzerland, by Ann Moore on Psalm. Back in action in time for the Olympic Games, he was only a shadow of his former self in Munich, but was

Janou Lefebvre, now Janou Tissot, on Rocket. The horse took off too close to the jump, but, being experienced, has kept out of trouble.

back on form by 1974 when Janou defended the world title in La Baule. Rocket proved to be on excellent form, and Janou retained her title, beating Michele McEvoy of the United States.

In the winter of 1972/3, Janou married and became Mme Tissot, under which name she won her second and last women's world title. After 1974 there is only one world championship, open to men and women alike. But Janou won two of the three Ladies' Championships to have been held, the first of which was captured by Marion Coakes, now Marion Mould.

Bradley, Caroline   Great Britain

Although slim and blonde and very feminine, Caroline Bradley, who took out a professional licence in 1973, is a great deal stronger than she looks and she is one of the top lady riders in Britain. Born in 1946, she has succeeded with a wide variety of horses—the hallmark of the expert.

She first joined the British team in Dublin in 1964, where she won two competitions with the little chestnut Russian horse, Ivanovitch. The following year she started a long and happy partnership with the late Robert Hanson's Franco, David Barker's mount in the 1960 Olympic Games, and at the end of a long and successful season they finished second to Harvey Smith with O'Malley in the New York Grand Prix. They went on winning speed competitions for many years.

In 1973, riding True Lass, Caroline was runner-up to Ann Moore and Psalm for the European championship in Vienna, and a year later she finished fourth for the world title in La Baule, behind Janou Tissot of France, Michele McEvoy of the United States, and Barbara Kerr of Canada.

A considerable puissance rider with immense courage, she rode Archie Thomlinson's New Yorker to win the puissance in Nice in 1973, and this same horse gave her the most prestigious home win of her career in 1974, when he carried her to victory in the Norwich Union puissance at Wembley's Horse of the Year show. It was her second major win of the week, for she also won the National Foxhunter Championship on the bay stallion Middle Road, which made her the champion lady rider of the show.

Caroline Bradley on Knowlton Tango. The horse is shown here as a novice and has got into difficulties, but the rider is in a perfect position nevertheless.

David Broome, on Mister Softee.

Broome, David   Great Britain

One of the world's most stylish, sympathetic and effective riders, David Broome was born in Cardiff in 1940 and started his riding career in the hunting field in Monmouthshire before graduating to jumping ponies. Very successful in his youth at the shows in South Wales, he attained national fame in 1959, at the age of nineteen, when he became the leading rider of the year in Britain in terms of prize money; he was riding the former King's Troop horse, Wildfire, bought very cheaply by his father, Fred Broome, because this temperamental performer had at that time a very determined 'stop'.

But every horse goes well for David Broome, and international recognition was soon to follow. In 1960, given the ride on another brilliant but by no means easy horse, Oliver Anderson's Sunsalve, he won the King George V Gold Cup only two weeks after starting to ride him. Short-listed and finally selected for the British Olympic team in the same year, he went on to win the individual bronze medal in Rome.

In 1961, on the same horse, he won the first of his three European Men's Championships in Aachen. The second came in 1967 in Rotterdam, when he rode John Massarella's legendary Mister Softee, and the third, on the same horse, at Hickstead two years later, where he successfully defended his title. In 1968, riding in his third Olympic Games, he won a second Olympic bronze medal on Mister Softee in Mexico City.

His greatest triumph was to come in 1970, when, riding Douglas Bunn's Beethoven, he won the Men's World title at La Baule in Brittany. The deciding factor was his masterly handling of the problem horse of the party, Graziano Mancinelli's German-bred Fidux, in the final when the four best-classified riders over the previous three days rode one another's horses.

Broome is the sort of rider who can get the best out of any horse, and the key to his success is an outstandingly good pair of hands which puts him in a class of his own. He excels on difficult horses; yet another was the Argentine Olympic horse Discutido, who was also a confirmed 'stopper' before joining Broome's string. He can also win major international competitions on horses which in any other hands would be considered moderate.

One of only four riders to have won the King George V Gold Cup on three occasions (the others being the late Colonel Jack Talbot-Ponsonby, Colonel Harry Llewellyn and Colonel Piero d'Inzeo), Broome won the British Jumping

Derby on Mister Softee in 1967, and has three European titles and World title to his credit, in addition to two Olympic bronze medals. He has ridden in four Olympic Games—in 1960, 1964, 1968 and 1972—but became a professional in 1973, riding for the Esso Petroleum Company on horses they had leased from him for the season. This sponsorship came to an end when the season was over, due to the oil crisis in the Middle East.

Perhaps the accolade which he values most, however, is the O.B.E., which he received from the Queen in 1970 for his services to show jumping, for which he is the best ambassador.

Broome defended his world title at the Men's World Championship held at Hickstead in July 1974. Riding Sportsman, he narrowly missed qualifying for the final of the four rounds which go to make up the championship. Later in the season, at the new Cardiff show, he had considerable consolation, for he won the first 'World Professional Championship', riding Philco, the American-bred grey.

Bunn, Douglas   Great Britain

Douglas Bunn.

Douglas Bunn, who started show jumping as a child rider before the war with considerable success, became an international rider when he left Cambridge and began practising law. In 1965 he won the Grand Prix at the Royal Winter Fair in Toronto riding Beethoven, on whom he only narrowly lost the King George V Gold Cup with a fault at the water in the barrage; but it is as the owner and founder of the All-England Jumping Course at Hickstead that he is best known.

For some years he had been conscious that British horses and riders laboured under some disadvantage when they went abroad because they lacked, at home, an international-type arena over which to practice, and were consequently at a loss when it came to negotiating permanent obstacles. So in May 1960 with foresight and enterprise and not a little courage, he opened the All England Jumping Course. From small beginnings Hickstead has become the most famous jumping course in the world. Home of the British Jumping Derby, it was quickly recognised by the International Equestrian Federation as an ideal place to hold international championships, and having staged two Junior European Championships, two Men's and one Ladies' European Championships, and two World Championships (the Ladies' in 1965 and the Men's in 1974), it has brought a new dimension to the sport in Britain.

A former chairman of the British Show Jumping Association, and *chef d'équipe* to the British team on numerous major international occasions, Douglas Bunn has also served as an international judge and course-builder; he is the man who will ensure that Britain remains in the first flight of the world's show-jumping nations.

Coakes, Marion *see* Mould, Marion

Dawes, Alison   Great Britain

Alison Westwood, as she was before her marriage, started her career in junior classes. Born in 1944, she began show jumping when she was eleven years old. Her first major successes were gained on The Maverick, an Irish horse which was first produced by the noted Northern Ireland rider and dealer, Jack Bamber, from Ballymena, Co. Antrim, ridden with great success by his son, Roddy Bamber; The Maverick was later sold to Douglas Bunn who sold him on in 1963.

Alison and The Maverick, coached by the late Colonel Jack Talbot-Ponsonby, first made their mark two years later, when Alison was leading rider at four official international horse shows, Aachen, London, Rotterdam and Geneva, and also at the unofficial international show at Enschede, in the Netherlands. That year they also finished third to Marion Mould and Stroller in the first Women's World Championship ever held.

Placed three times in the Queen Elizabeth Cup, which they eventually won in 1969, Alison and The Maverick finished third in the Women's European Championship in Dublin in the same year. In 1968 they had done exceptionally well at the Midlands International show at Stoneleigh, and their victory shortly afterwards in the W.D. & H.O. Wills British Jumping Derby at Hickstead finally won them the reserve position in the British Olympic team, and a trip to Mexico.

In 1971 they were second in the Women's European Championship in St Gall, Switzerland, and only a controversial decision at the water (that originator of controversial verdicts in show jumping at all levels) put them behind Ann Moore and Psalm. They had to pull out of the Olympic short-list because the horse was not sound, but in 1973, when Alison turned professional and The Maverick was re-named Mr Banbury, they won their second British Jumping Derby at Hickstead with the only clear round of the day.

Alison Dawes.

Drummond-Hay, Anneli *see* Wucherpfennig, Anneli

Fletcher, Graham   Great Britain

Born in 1951, the son of Mr and Mrs Kenneth Fletcher, who farm near Thirsk in Yorkshire, Graham is the best prospect to have come out of Yorkshire—or out of England, for that matter—since Harvey Smith. He has something of the style of David Broome, an excellent eye and sense of timing, and he has passed the acid test of taking horses from the hunting field, at hunter price, and schooling them on to become top-class international competitors.

Graham Fletcher.

His best horse, Buttevant Boy, bred in Ireland, came out as a four-year-old when Graham was still in Young Riders' classes, and was responsible for Graham's meteoric rise to fame at the Horse of the Year Show at Wembley in 1970, when he won the Cortina Crown for points gained throughout the show. The following year he joined the British team for Rome, Fontainebleau and Aachen, and finally won the richly endowed Dublin Grand Prix for the Irish Trophy, in addition to the Olympic Trial at the British Timken Show.

Short-listed for the British Olympic team the following year, he was deemed in the last analysis to be too young and to lack experience commensurate with that of some of his older rivals. But as one of the few top British riders to have retained his amateur status, he is a very hot tip for the British Olympic team in Montreal in 1976.

Perhaps Graham Fletcher's best win in 1973 was the Grand Prix at the Dunhill Show at Olympia. Had the British selection for the Men's World Championship pair in 1974 been postponed until after the Great Yorkshire show, where he swept the board, he might well have take precedence as one of Britain's selected pair of riders. But he is still in his early twenties; and has many years and multiple victories before him; the fact that he hunts regularly with the Bedale Hounds must stand him in good stead in the future, as it has so many other top British riders in the past.

In 1974 he won the Leading Show Jumper of the Year competition on Tauna Dora at Wembley.

opposite: *Harvey Smith of Great Britain, riding Salvador.*

Koechlin-Smythe, Pat   Great Britain

Pat Smythe (as she was known in her riding days), who was born in 1928, first won at the Richmond Royal Show in 1939 on a diminutive pony called Pixie, but it was after the war that she made her name when, riding a small bay mare called Finality, she won the Ladies' Championship in Paris in 1949, the Grand Prix in Brussels, and was leading lady rider in Geneva.

Her father died when she was small and her mother, who ran a riding school near Bath and had played polo before the war, found her horses and helped considerably with their schooling. Finality, who won the leading show-jumper title at the Horse of the Year Show at Harringay in 1950, was followed by Tosca and Prince Hal. Tosca became the leading money-winner in Britain in 1952, winning the then-record sum of £2,000 in prize money, and Prince Hal became a very successful international horse.

In 1956 she started to ride the former three-day-event horse Flanagan for the late Robert Hanson, and later that year became not only the first woman ever to ride in the Olympic Games, but the first to win a medal, when, with Wilf White's Nizefela and Peter Robeson on Scorchin', the British team finished third in Stockholm. Four years later, still riding Flanagan, she finished eleventh individually in the Rome Olympics.

In 1957 she won her first European title, at Spa, and in 1961 she initiated her hat-trick of victories in the European Championship at Deauville; there followed successes at Madrid and Hickstead, where she also won the British Jumping Derby. In 1958, after many years of trying, she won the Queen Elizabeth II Cup on Mr Pollard.

She retired from the sport in 1963, when she married Dr Sam Koechlin, a Swiss industrialist and former three-day-event rider. She now divides her time between her adopted country and Gloucestershire, but is still on the international committee of the B.S.J.A. and is a selector and sometime *chef d'équipe*.

Pat Smythe, on Prince Hal.

Llewellyn, Lt-Col. Harry   Great Britain

Harry Llewellyn was the man who put show jumping on the map in Britain after the war, and his partnership with the legendary Foxhunter won Britain a team bronze medal in the 1948 Olympic Games, and a gold medal in Helsinki four years later.

But his equestrian career goes back further. In the 1930s, as a Cambridge undergraduate, he rode Ego to finish second and fourth in two Grand Nationals, and after the war, when he was a member of Field-Marshal Montgomery's staff, he won two important amateur races on Bay Marble and State Control—the latter named after the take-over of his family's mining interests in Wales by the socialist government of the time. When he became too heavy to ride in racing, he turned his attention to show jumping, and on Kilgeddin he achieved important international victories before, in 1948, he provided all three of the horses—Foxhunter, Kilgeddin and Monty—which won the bronze medals in the Olympic Games at Wembley. In the same year he won the King George V Gold Cup for the first time on Foxhunter, and he completed his treble on the same horse in 1950 and 1953—they were the only combination ever to win this coveted trophy on three occasions.

Llewellyn and Foxhunter competed at top international level from 1947 until 1956, and won no fewer than seventy-eight competitions against the rest of the world. Foxhunter won his last-ever competition in Dublin, and after he retired he was hunted with the Monmouthshire Hounds, of which his owner-rider was joint-Master. He died in 1959, but Harry Llewellyn did not hang up his boots until he had won internationally on the Irish mare Aherlow.

When he retired from the international arena, he by no means forsook the sport which had made him a household name. He was chairman of the British Show Jumping Association for two·years, and on many occasions *chef d'équipe* to British teams abroad; he then became chairman of the International Affairs Committee of the B.S.J.A., in addition to being a member of the Bureau of the International Equestrian Federation and chairman of the Sports Council for Wales. In 1974 he became President of the British Show Jumping Association.

Harry Llewellyn.

McMahon, Paddy   Great Britain

Paddy McMahon, who was brought up in Derby, started riding ponies belonging to scrap-iron dealer Tom Mulholland when he was still at school. He rode Mulholland's team of horses after leaving school, and the best of them, Ted Williams's former horse Timm II, was the first top horse he rode.

His first international horse at the modern level was Hideaway, whom he produced for Trevor Banks. But the best he has ever ridden is Pennwood Forgemill, owned by the Staffordshire dealer, Fred Hartill.

McMahon and Forgemill were unlucky not to be selected for the British Olympic team in 1972, but compensation came their way in the following year, when they won the Men's European Championship, sponsored by W.D. & H.O. Wills, at Hickstead and the King George V Gold Cup shortly afterwards at the Royal International Horse Show at Wembley. A year earlier they had won the Victor Ludorum for the Ronson Trophy at the Horse of the Year Show, to tumultuous applause, and Forgemill was the equine pin-up in England throughout 1973. Fame is, however, always ephemeral; after his victory in the men's European title at Hickstead McMahon declared, prophetically, that in show jumping one is only 'king for a day'.

A year later, when well in touch for the men's world title at Hickstead, lying fourth after the first two legs and thus well in the running to contest the final,

opposite above: Piero d'Inzeo of Italy, riding Easter Light.

opposite below: William 'Buddy' Brown of the United States, riding Sandsablaze at Lucerne.

he was beaten in the third phase by the final combination fence in the Nations' Cup-type course by a massive spread coming out of the treble.

Moore, Ann   Great Britain

Ann Moore.

Britain's second Olympic individual silver medallist, following in the footsteps of Marion Mould in the Mexico City Games of 1968, Ann Moore won her Olympic medal on Psalm at Munich in 1972. The eldest of the six children of West Midlands industrialist Norman Moore, she too was a successful child rider and attained international status as a member of the British junior team in 1968, when she won the European junior title at Stoneleigh; she made it a hat-trick for her age group when she also cornered the W.D. & H.O. Wills Young Riders' Championship of Great Britain at Hickstead and the Young Rider of the Year title at the Horse of the Year Show at Wembley.

Reserve for the Ladies' World Championship at Copenhagen in 1970, the following year she won her first European title, on Psalm, at the Swiss show of St Gall, and retained her title two years later in Vienna. In the interim, she won her Olympic medal in Munich, with Graziano Mancinelli taking the gold on Ambassador for Italy, and Neal Shapiro and Sloopy gaining the bronze for the U.S.A.

In 1971, her best international season, she was Britain's only winner in Rome and Fontainebleau and did more than her share in Aachen. She was equally hard to beat at home and few of the big prizes eluded her; she won the Queen Elizabeth II Cup in 1972 and retained it in 1973, though this time it was a shared win with Alison Dawes on The Maverick.

In 1974 she won one of the few titles that had so far escaped her net, the Ladies' National Championship at Royal Windsor, and she was an obvious choice for the Ladies' World Championship in La Baule. But a week after Windsor Psalm was taken home after jumping only one day at Devon County; he was not jumping with his old elan, and it was later announced that he was resting with a strained foreleg. He jumped his last round at Arena North in June, and though he achieved a double clear, on the next day the decision was made not to jump him again.

Two days later, Ann Moore declared that she was retiring from the sport which made her famous before she was twenty. Twenty-three years old, she entered the fashion business and opened a boutique near Birmingham, and is also under contract to the B.B.C. as a television commentator on the sport.

Mould, Marion   Great Britain

Marion Coakes, as she was when she won the first-ever F.E.I. Ladies' World Championship at Hickstead in 1965 at the age of seventeen, was a successful child rider and a valued member of the British junior team; but it was when she graduated to the adult competitions with her phenomenal Irish-bred pony Stroller, that she achieved international fame which culminated, in 1968, in an Olympic individual silver medal in Mexico City.

The daughter of a Hampshire farmer, Ralph Coakes, who used to breed Shire horses at his farm near Milford-on-Sea, she followed her two older brothers, John and Douglas, into the British junior team. Then, in 1965, she won her world title from under the nose of the favourite, Kathy Kusner of the United States on Untouchable, at the start of an enviable international career during which she won at most of the leading shows in Europe as well as in the United States, where her 14.2 hands pony Stroller was a major sensation.

When Marion graduated from the junior classes, her father intended to sell Stroller to another juvenile rider, but she persuaded him to let her have a season with the pony in open competition, having a pretty shrewd idea of his capabilities. It proved to be a masterly decision, for the bigger the obstacles, the better this lion-hearted pony performed. His rider soon proved that her world title victory was far from a flash in the pan, for she went on to win the Queen Elizabeth cup and a great many top international competitions against the best male riders in the world, with Stroller often giving away two hands (eight inches) in height.

Her consistency at Hickstead was proverbial, and she won the Wills Hickstead Gold Medal, awarded for consistency in the major international competitions throughout the season in no fewer than five consecutive years—a record which seems likely to stand unrivalled for some time. In 1973 Stroller was honoured in a ceremony, marking his retirement, on the All England Jumping Course, the scene of so many of his triumphs, including the British Jumping Derby in 1967.

Since her marriage to David Mould, the stylish and highly successful steeplechase jockey, Marion has brought out several useful horses, among them Bandalero and Dunlynne. But Stroller was her once-in-a-lifetime show jumper; on him she reached the height of her riding career.

Oliver, Alan   Great Britain

Alan Oliver's father, Phil Oliver, a small farmer in Buckinghamshire, used to boast in pre-war years that he would one day own the best string of show jumpers in England; twenty years later Alan started riding his father's horses after the war as a slim, slight lad of eleven, and very soon arrived at the top. Born into a family of hunting farmers, he learned to ride almost before he could walk.

Born in 1932, he had many successes as a junior on the pony Thumbs Up, and his first good horse was Red Star II, owned by the late A.H. Payne, his father's patron for many years. His first top international horse was Red Admiral, on whom, in the Moss Bros. (later Lonsdale) Puissance at the Royal International Horse Show at the White City he had many a duel with the top Italian, Piero d'Inzeo, on The Rock.

In 1951, the year in which, aged nineteen, he first joined the British team—and cut a field of corn at home soon after dawn on the day when he first rode in the Prince of Wales (Nations') Cup—Alan won the National Championship jointly with Red Knight and Red Admiral, in addition to riding the top money-winner of the year, Red Star II. Two years later, Red Admiral was the Leading Show Jumper title winner at the Horse of the Year Show at Harringay.

Every show-jumping rider of any standing knows that the interval between top horses which they all experience will mean a period in the wilderness when nothing seems to go right. This happened to Alan at the end of the 'Red' dynasty which had been so successful in the 1950s; and when this great team went over the hill he relinquished his previous aerobatic style, which never found favour with the purists, and opted for classicism and convention.

This was no bad ploy, for in the late 1960s he came storming back on Sweep III and Piz Palu. Content hitherto to campaign in the main in Britain, he won two events in Rome in 1969, helped to win the Nations' Cup in Barcelona, and on Piz Palu won his second Ronson Trophy for the Victor Ludorum.

An accomplished point-to-point jockey in addition to his show-jumping activities, Alan has now retired from top-class jumping and assists his wife Alison in the training of the three-day event horses ridden by H.R.H. The Princess Anne and her husband, Captain Mark Phillips.

Marion Mould.

Alan Oliver.

Pyrah, Malcolm   Great Britain

Malcolm Pyrah.

Malcolm Pyrah, born in 1940 in Hull, is the son of a Battle of Britain pilot who was shot down during the Second World War. His step-father provided him with ponies and eventually with a show jumper, Dark Night, but Malcolm, who was educated at the local grammar school, went to work in a government office as a civil servant and it was not until some ten years ago that he decided that office life was not for him, and that he would chance his luck as a rider of show jumpers.

He gave himself ten years to reach the top, and he achieved his target. He started riding for Trevor Banks, then moved to the Massarellas at Doncaster, and during the time that he was there he learned a great deal about the game and saved enough money to open three dry-cleaning shops in Hull, which are managed by his step-brother.

When he married the former Judy Boulter he opened his own yard in Nottinghamshire, where he runs a very successful business. Some of his best international victories—notably dividing the puissance at the Horse of the Year show in 1971 with Raimondo d'Inzeo on Fiorello, clearing 7 ft 2 in—were gained on the Massarellas' former champion show hack, Lucky Strike, who was retired after the same show in 1974. The last fence he ever jumped stood at 6 ft 8 in and he was nineteen years of age.

Malcolm first joined the British team in 1972 in Madrid and on Trevarrion won the classic Generalissimo Franco Cup, as well as helping Britain to win the Nations' Cup. He was unlucky not to be selected as one of Britain's pair for the European championship in that year, and also for the world title in 1974. In Rome, riding Law Court leased from the Massarellas, he won the puissance and was the best-classified non-Italian rider. He has forged a good partnership with April Love, the little grey Australian mare who was formerly ridden by Ann Moore, and together they won at the Horse of the Year and Courvoisier Cognac shows.

Robeson, Peter   Great Britain

Robeson is veteran of the British international riders, although still several years short of his half-century; his father, the late Mr Toby Robeson, preceded him as a member of the British team, for whom he rode Rufus II in the Low Countries in 1947, the first post-war international season. Peter himself first joined the team on his home-bred bay Craven A, a mare who was only one generation removed from a Shire horse and who, foaled in the war years, is not only still alive and well, living out a well-earned retirement on her owner's home near Newport Pagnell, but not so long ago took part in a sponsored ride (or walk) for charity.

With a series of enviable national and international victories under his belt, Robeson was reserve for the British Olympic team in 1952, travelling with them to Helsinki. Four years later, when Craven A was past her best, he rode the late Hon. Dorothy Paget's Scorchin' in Stockholm, in the team which won the Olympic bronze medals. An interregnum without a horse of Olympic calibre kept him out of the team until Tokyo, in 1964, when he won the individual bronze medal, after a jump-off with John Fahey of Australia on Bonvale, riding Firecrest.

He achieved a long-held ambition in 1967 when, after many abortive attempts, he finally won the King George V Gold Cup at the White City.

Short-listed for the 1972 Olympic team with Grebe, who had been going exceptionally well abroad, he did not ride at Munich but seven months later in

Rome he showed the selectors that it would have been better for British interests if he had. He was the decisive factor in the Nations' Cup victory there, and he has always been an excellent team member, while his wife, the former Renée de Rothschild, is also an asset to any team which goes abroad.

Robeson is currently bringing on a string of young horses with considerable success.

Smith, Harvey   Great Britain

Harvey Smith.

Harvey Smith, born in Yorkshire in 1938, is one of the most colourful personalities in show jumping as well as one of its stars. He first came to fame on Farmer's Boy, bought for £40 at York Repository as a four-year-old in 1954. Four years later he was invited to join the British team in Dublin, and helped to win the Aga Khan Trophy; since this time his rise has been meteoric—first on a succession of horses which other riders had tried and given up, such as Warpaint, Montana, The Frame, and The Sea Hawk, later on horses such as the Canadian-bred O'Malley, who was brilliant but difficult, Harvester, Madison Time, Evan Jones, Mattie Brown, Johnny Walker, Summertime, Lights Out—and more recently with the German-bred Salvador.

Overlooked by the British selectors for the Tokyo Olympics, Harvey Smith went with the next Olympic team to Mexico City and rode Madison Time, and was in the British team with Summertime in Munich. But here his career as an Olympic rider came to an end, for early in 1973 he was the first British international rider to turn professional, and in the spring he went into a dealing, owning and riding partnership with another Yorkshireman, Trevor Banks.

Harvey also became a professional wrestler in 1974, and seems to take it seriously. Though he has yet to win an Olympic medal or a world or European title, he has been well placed in many continental championships, second on Harvester in 1967 and also on Evan Jones in 1971. He has won the John Player Trophy, the British Grand Prix, on six occasions and the Wills British Jumping Derby three times.

Smythe, Pat *see* Koechlin-Smythe, Pat

Talbot-Ponsonby, Lt-Col. Jack   Great Britain

Jack Talbot-Ponsonby, whose father was a regular soldier and Master of several packs of hounds, was born in Ireland near Kilcullen, Co. Kildare, and the first fourteen years of his life were spent in that country, where he was able to nurture his inherited love of horses and hunting. 'To me,' he said many years later, 'the Emerald Isle will always mean horses and hounds, and anything else that happens there will always seem entirely subsidiary to these two.'

He started hunting when he was eight, on a three-year-old cob called Tommy. When he had left Harrow School he went to the military college at Sandhurst, where Colonel Joe Hume Dudgeon was then in charge of equitation, and had his first introduction to show jumping under the tutelage of this very keen jumping rider.

He was commissioned to the 7th Queen's Own Hussars in 1927, and a year later he rode for the first time at Olympia, where he was to win the King George V Gold Cup three times. In 1929 he was sent on a course to the Army Equitation School at Weedon, where he was subsequently an instructor and a regular member of the British army team.

He trained the winning British Olympic team in 1952, and was trainer until after the 1960 Olympic Games in Rome, when be became the most erudite builder of international courses in the world, with a great penchant for distance problems as an alternative to overfacing horses over enormous fences, or deciding every competition against the clock. He ran a very successful instructional establishment at Todenham, in Gloucestershire, and when he died in the hunting field in December 1969 at the early age of 61, British show jumping was very much the poorer for the loss of a distinguished, intelligent and witty man.

Westwood, Alison *see* Dawes, Alison

Wucherpfennig, Anneli   Great Britain

Anneli Drummond-Hay (now Wucherpfennig) was born in 1937 and is one of the very few three-day-event riders to have made a successful transition to show jumping at the top international level. A grand-daughter of the late Duke of Hamilton, she was born in Dorset but spent much of her childhood near Perth. She was preceded into the horse world by her elder sister Jane—now Mrs Timothy Whiteley—who finished second, riding the late lamented Happy Knight, at the Badminton Horse Trials in 1951. Anneli, too, first made her name in three-day events and won the first-ever Burghley Horse Trials in 1961, riding Merely-a-Monarch. This remarkable horse soon adapted himself to show jumping, and one of his earliest international victories was to win the Imperial Cup at the Royal International Horse Show.

This was the start of a successful European career, which culminated in winning the Womens' European Championship in Rome in 1968. But the horse had a difficult temperament, and Anneli never succeeded in making an Olympic team, the ambition of every rider of either sex. She did, however, win Grand Prix competitions in Geneva and elsewhere, and on the fiery chestnut Xanthos, who started his working life as a hunt horse in the stable of Captain Brian Fanshawe, who was then Master of the Warwickshire Hounds, Anneli twice won

Anneli Wucherpfennig (formerly Drummond-Hay).

168

the gruelling Olgiata Jumping Derby, a cross-country-cum-show-jumping competition held during the Rome International Horse Show. But Merely-a-Monarch was her most successful horse, and to prove his versatility he followed up his Burghley victory by winning the Badminton three-day event the following spring.

Having finally won the Queen Elizabeth II Cup at the Royal International in 1970, Anneli finished third in the Women's World Championship in Copenhagen. She is now married to the South African rider, Errol Wucherpfennig, and lives for the most of the year in South Africa.

Campion, Edward ('Ned')   Ireland

Ned Campion.

Ned Campion, born in 1937, lives with his wife and family in South County Dublin. He joined the Army Equitation School at McKee Barracks, in Dublin's Phoenix Park, in 1958, and three years later started competing in international competitions.

He has won in London, New York, Vienna, Nice, Rome and Ostend, and has helped to win several Nations' Cups, including the Aga Khan Trophy in Dublin, his home show, in 1967. In the same year he was leading rider in Nice.

His most successful horse is Garrai Eoin (pronounced Garry Owen), a chestnut mare, foaled in 1962, by Candelabra. Bought by the Irish Army from the late Lady Daresbury in 1962, she was one of the most successful army horses for some years and in 1971 was in the winning Nations' Cup team in Ostend, where she also won the Prix du Rhin, and was in the winning team for the Military Cup at Fontainebleau, where she jumped two clear rounds.

Hayes, Seamus   Ireland

Born in 1925, Seamus Hayes is the son of the late Major-General Liam Hayes, the man who while his son was still a small boy bought most of the good horses that brought the Irish Army Jumping Team to the top of the European league in the 1930s; they were trained at McKee Barracks in Phoenix Park, Dublin, by the legendary White Russian cavalry officer Colonel Paul Rodzianko.

Seamus left home, and Ireland, in 1946, bringing with him a splendid little horse called Snowstorm, and went to ride for Yorkshire owner Tommy Makin, himself a former rider, who had a strong team of jumpers. Seamus Hayes was leading rider in England in 1949, 1950 and 1952, among his greatest triumphs being the 1950 Royal International Grand Prix on Sheila. Then he transferred to another Yorkshire stable, that of Andrew Massarella Senior at Doncaster.

Seamus Hayes.

In the mid-1950s he returned to Ireland as civilian instructor to the Irish Army Jumping Team, but the lure of the ring grew too strong to be denied, and he returned to competitive riding first with Joe McGrath, later with Belgian-born Omer van Landeghem. In 1960, married to Mary Rose Robinson (sister of steeplechase jockey Willie Robinson), he set up his own establishment and first rode the brilliantly successful chestnut gelding Goodbye, by Renwood, for Lord Hartington's daughter, Lady Jane Stanhope.

Goodbye and Seamus won throughout the continent of Europe, but in England they are best remembered for their victory, with only one clear round, in the inaugural British Jumping Derby at Hickstead in 1961. Three years later they won it again after jumping off with Marion Coakes, as she then was, on the pony Stroller.

Seamus and Goodbye cleared 7 ft 2 in on six occasions before the horse was retired at the end of 1967. In 1968 Seamus won the Imperial Cup at the Royal

International on Ardmore, who was then sold to Italy; but Goodbye was the last top-class horse with which he was associated.

Kellett, Iris   Ireland

Iris Kellett, the daughter of a Dublin veterinary surgeon who also owned a flourishing riding school in Dublin, first attained international fame in 1969, when she won the Ladies' European Championship at the summer horse show of the Royal Dublin Society at Ball's Bridge riding her chestnut gelding, Morning Light. This horse was later sold to France for some £35,000, to be ridden by the dual Olympic champion, Pierre Jonquères d'Oriola.

Iris Kellett's first international success outside Ireland was at the White City, then the home of Britain's international horse show, in 1949, when she won the first-ever ladies' championship for the Queen Elizabeth II Cup (known until the year 1953 as the Princess Elizabeth Cup) on her outstanding horse Rusty II. Two years later, she won it again.

Morning Light's European Championship victory was, however, only a harbinger of the success which was later to attend Iris Kellett—now no longer a rider, but a trainer at top European and world level. She ceased to ride internationally for some years, though she made a gallant return to the ring after a bad accident in 1952. Schooling a horse at home—or, more precisely, at the riding school in Mespil Road, Dublin, which she ran with her father, the late Harry Kellett—she sustained a compound fracture of the leg and later, in hospital, contracted tetanus.

Iris, who has moved her riding establishment out to Co. Meath, is now best known as an owner of international horses which are ridden by twenty-four-year-old Eddie Macken. Having trained and produced the rider and the horses, she now has the top Irish team of which the star is the chestnut Pele, a former champion hunter at the Royal Ulster Show in Belfast, who finished second for the Men's World Championship at Hickstead in 1974.

Iris Kellett.

Kiely, Capt. Larry   Ireland

Captain Larry Kiely was born in 1941 and is a former Tipperary All Ireland Hurler. He joined the Irish Army Equitation School in 1962 and started to ride in international competitions four years later. His first major international victory was gained in the puissance at Ludwigsburg in 1969. Two years later he broke a leg in the early part of the season and then rejoined the team at Wulfrath, where he celebrated his return to the fray by winning the Grand Prix. In 1971 he was also in the winning Nations' Cup team in Ostend.

His most successful horse is Inis Cara, a bay horse foaled in 1961 by the well known Irish sire Golden Years, and bought by the Army in 1965 from Jerry Rohan in Midleton, Co. Cork. Inis Cara first competed internationally in 1968 and won the puissance in Ludwigsburg and Ostend in 1969, clearing 7 ft 2 in. In 1971 he was in the winning cup team in the military event in Fontainebleau and won the Grand Prix in Wulfrath.

In Rome in 1972 he finished second to Raimondo d'Inzeo and Bellevue in the puissance, and he has been one of the younger d'Inzeo brother's most formidable opponents in puissance competitions for some years past, in particular in Rome and also in Dublin, where in 1974 they shared first place in the Shell Puissance.

Larry Kiely.

Macken, Edward ('Eddie')   Ireland

Eddie Macken, who was born in 1950, comes from Granard, in Co. Longford, and is a living testimony to the instructional ability of Iris Kellett, who competed at top level for more than twenty years before she won the Women's European Championship in Dublin in 1969, riding Morning Light.

Iris Kellett has had many pupils through her hands during the course of the last quarter of a century, but in Eddie Macken she has produced an exceptional rider who is capable of taking on, and beating, many of the top Continental riders. But every rider is only as good as his horses, and though he had many international victories on Easter Parade and Oatfield Hills, it was on Pele that Macken really made his name.

Eddie Macken, on Pele.

Billy Ringrose.

Pele, who was bred in Co. Cork by the little-known hunter sire, Go Tabaan, was first owned by Fiona Kinnear, for whom as a four-year-old he won the Royal Ulster Hunter Championship in Belfast. A year later, in 1972, he was champion ladies' hunter under side-saddle at the Dublin Horse Show. But he was at the same time acquiring a reputation as a show jumper, and it was thus that he caught the attention of the most experienced dealer in hunters and show jumpers in Northern Ireland, Jack Bamber, who has produced so many brilliant performers from his establishment in Ballymena, Co. Antrim.

He was subsequently bought by Iris Kellett, who saw in him the raw material of an international champion. Her judgement was proved beyond all doubt when she trained both horse and rider to qualify for the final seeding in the Men's World Championship at Hickstead in 1974, where it took a jump-off to divide Macken from the eventual winner of the title, Hartwig Steenken of West Germany. But given another Pele, Macken, now riding for West Germany, has all the attributes which could bring him the title in 1978.

Ringrose, Lt-Col. William ('Billy')   Ireland

Billy Ringrose, who rode in his first International Horse Show in 1954, became the most successful Irish Army rider of the post-war era—with the possible exception of Captain Michael Tubridy, who died when schooling a horse in the early 1950s—when he took over the best of the Irish army's post-war horses, the chestnut Loch an Easpaig, in 1958.

The Irish army had changed its qualifications for riders after the World War II, not with entirely happy results. In the pre-war period, young men who had been born and brought up with horses, and who showed the necessary aptitude, did not find it hard to get a riding commission with the Irish army jumping team—any more than the d'Inzeo brothers did in Italy after the war. But in Ireland there were suddenly certain educational requirements that had to be met—including, the most difficult of all, the ability to speak Erse, or Irish Gaelic. As the late Colonel Fred Ahern once said: 'Before the war, we had the farmers' sons who had grown up with horses. Afterwards, we had the sons of Dublin shop-keepers—and many of them had never had their leg over a horse until they came to us.'

Billy Ringrose, who is now the Irish *chef d'équipe* on important international occasions, won the Rome Grand Prix in 1961 on Loch an Easpaig, and won too in Nice, London, Washington, New York and Toronto. Two years later they won the first leg of the European Championship in Rome, and won again on the North American Fall Circuit. In 1965 they took the Grand Prix in Nice and in London a year later, when the horse had attained the respectable age of fifteen, they won the *Daily Mail* Cup.

The partnership also helped Ireland to many Nations' Cup victories, finally in the Aga Khan Trophy in Dublin in 1967. Sadly, only a few weeks later, the horse, who had gone clear in the first round of the Nations' Cup in Ostend, sustained a heart attack and died in the second round.

Caprilli, Federico   Italy

The originator of the 'forward seat', and thus the man who revolutionised the art of jumping fences on horseback, Federico Caprilli was born in 1868 at Leghorn in Italy. The son of a wealthy ship-builder, he graduated from the cavalry school at Modena and in 1904 was given a class of recruits at the cavalry school at Pinerolo.

He had spent considerable time in studying the centre of balance of the horse, both on the flat and over fences, with a rider and without one, and he was then able to put his theories into practice. Briefly, they were based on the idea that the rider, instead of sitting forward going into a fence and then sitting back on landing, which was at that time the accepted practice, should assist the horse by taking the weight off his loins and remain in a forward position throughout the entire leap.

He achieved quite remarkable results with his young pupils in a very short space of time, and on the strength of them was posted to Tor di Quinto—a cavalry school on the outskirts of Rome, just across the River Tiber from the city. Here he continued his experiments, which were so well received and so marked a success, that soon he was taking pupils from the leading cavalries of the world, including Germany, France, Russia, Britain and the United States.

Caprilli took a number of falls in proving his point and when he was only thirty-nine years of age he suffered a fatal accident. Unfortunately he had not had time to commit his ideas comprehensively to paper, but a friend and pupil, Captain Piero Santini (1881-1960), rectified the omission with two famous books, *The Forward Seat* and *Riding Reflections*. In 1951 he edited an English translation of Caprilli's random papers under the title *The Caprilli Papers*.

Although his ideas have been modified in the light of experience, and with the ever-increasing size of show-jumping fences, Caprilli was the originator of a concept which completely altered every form of riding technique.

d'Inzeo, Lt-Col. Piero   Italy

Piero d'Inzeo, on The Rock.

The elder of two sons of Constante d'Inzeo, a rough-riding sergeant in the Italian Cavalry, Piero d'Inzeo, born in 1923, rode from his boyhood and joined the army as an officer cadet. He passed out in 1946 and has since spent his life in finding, schooling and campaigning top-class international show jumpers, bringing himself world fame in the process as the best exponent of Caprilli's teachings; onto this classical foundation he has grafted his own ability and experience.

He first started to make a name for himself in the early 1950s, and in 1956 he won an individual bronze medal in the Olympic Games at Stockholm, helping his team to a silver medal in the process, riding the chestnut Uruguay. On the same horse he won the Men's European Championship three years later.

At the Rome Olympics in 1960 he rode The Rock to a team bronze and an individual silver medal. By 1964 he had risen to the rank of major and, riding Sunbeam, he helped to win another team bronze medal in Tokyo.

He has won the King George V Gold Cup in London on three occasions, and his best horses have all been Irish with the exception of Uruguay, who was bred in France. The Rock, Sunbeam, Ballyblack, Red Fox and his most recent Olympic horse Easter Light all came from Ireland.

In 1973 he made a great comeback with Easter Light to win four competitions, including the Grand Prix, in Rome, and was selected with his brother to stake Italy's claim to the Men's World Championship a year later. More of a stylist than his brother Raimondo, he has nevertheless failed to attain the same degree of success, perhaps because he is never averse to disagreement with the Italian federation. He is now in command of a tank regiment near Naples.

d'Inzeo, Maj. Raimondo   Italy

Born in 1925, the younger of the two d'Inzeo brothers is a completely different character from Piero, as gentle and retiring as Piero is flinty and self-assured. He is no stylist, in fact he is at times an untidy rider, but his horses all give of their best for him and he has been far more successful than Piero over the years.

Initially less keen on riding, and unable to bother himself with the classically correct position in the saddle, he studied at Rome University before he too decided to join the army, later transferring to the Carabinieri, the mounted police.

His Olympic record is outstanding, including as it does a team and individual silver medal on Merano in 1956, a team bronze and an individual gold on Posillipo in 1960, and a team bronze on the same horse four years later. He won the World Championship in 1956 on Merano and retained it four years later on Gowran Girl. With the exception of Merano and Posillipo, who were bred in Italy, all his best horses have been Irish-bred—horses such as The Quiet Man, Bellevue and Gone Away.

When his young daughter had a fatal accident while skiing, Raimondo could not bring himself to compete for a couple of seasons, but the sport is too deeply embedded in his personality for him ever to be able to give it up.

Raimondo d'Inzeo, on Posillipo.

Mancinelli, Graziano   Italy

Graziano Mancinelli's career started with his membership of the Italian junior team, with which he rode for four years. Born in 1937, he joined the junior team in 1952 and graduated to the senior team in 1958 with the grey Irish mare Rockette, who was reputed to be by Water Serpent and a full sister to The Rock.

For many years Mancinelli rode for the Milan horse-dealing firm of Fratelli Rivolta, and was in fact considered by his fellow riders to come into the professional category. It was a surprise to many, indeed, when he turned up in

Tokyo as a member of the Italian Olympic team in 1964; but it transpired that he was an adopted son of one of the Rivolta brothers, and that, as he was thus riding for a parent, he could not be considered to be a professional.

Riding Rockette, he helped Italy to win the team bronze medals, and on the same mare he won the Men's European title in Rome in 1963. He subsequently got together the most formidable string of international horses in Italy, all of them Irish-bred, of which the most famous was the grey Ambassador, by Nordlys, which he bought from Tommy Brennan with the express intention of winning the Olympic gold medal in Munich in 1972. He duly achieved his ambition, and won a team bronze medal to boot.

His wife, the former Nelly Pasotti, is also a rider and has often been a team member as well, as for example on the North American fall circuit in 1973. Mancinelli's star has waned somewhat in the interim. He was not selected to jump for the European championship in 1973, nor for the world title the following year.

Mancinelli is undoubtedly a strong and effective rider, but his rough checking nevertheless brings him under fire from the classicists.

Graziano Mancinelli on The Turvey.

Novo, Lalla   Italy

Lalla Novo on Rabin.

Lalla Novo, the law-student daughter of a wealthy Italian family who live near Turin, was born in 1938, and first joined the Italian team in Nice in 1963, riding the Irish horse, Rahin. Rahin had competed in the Olympic Games in Rome three years earlier in the Italian three-day event team. Though denied any really spectacular individual victories during the ten years in which she rode for Italy, she was a reliable team member who helped her country to win many Nations' Cups, including that at her inaugural international show.

Three years later she took over another Irish horse, Oxo Bob, and finished third behind Janou Lefebvre (now Tissot) of France and Monica Bachmann (now Weier) of Switzerland in the Ladies' European Championship in Gijon.

A year later she rode a French-bred horse, Prédestiné, to win the last log of the Ladies' European Championship at Fontainebleau, and her consistency throughout the competition left her runner-up for the title to Kathy Kusner of the United States.

But, unlike many riders who have virtually retired from the international field, she retains her interest in the sport and still accompanies the Italian team to many of their major fixtures, where her experience and her sound common sense make her as invaluable in an advisory capacity as she was previously as a rider. Few women are capable of sinking self-interest to such a degree that they continue to care about their team in an active capacity when they are no longer a part of it; Lalla Novo is one of them.

Orlandi, Dr Vittorio   Italy

Dr Vittorio Orlandi, whose family owns a textile factory in Milan, was born in 1940; he first joined the Italian team in the late 1960s as a comparatively novice international rider, and he has retained his place in it on merit.

His first good horse—and the horse 'arrived' after he took it over—was Fulmer Feather Duster, an Irish-bred chestnut whose original owner, Juliet Jobling-Purser, rode him in the Ladies' World Championship in Copenhagen in 1970.

Orlandi first proved himself as a team rider, and made his mark fairly rapidly in this field. At the Munich Olympics he rode two splendid 4-fault rounds in the team event to lead his more famous team-mates, including the individual title-holder, to the team bronze medal. A number of good individual successes followed, and during the winter of 1972, after the Munich games, he bought the chestnut Fiorello from Major Raimondo d'Inzeo—but who could hope to succeed where a d'Inzeo had failed?

Though selected by his national federation to represent Italy in the European championship at Hickstead in 1973, Orlandi was overlooked for the World Championship in 1974, when the Italian federation pinned its hopes on the d'Inzeo brothers.

Serventi, Giulia   Italy

Giulia Serventi first joined the Italian team as long ago as 1950, and was a member of it for twenty years, which is something of a record for lady riders.

Her career in the ring started with the French-bred chestnut, Doly, who was by that phenomenal sire of jumpers, Furioso. She finished second to Pat Smythe in the first women's European Championship in 1957, and the following year won the title in Palermo, beating Anna Clement of West Germany.

Doly was a good servant to his owner, but when he finally lost his form she remained without a top-class horse for some time, until she found in Ireland the chestnut Gay Monarch. Sometimes gayer than his new owner might have desired—especially one year at Rome, when he 'took off' round the sand track which borders the course, and took a good deal of stopping and catching, he came into his own in 1968. On the home ground of his adoptive country, he brought Giulia into the position of runner-up for the European title to Anneli Drummond-Hay of Britain on Merely-a-Monarch, with Marion Coakes on Stroller and Janou Lefebvre on Rocket following on.

Like Lalla Novo, Giulia Serventi was a first-class team rider, and her performances in Nations' Cups helped Italy on occasions too numerous to count. She was perhaps more effective than elegant, but elegance has never won competitions, and she often played a vital part in supplying the missing link to the legendary d'Inzeo brothers and keeping Italy well in the forefront of the Nations' Cup competitions from 1950 onwards.

Mariles, Gen. Humberto   Mexico

General Humberto Mariles Cortes was born in 1913 and was responsible for his team's remarkable victory at the 1948 Olympic Games in London's Wembley Stadium, where he also himself won the individual gold medal on a little one-eyed horse called Arete.

The son of Captain Antonio Mariles of the Mexican cavalry, he was born in Parral, Chihuahua, and spent his youth on his father's ranch, where he rode horses from his earliest childhood. When he was thirteen he became a cadet at the Military Academy, whence he graduated five years later, to be taken on the staff as an instructor for three years. The next two years were spent at another cavalry school, where he was mainly responsible for training the Mexican jumping team.

A private visit to the Olympic Games in Berlin in 1936 brought him into contact with the brilliant German team who were then dominating European competitions, and he based his style and his methods of instruction from that time onwards upon a combination of German discipline and a more Italian position over fences.

In 1938 he was made commandant of the new Military Riding Academy, and captained the Mexican team for the next eighteen years. During the war years he took his team to jump in North America with great success. In 1955 he gave the home crowds a success of near-Olympic dimensions when he led his team to win the gold medals in the Pan-American Games in Mexico City, beating the Argentine, Chile and the United States, and taking individual gold and bronze medals for good measure.

An outstanding career came to a sad end in 1964, while he was training riders for the Olympic Games. On the night of August 14 after a party commemorating his Olympic victory he was driving home on Mexico City's Via Periferico when another motorist tried to push him off the road. At the next traffic lights, Mariles shot him and was sent to prison. Though later released by presidential pardon, Mariles was arrested in 1973 in Paris on drug-smuggling charges, and died there in prison before coming to trial.

Humberto Mariles.

Ebben, Antoon ('Toni')   Netherlands

Toni Ebben, a pupil of the late Col. J.A. Talbot-Ponsonby, was born in 1930 and did not start show jumping until he was twenty-one-years old. Three years later he competed at his first international show in Germany.

In 1964 he went particularly well at the Horse of the Year Show at Wembley, in London, to win the Harringay Spurs, the points championship, riding his good horse Kairouan. Kairouan was a son of that prolific sire of show jumper of top class all over Europe, the French-bred Furioso, who stood at the French stud at Haras du Pin, near Argentan in Normandy.

A businessman in Hilversum, Ebben has also won several important competitions in Europe on Prins Ajax, who was foaled in Holland and is by a very common albino horse of unknown ancestry who is so unattractive that he only got a license to stand at stud by the skin of his teeth. He has sired a number of good jumpers, however, and a lot of breeders have sent mares to him in the hope of producing an international show jumper.

Callado, Col. Henrique   Portugal

In addition to being the most successful rider in Portugal, General Henrique Callado is a former director of the Portuguese Cavalry School at Mafra, which is *opposite: Michael Matz of the United States on Mighty Ruler at the Nassau A.H.R.C. Horse Show.*

now integrated with the Military Centre of Physical Education and Sport. In 1958 it opened its doors to civilian riders and included, for the first time, sports other than riding.

Henrique Callado joined the Portuguese team in 1943, when he was twenty-three, and he was still riding at top level when he led his team in the Tokyo Olympic Games in 1964. One of the best horses he rode during recent years was the French-bred Joc de l'Ile, on which he won a leg of the European Championship in 1963. Joc de l'Ile is yet another son of Furioso.

Rodzianko, Col. Paul   Russia

Paul Rodzianko.

Born in Russia in the last century, Paul Rodzianko followed his father—who owned an estate as big as England—into the Russian cavalry. As a young soldier he was privileged to study equitation under the celebrated English instructor James Fillis, and later in Italy, at Pinerolo and Tor di Quinto.

The two styles were totally opposed, and Rodzianko, the only man living then to have been taught by both, was able to supply the missing link. He trained and rode with the Russian team which won the King Edward VII (Nations') Cup, later to be the Prince of Wales Cup, at the International Horse Show at London's Olympia in 1912, 1913 and outright in 1914.

He was attached to the Russian embassy in Rome when the revolution broke out in his country in 1917, and came to England to join the British Army. He accompanied them with an expeditionary force to Siberia, was able to rescue the little spaniel belonging to the murdered Romanovs, and brought it back to England, where it lived out its life at the riding establishment which he started at Windsor.

Between the wars he went to Dublin to train what was to become the world-beating Irish Army show-jumping team. In World War II he joined the British army again, and afterwards returned to Dublin. One of the greatest instructors in the world, he had enormous influence on the training of British riders too, after he opened his final school near Olney in Buckinghamshire. He was a splendid character, and his book *Modern Horsemanship* is a classic. He also wrote an interesting autobiographical note entitled *Tattered Banners*.

Betrix, Gonda   South Africa

Gonda Betrix, or Butters as she was known before her marriage, was born in 1944, and was the outstanding rider in the only South African team that ever toured Europe, in 1958 before the African horse sickness ban came into force.

Only fourteen years old, she made a great impression with her two horses Gunga Din and the little chestnut Oorskiet, whom she sold to Lady Sarah FitzAlan Howard before she left and on whom his new owner won the Queen Elizabeth II Cup at the Royal International Horse Show in London in 1961. The team, which was a junior one, finished second to Britain in that year's Junior European Championship in Hanover, West Germany. Since then she has won innumerable championships at home with such brilliant performers as Flybridge, Ratification, and Eldorado, including two Derby wins at Johannesburg. In the autumn of 1973 she won the Washington D.C. Women's Invitational Championship in the U.S., shortly after her marriage to Desmond Betrix.

Butters, Gonda *see* Betrix, Gonda

Grayston, Robert ('Bob') South Africa

Though he was born in England, in 1912, the youngest of three riding brothers, Bob Grayston emigrated to South Africa in the 1930s, opened a riding school in Johannesburg and even fought with the South African army during the war. But he returned to England on several occasions after the war, until the travel of horses from Africa was forbidden.

His first visit was in 1953 with Guardsman, and he returned in subsequent years with Buccaneer, Captain Bligh and The Sea Hawk, a former champion hack in South Africa, whom he sold to Peter Robeson and who was eventually owned and ridden by Harvey Smith to win many speed competitions, all over Europe.

When African horse sickness led to a ban on the transport of horses to Europe he confined himself to his own country for some time, and was very successful there on a horse called Sabre. In 1965 he bought Royal Searcher in England—a horse he had tried in vain to buy five years earlier. He thus had a top horse in each country and achieved success with both. The two seasons were at opposite ends of the year, so if their rider was overworked, they themselves were not.

After selling Royal Searcher to Warren Wofford in 1967, he confined his activities to South Africa, where his King Cole and King Canute were outstandingly successful, mostly ridden by his wife Wendy. Although he did little show riding himself in later years, Bob won the last competition in which he ever rode, at the Pietermaritzburg show in 1973, and he died literally in the saddle, of a heart attack when he had completed the winning round.

Bob Grayston.

Louw, Mickey South Africa

Mickey Louw was born in 1944 and is an insurance broker in Johannesburg; but show jumping is his sport and his hobby and he was South African champion in 1964 on Jurigo. In the same year he was awarded his Springbok colours.

In 1966, at the suggestion of Jack Talbot-Ponsonby, he went to England to widen his experience, and rode the late Len Carter's Trigger Hill with great success to win many major competitions throughout the season. Included among them were the *Horse and Hound* Cup at the Royal International, the *News of the World* Championship at Ascot, and two competitions at the Horse of the Year Show.

Mickey Louw, on Trigger Hill.

opposite: Frank Chapot of the United States jumping at Hickstead on San Lucas.

He was a regular member of the team at Lourenco Marques, the only international show to which South Africans could take their horses, due to the ban on the travel of horses who may have been exposed to African horse sickness. At home his record in recent years has been outstanding, and he is now not only the leading male rider in South Africa, but surely one of the best in the world as well. In 1973 he won all but three of the eleven jumper competitions at Johannesburg, surely a record for a top-class show, riding Torch Sign and Fancy That, and he is the only three-time winner of the Rothman's Show Jumping Derby at Johannesburg.

Goyoaga, Francisco ('Paco')   Spain

'Paco' Goyoaga, who owns a dry-cleaning business in Madrid and is the nephew of one of the greatest Spanish military riders of all time, the late Colonel Jaime Garcia-Cruz, is the best civilian rider that Spain has produced since the war. In 1953 he won the first-ever world championship for men, in Paris, riding the former Olympic horse Quorum.

He qualified for the final by the narrowest of margins, but though he was matched against three giants of the game in the Helsinki gold medalist Pierre Jonquères d'Oriola riding Ali Baba for France, Fritz Thiedemann of West Germany on Diamant (this horse was later sold to America and ridden by Frank Chapot in the U.S. team), and Captain Piero d'Inzeo riding Uruguay for Italy, he had only two fences down and scraped home by a quarter of a fault, with Thiedemann as runner-up.

In 1956 in Aachen, Goyoaga, riding the German horse Fahnenkönig, was second in the world championship to Captain Raimondo d'Inzeo of Italy on Merano, and he also won the Grand Prix at the same meeting. Two years earlier, in Madrid, he finished third in defence of his title, behind Hans Günter Winkler on Halla for West Germany and d'Oriola on Arlequin D for France.

Goyoaga favoured the heavy type of German horses that were then in vogue, following the German victory in the 1956 Olympic Games, and he did well on the black mare Toscanella, who later went to Ireland as the mount of Diana Conolly-Carew, and Baden, but he also had considerable success on the French-bred Kif-Kif, and she won him the Spanish championship in 1960, 1961 and 1964, as well as the Geneva Grand Prix. A heart operation put him out of action, but before he retired he led his team to victory in the Geneva Nations' Cup in 1965. He sold Kif-Kif to the Spanish Government for a record sum of £20,000, and now he is often *chef d'équipe* to the Spanish team.

Francisco Goyoaga, on Sea Leopard.

Segovia, Alfonso   Spain

The best of the present-day Spanish riders, Alfonso Segovia was born in 1945 and first joined the Spanish team in the early 1970s, after which he finished eighth individually with Fritz Ligges of West Germany for the Olympic Grand Prix in Munich, riding Tic Tac, with a score of sixteen faults. In the team event he was the joint-best of his squad, which finished in seventh place.

Tic Tac, his most successful horse, was runner-up to Raimondo d'Inzeo on Gone Away in the Rome Grand Prix in 1974, these two having the only double clear rounds.

Weier, Maj. Paul, and Monica   Switzerland

Major Paul Weier, who was born in 1934, has been the Swiss champion almost permanently since 1959 and is still in a class of his own. He first rode in the Rome Olympic Games in 1960 on Centurion, competing as an individual, and in Tokyo four years later he finished fourteenth individually on Satan; and in the Mexico Olympics he rode Satan and Wildfeuer.

Perhaps his best horse of all has been the big grey German-bred Wulf, who carried him to third place in the Men's European Championship in Aachen in 1971, behind Hartwig Steenken and Harvey Smith, and into twenty-second place in the Munich Olympics in 1972.

Paul Weier owns an hotel, where he takes pupils for instruction in riding, and having trained the most successful woman rider in Switzerland, the former Monica Bachmann, he married her in 1972. She was born in 1942 and was the overall Swiss champion in 1966 and 1970, beating her future husband.

Her first major international appearance was in the Women's World Championship at Hickstead in 1965, the first in the series of three—for after La Baule in 1974, where the final women's championship was held, the F.E.I. decided to hold only one world title, open to both men and women. In 1965 she finished fourth on the German-bred Sandro. A year later she was runner-up to the future double world champion, Janou Lefebvre of France (now Janou Tissot) riding Sandro again.

Now her best horse is Erbach, on whom she finished seventh individually in the Mexico Olympics, third in the 1967 European championship in 1966 in Fontainebleau, behind Kathy Kusner of the U.S.A. and Lalla Novo of Italy, and third again in Vienna in 1973, behind two British girls, Ann Moore and Caroline Bradley.

Alfonso Segovia, on Tic-Tac.

Monica Weier.

Bachmann, Monica *see* Weier, Monica

Brown, William ('Buddy')   U.S.A.

Next to Rodney Jenkins and Frank Chapot, the most successful American rider in Europe during the U.S.E.T.'s tour in 1974 was eighteen-year-old Buddy Brown.

He started riding show ponies for Mr and Mrs Thomas K. Waller's famous stud at Tanrackin Farm, Bedford Hills, New York, and later rode hunters for Bob Freels, a former U.S.E.T. stable-manager. He lives not far away with his parents, in South Salem, New York, some forty miles north of New York City. One of the most successful junior riders in the United States, he won the junior hunter championship at the National Horse Show in Madison Square Garden in 1972

Buddy Brown, on Aires.

and again in 1973, and is a product of the U.S.E.T.'s nationwide screening trials.

Brown's best horse, the six-year-old grey gelding A Little Bit, by Grey Cage out of Dolorus, was loaned to the team by his parents, Mr and Mrs Graham Brown. A former racehorse who won a race on the West Coast only seven months before he came to Europe, A Little Bit has exceptional ability and was a good winner in England and in Dublin in 1974.

Buddy Brown, a delightful personality but a tenacious competitor, also did well in Europe on his parents' chestnut seven-year-old Sandsablaze, by Blazing Count out of Sandy Atlas, who was campaigned successfully at home for three seasons before joining the team. Sandsablaze gave him the biggest win of his career in the Irish Trophy for the Grand Prix, worth £7,000 in stakes with £2,000 to the winner.

Chamberlin, Gen. Harry U.S.A.

General Harry Chamberlin, unquestionably the most brilliant of all the U.S. military horsemen, was born in Elgin, Illinois in 1887 and died in 1944 from an illness contracted while commanding a task force in the New Hebrides. A West Pointer who served with the Infantry in France during World War I, Chamberlin afterwards became an horsemanship instructor at the Cavalry School at Fort Riley, Kansas, and a competitor in the 1920 Olympic Games in Antwerp. His experiences there, and later at Saumur and Pinerolo, enabled him to take a leading role in revamping the doctrines taught at the Cavalry School, which he both helped to formulate and himself demonstrated with unequalled success. Winner of two Olympic medals in 1932—an individual silver in the Prize of Nations and a team gold in the three-day event—Chamberlin also rode Grand Prix dressage and was a fine polo player. His second book, *Training Hunters, Jumpers and Hacks,* has remained in print almost continuously since its initial appearance in 1937.

Chapot, Frank U.S.A.

Born in 1934, Frank Chapot started riding in the show ring at the age of ten. He graduated from the University of Pennsylvania and then saw service in the United States Air Force. Since then he has worked as a salesman of small leather goods, and more recently has run his own farm in New Jersey.

Riding has always been his major preoccupation and he has had a good deal of success as an amateur steeplechase rider, in addition to pursuing a highly successful career in international show jumping. He first joined the United States Equestrian Team in 1955, and has competed in the Olympic Games in Stockholm (1956), Rome (1960), Tokyo (1964), Mexico City (1968) and Munich (1972).

Chapot's first season with the team coincided with that of their brilliant coach, Bertalan de Nemethy, a former Hungarian cavalry officer, who was selected as a member of the Hungarian Olympic team for the 1940 games, which were ultimately cancelled due to the outbreak of World War II. (Although Nemethy never performed himself at the Olympic Games, he has trained five Olympic teams, winning silver medals in 1960 and again in 1972.)

Frank Chapot's first Olympic horse was Belair, whom he rode in the team which finished fifth behind Germany, Italy and Great Britain. Then he took over the German horse Diamant, formerly the mount of Fritz Thiedemann, who helped to win a team gold medal in the Pan-American Games in 1959. A year later, at the Rome Olympics, he rode the twenty-year-old veteran Trail Guide to a team silver medal. In 1961 he took the ride on what was to prove his best horse, the gargantuan chestnut thoroughbred San Lucas (*q.v.*), on whom he was runner-up for the men's European title at Lucerne in 1966, the corner-stone of the American team, and the winner of countless international puissance and Grand Prix competitions.

Since the retirement of Bill Steinkraus after the 1972 Olympic Games, Frank Chapot has captained the American team. His achievements in 1974 included third place in the Men's World Championship, and winning the King George V Gold Cup in London.

Frank Chapot, on San Lucas.

Chapot, Mary U.S.A.

As Mary Mairs, born in 1944, Frank Chapot's wife joined the U.S.E.T. in 1962. She was already a champion rider, having won the American Horse Shows Association Medal finals at the National Horse Show in Madison Square Garden, New York, in 1960. She comes from Pasadena, California, where she was a pupil of Jimmy Williams, and became the first American rider ever to win a Games gold medal in show jumping when she took the individual title at the Pan-American Games in Sao Paulo in 1963. She was riding her chestnut mare, Tomboy, a thoroughbred by Wait-a-Bit out of Jane Tana, who a few weeks later won the Grand Champion Jumper title at the Washington, D.C. international show.

Mary Chapot.

Perhaps the most stylish of all the American girls, Mary represented the United States in the Tokyo and Mexico Olympic Games. In 1968, riding White Lightning—the grey thoroughbred which her husband rode in the 1972 Olympic Games in Munich—she won the Queen Elizabeth II Cup at the Royal International at Wembley Stadium in 1968. She had already made her first trip to Europe four years earlier, winning the John Player Grand Prix on Tomboy and the Imperial Cup on her German-bred grey mare, Anakonda, bought towards the end of her first European tour.

She married Frank Chapot during the winter of 1965 and this husband-and-wife team has continued to compete together since then, as also do two other well known couples, Britain's Ted and Elizabeth (née Broome) Edgar and Switzerland's Paul and Monica (Bachmann) Weier.

d'Ambrosio, Anthony ('Tony')   U.S.A.

Born in 1956, Tony was hardly out of junior classes when he won the Leading Rider Award at New York's National Horse Show in 1972, riding The Phoenix and Alligator Farm's dazzling Sympatico. A native of Pelham Manor, New York, Tony had already accounted for the Orange Coast Grand Prix in California with Sympatico the same year, and the combination has recorded many important wins since then, including a record 7 ft 4 in puissance victory in New York in 1973 and the puissance at the Washington International in 1974.

Hofmann, Carol   U.S.A.

Carol Hofmann.

Born in New Jersey in 1943, the daughter of the chairman of Johnson & Johnson, the pharmaceutical company, Carol Hofmann had the ambition when she was still in the Pony Club to be a member of the United States Equestrian Team. At the early age of fourteen she came to the attention of the team selectors when she won the U.S.E.T. Combined Test finals of the American Horse Shows Association Medal class at the National Horse Show in Madison Square Garden, New York. She joined the team for the full circuit in 1962, and riding in her first international show at Washington D.C. she was a winner already.

One of her earliest international horses was Can't Tell, a chestnut mare by Curate, on whom she made her first appearance in Europe in 1964. She was later to achieve success on a grey thoroughbred called Out Late.

An all-round horsewoman, Carol also devotes considerable time and enthusiasm to the exhibiting of hunters, in recent years this has occupied more of her time than riding international show jumpers. Her father, Philip Hofmann, is an international driving enthusiast who regularly takes a team of coach horses across the Atlantic to complete in the driving championships in Europe, particularly in England, West Germany and Switzerland.

Carol was educated at the Kent-Place School in Summit, New Jersey, and until she graduated she was only able to concentrate on her riding during the holidays. Her last competitive appearance in Europe was in 1968, when she and Out Late won two competitions in Dublin and three, including the Grand Prix, in Rotterdam. In 1974 she married J. Willard Thompson, a former Steeplechase rider who now trains race-horses.

Jenkins, Rodney   U.S.A.

Born in 1944, the son of a farmer and professional huntsman to a pack of foxhounds in Orange, Virginia, in the American South, red-haired Rodney Jenkins became the first professional rider ever to join the United States Equestrian Team when he was selected for the North American indoor circuit in 1973.

He grew up in the hunting field, whipping-in to his father from the age of eight, until, eleven years later, he decided to take up riding as a professional. He now has from fifty to sixty horses, his own and other people's, and it is by no means unusual for him to arrive at one of the big American shows with a string of ten or twelve horses—and to win with most, if not all, of them.

His most famous horse is Harry Gill's thoroughbred Idle Dice, who is almost a legend in the United States, having won well over $125,000 in prize money in the show ring, and who was considered by all the British riders in New York and Toronto in 1973 to be one of the most outstanding performers they had seen for years; but he has been associated with a large number of outstanding hunters and jumpers, among them Gustavus, Brendan, Mainspring, and Number One Spy. Winner of a dozen major U.S. Grand Prix titles, Jenkins added to them the John Player Trophy for the Grand Prix of Great Britain in 1974, as well as the reserve Championship to David Broome in the Professional Show Jumping Championship at Cardiff—both these victories achieved on Number One Spy.

Kusner, Kathryn ('Kathy')   U.S.A.

Born in 1940 in Arlington, Virginia, into a non-horsey family—both her parents have been school teachers—Kathy Kusner took her own line with a vengeance and became a champion woman rider both in show jumping and in racing over fences. Having started her race-riding career in point-to-points, she eventually became the first woman in the United States to hold a jockey's licence, and had to take the authorities to court in order to do so.

When she was only eighteen she rode a mare called Freckles to set up the American women's high jump record, clearing 7 ft 3 in and she joined the U.S.E.T. four years later. In 1963 she was a member of the team which won the Pan American gold medals, riding Unusual, a half-brother to Arthur McCashin's former Olympic mare, Miss Budweiser. She also won the international championship in New York.

Her greatest successes were gained on the chestnut thoroughbred gelding Untouchable (q.v.), on whom she won the Irish Grand Prix in Dublin for two successive years, 1964 and 1965. She also won the Olympic Trial in Rotterdam in 1964, and finished in thirteenth place individually in the Olympic Games in Tokyo.

In 1965, when the Women's World Championship was held at the All England Jumping Course at Hickstead, Kathy Kusner and Untouchable were runners-up for the title to Britain's Marion Mould and Stroller. Two years later, Kathy won the Women's European Championship at Fontainebleau, to become the only American woman ever to take this title—a record which she will hold in perpetuity, for non-Europeans are no longer eligible to compete for either the men's or the women's title.

In the Mexico Olympics, riding with the Chapots, Kathy missed the team bronze medal by only a quarter of a fault, the margin by which the U.S. team finished fourth behind West Germany. On the former Irish horse Fru she had a fall and broke her leg in New York shortly afterwards, but the following season she made a successful tour of several continental shows.

She holds a commercial pilot's licence with instrument and jet ratings and loves to fly an aeroplane, and she also plays folk music on a guitar.

McEvoy, Michele   U.S.A.

Born in 1953, Michele McEvoy lives in Summit, New Jersey, and is the daughter of a highly successful transport executive. She started her riding career as a child with a working pony, given her as a Christmas present. At New York in 1973 she won the National Championship, and she won the Invitation Championship on the Sunshine Circuit in Florida the following Spring, riding the chestnut thoroughbred Sundancer, bought from the Canadian Olympic rider, Jimmy Day.

Michele made her first trip to Europe in 1974, accompanied by her trainer, Carl Knee, who produces her horses from his stable at Lagrangeville, New York. She competed at the W.D. & H.O. Wills Spring Tournament at Hickstead over Easter, and appeared next in Rome, where she won the opening competition on

Rodney Jenkins.

Kathy Kusner.

Michele McEvoy.

the ill-fated Mister Muskie, a quarter horse owned by the American trumpeter and bandleader, Doc Severinsen and won two other competitions during the week. The Roman crowd always love to see a girl in the winner's enclosure, and she soon became the toast of the Piazza di Siena.

Returning home to compete in a few major international shows, she crossed back to Europe to join the United States team, accompanied by her parents. Though neither was interested in horses before their daughter started riding, her father learned to ride in order to be able to understand what Michele was talking about, and now enjoys foxhunting in New Jersey. In La Baule Michele met her match in Janou Tissot, who retained her world title, but she was runner-up on Mister Muskie. The visit to Europe was sadly marred when Mister Muskie caught pneumonia and died.

Mairs, Mary *see* Chapot, Mary

Matz, Michael   U.S.A.

Born in 1951, Matz is another member of the U.S. Equestrian Team's youth movement who has represented his country abroad while hardly past his majority. A versatile rider who is just as much at home on show hunters as jumpers, Matz first attracted notice while riding J. Basil Ward's horses for trainer D. Gerry Baker, winning the Cleveland Grand Prix on Rosie Report in 1972 and the North American Championship at Detroit on Mighty Ruler the following year. Named to the U.S. Equestrian Team squad for the fall circuit in 1973, Matz made his first European tour in 1974, and also represented the United States at the Johannesburg, South Africa, C.H.I.O. the same year.

Ridland, Robert   U.S.A.

Born in 1951, Rob Ridland was the youngest member of the U.S. Equestrian Team when he was named to the 1972 Olympic squad. Although a native of California where he developed under the tutelage of Jimmy Williams (who had also coached Mary Mairs), Ridland went to college in the East, graduating from Yale College. A veteran of four European tours with the U.S. team (1970, 1971, 1972 and 1974) Ridland has accounted for two major Grands Prix on his favorite mount, Mrs W.K. Day's Almost Persuaded—New York in 1971, and Lucerne in 1974. In addition, he was the individual champion at the Caracas, Venezuela, Invitational in 1973.

Shapiro, Neal   U.S.A.

Neal Shapiro was born in 1946 and joined the United States Equestrian Team in 1964, when he was eighteen years old, making his first trip to Europe with the squad two years later. He distinguished himself very early on by winning the Grand Prix in Aachen, one of the most prestigious competitions in Europe, on Jacks or Better.

He was born into a horse-minded family, and started riding when he was seven years old. His father owns a stable of trotters, which Neal drives successfully when he is not away with the team.

Shapiro had considerable success in the U.S. with the grey ex-rodeo horse Uncle Max, before he sold him to Ted Edgar in 1968. He piloted this ebullient and headstrong animal to the P.H.A. National High-Score Award and several major championships. But in 1971 he acquired an enviable and even more appropriate partner in the bay thoroughbred Sloopy (*q.v.*), on whom he won an Olympic individual bronze medal in the Munich games in 1972, and a team silver medal.

When he is not touring with the team, Neal works in his father's business, which includes a string of restaurants. He lives in Glen's Head, Long Island, and was married in 1971. Like Kathy Kusner and Frank Chapot, he is a licensed pilot, with several thousand hours to his credit.

Steinkraus, William ('Bill')   U.S.A.

Bill Steinkraus, the captain and senior member of the United States Equestrian Team for so many triumphant years, was the first and at the time of writing remains the only American rider ever to win an Olympic gold medal for show jumping. He achieved this feat in Mexico City in 1968, riding Snowbound (*q.v.*).

Born in 1925, he has been a member of no fewer than six Olympic squads, the last occasion being the Munich Olympics in 1972, where his team won the silver medals, only a quarter of a fault behind the victorious West Germans. On Mainspring, he jumped one of the only three clear rounds of the day in the Olympic stadium, and finished with the best individual score, a total of only four faults, incurred when Mainspring jumped the water quite disastrously.

Bill Steinkraus started riding when he was ten, and was a successful show jumping rider before the war, with his own horse Salmo and Gordon Wright's Sonny. He won both national equitation titles as a junior in 1941. He served in World War II, later graduated from Yale University, and first joined the U.S.E.T. in 1951. A year later he rode Hollandia with the team which won the Olympic bronze medals at Helsinki.

Among the top-class competitions which he has won in Europe and on the American continent, he especially prizes the King George V Gold Cup, which he took for the first time in 1956, riding First Boy, and again in 1964 on Sinjon, the International Championship of Germany, which he won on Riviera Wonder in 1959, and a number of Grands Prix.

A New Englander from Connecticut, he worked for some years on Wall Street, but has spent the past ten years in book-publishing. Collecting books is one of his principal hobbies, and another is music—an accomplished violist, he has played in symphony orchestras, but now prefers to play chamber music.

Married, with three young sons, he has retired from international sport in order to spend more time with his wife Sis, and their family. But he has by no means hung up his boots, and still rides daily.

Wiley, Hugh   U.S.A.

One of the most colourful members of the United States Equestrian Team during a relatively short but highly successful period as an international rider, Hugh Wiley, born in 1927, started jumping Shetland ponies at the age of six in Maryland and joined the team in 1950.

At the same time as running a constructional engineering business in Baltimore, Hugh was able to indulge the love of horses which he inherited from his grandfather. On the family farm he not only rode horses but also bred them, perhaps his most outstanding product being the grey Ksar d'Esprit (*q.v.*), who was foaled in 1946 and sold to Canada as a young horse, jumping for the Canadian team before being bought back to become a mainstay of the U.S.E.T.

Neal Shapiro, on Sloopy.

Bill Steinkraus.

Hugh's biggest successes were gained on the palomino, Nautical (q.v.), a remarkable horse with china-blue eyes who was bred in New Mexico and passed through many hands before his last owner found him in Pennsylvania and took him to Gladstone, New Jersey, to the team training-centre; there Bert de Nemethy helped form a combination of horse and rider that won London's Saddle of Honour and Loliners' Cup in 1959 and many other international triumphs.

Nautical was not, however, the vehicle for Hugh Wiley's first major international victory in Europe. It was on the grey thoroughbred Master William, who raced as a two- and three-year-old and was hunted for several seasons before being loaned to the team, that Hugh Wiley won the King George V Gold Cup in 1958. But it was on Nautical, who first came to Europe in 1955, that he retained the cup in 1959.

Seventh individually on Master William in the 1960 Olympic Games in Rome, Wiley was not selected to compete in the team event, and the following year he turned professional. He now teaches riding in southern Virginia, and is also well known for conducting clinics.

Hugh Wiley, on Nautical.

Brinckmann, Hans Heinrich   West Germany

A highly successful German cavalry rider in the 1930s, 'Mickey' Brinckman is now the most famous and successful course-builder in the world. He is the resident architect at the Aachen show, whose courses have long been renowned as the toughest, though also the fairest, in Europe, and he built exceptionally brilliant courses for the 1972 Olympic Games in Munich.

Brinckmann has the inestimable advantage of having ridden with the crack German team for six years before the war. He was born at Ratzeburg, near Lübeck, the son of an officer in the Jäeger regiment. As a boy he rode at a riding-school under the instruction of an ex-cavalry sergeant-major, and by the time he was fourteen he was determined to join the cavalry. Three years later, having passed out of his public school with honours in four languages, including Latin and Greek, he joined the 14th Cavalry Regiment at Mecklenberg, near Berlin, now in East Germany.

He first joined the German team in 1935, but was too young to be considered for the Olympic team the following year and gained his fame from 1937 to 1939. Among his successes were the Grands Prix in Rome, Aachen and Amsterdam, and the German Grand Prix in Berlin in 1937, held in the Olympic stadium under the new formula of a two-round competition, then in its experimental stage but now accepted. He was nominated for the 1940 Olympic team, but war intervened to cancel these games.

After the war was over Brinckmann helped to rebuild the sport in West Germany and rode with the German team from 1952 until 1954. Then he went to Egypt and schooled the Egyptian team for two years, accompanying them to the Olympic Games in Rome, where they finished fourth on German horses. On his return home he instructed at the German school at Warendorf, became a member of the Olympic committee and is now its chief instructor, a post he has held since 1969. A year earlier, he was *chef d'équipe* to the German Olympic team in Mexico, where they won the bronze medals.

He has also ridden in racing, and in three-day events as a member of the Hanover Cavalry School.

Ligges, Fritz   West Germany

An exceptionally versatile rider, Fritz Ligges, who was a member of the West German team which won the Olympic gold medals at Munich in 1972, riding the grey Hanoverian, Robin, who died the following winter. He was formerly involved in three-day events.

In 1964, at the Olympic Games in Tokyo, he was a member of the West German three-day-event team and won the individual bronze medal riding Donkosak.

Ligges was following in the tradition of many of his team mates, who started their riding careers in what is known on the Continent as the *Military* before turning their attention to show jumping, where they confess to finding the ultimate precision that is required to be more of a challenge than riding at speed across country.

Since losing Robin, Ligges has reinforced his string with Genius and the stallion Ramiro, an exceptionally well made, quality horse who is out of a mare by the Irish 'chasing sire, Cottage Son. When his jumping career is over, Ramiro will be retired to stud and it is hoped that he will prove to be a useful sire of show jumpers.

Born in 1938, Ligges is a product of the West German federation's training establishment at Warendorf, Westphalia.

Jarasinski, Kurt   West Germany

The most distinguished pupil of Fritz Thiedemann at the Holstein Stud at Elmshorn, Kurt Jarasinski was born in 1938 and, having ridden Torro in the winning West German team in the Tokyo Olympic Games in 1964, became editor of the Holstein Stud Book in later years. He farms near Elmshorn and breeds horses which, predominantly Holstein in origin, have now achieved more quality with the addition of thoroughbred blood.

Although never a big individual winner, Jarasinski was a reliable team rider and filled the gap left by Thiedemann when he retired.

Fritz Ligges.

Merkel, Lutz   West Germany

Born in 1937, Lutz Merkel works as a butcher in a sausage-making firm near Warendorf when he is not touring with the West German team. Although the big prizes in the Grand Prix category have so far eluded him, he is a reliable team member and an asset in Nations' Cups, always in evidence in the major competitions.

He was in the team in 1969, making a major contribution to the first German victory in the President's Cup, the world team championship, presented by Prince Philip in his capacity of President of the F.E.I. (International Equestrian Federation). On Sir, he was a member of the team which won the Aga Khan Trophy after a jump-off with Britain in Dublin, and at the end of that European season, in Geneva, he rode the same horse to assist in the German victory over the Italians, with whom until then they had been lying neck-and-neck.

A quiet horseman with a cool, unflappable temperament, he is at his best jumping big fences without undue regard for the time element. Were he more of a go-getter against the clock he would win more individual competitions, and his compatriots often accuse him of going to sleep in the middle of a round.

Out of the saddle he is a witty, unassuming and unfailingly pleasant personality, who at the annual dinners given by the British for the Germans and vice versa, is frequently called upon to entertain the company with his unique rendering of an aria from *Tosca*, delivered in a note-true falsetto.

He has recently been made public-relations officer for his firm, which owns three prominent sausage-factories in West Germany.

Lutz Merkel, on Sperber.

Alwin Schockemöhle.

Schockemöhle, Alwin   West Germany

Alwin Schockemöhle, born in 1937, was Hans Gunter Winkler's star pupil from the time he was seventeen, and at Stockholm in 1956 was reserve for both the show jumping and the three-day event Olympic teams. A year later he won his first international class at Aachen, and three years later, riding Ferdl, was a member of the winning Olympic team in Rome. Placed in the first four in three European championships, he was the German champion on three occasions and set up the German high-jump record in 1965, clearing 2.25 metres (7 ft 4 in) on Exakt.

In 1968 he won the Aachen Grand Prix on Donald Rex, and the same horse was the best individual that year in the Olympic team event in Mexico City, after which Donald Rex was hailed as the best horse in Europe. A year later, having won Grand Prix competitions all over Europe, Schockemöhle just lost the Men's European title to David Broome at Hickstead, and was second to Harvey Smith on Mattie Brown in the Wills British Jumping Derby a year later.

A fall sustained here laid both him and his horse off with back injuries in 1971, and when he reappeared a year later it was with one of Donald Rex's relations, the grey Rex the Robber, among whose successes were the Irish Grand Prix in Dublin. On the same horse he was runner-up again for the Men's European Championship at Hickstead the following year, beaten by Paddy McMahon on Pennwood Forgemill. Rex the Robber also won the Grand Prix of Europe, the President's Cup in Washington and the amateur title in Cardiff.

A martyr to back troubles, Alwin Schockemöhle often suffers considerable pain while he is riding, but he has a philosophical attitude to life which was never more in evidence than in 1973, when he had £3000 in prize money, won at Hickstead and Wembley, stolen from his luggage at London Airport while he was waiting for his flight back to Germany after the two shows.

The owner of a factory and a man of considerable private means, Alwin also runs a stud with his two brothers, Werner and Paul, specialising in the breeding of show jumpers.

Schockemöhle, Paul   West Germany

Born in 1944, Paul Schockemöhle first joined the German team in 1971, and has had considerable success with the grey Hanoverian Abadir, the chestnut Talisman and the bay Gonzales.

But the horse with which he will always be associated is the grey Askan—not for riding him to victory in an important competition so much as for having sold him for the then-record price of £56,000 to the Ruhr industrialist, Josef Kun, in 1971.

Something of a rebel against all kinds of authority, including that of his brother and his federation, Paul is a very determined rider who demands the maximum of his horses; but he dominates them less than do many of his compatriots during the riding-in period and they are seldom strapped down and overbent.

Paul Schockemöhle.

Schridde, Hermann   West Germany

Born in 1937 and a farmer from Westphalia, Hermann Schridde is a pupil of Hans Gunter Winkler; he won the German international championship in Aachen in 1963, riding Ilona. The following year he won the Hamburg Jumping Derby on Dozent, a horse he had taken over from Lutz Merkel and Alwin Schockemöhle, before going on to take the Olympic individual silver medal in Tokyo. They gained it by virtue of a clear second round, a feat emulated by the winner of the gold medal, Pierre Jonqueres d'Oriola of France with Lutteur B.

Schridde also helped the German team to win the gold medals on the same big chestnut Hanoverian, and the following year he won the Men's European championship on him in Aachen, with Queipo de Llano second for Spain on Infernal and Alwin Schockemöhle third for the host nation on Exakt.

The next Olympic Games in Mexico City in 1968 saw Schridde and Dozent left out of the individual competition, but in spite of their total of 70¼ faults in the team event the West German team won the bronze medals.

Hermann Schridde, on Dozent.

Snoek, Hendrik and Marion   West Germany

Hendrik Snoek.

The son of a prominent West German industrialist, Hendrik Snoek was still a university student when in 1972, having a year earlier been the leading rider in Dublin, he won the British Jumping Derby at Hickstead on Shirokko after a jump-off with Paddy McMahon on Pennwood Forgemill.

A great hero among the young of his own country, where poster-size portraits of him are on sale, he has a wide choice of horses, for his family breed a good many, often using Irish stock as foundation mares. His greatest successes have been gained on Shirokko, and on Rasputin.

Born in 1948, Hendrik rode Dorina to share the Aachen Grand Prix with Alwin Schockemöhle on the great Donald Rex early in his career, in 1968.

His younger sister Marion was the individual Junior European Champion, and a member of the team which finished second for the title, at Hickstead in 1971. Two years later she was selected to represent her country for the European Ladies' Championship in Vienna, still riding the grey home-bred Janeau, who

looks like an Irish horse. Second to Ann Moore and Psalm in the first leg over a speed course, she was in fourth place overall at the end of the week, behind the two British girls and Monica Weier of Switzerland.

Steenken, Hartwig West Germany

Hartwig Steenken on Simona.

The most sympathetic and tactful horseman among all the younger generation of German riders, Hartwig Steenken, who is himself a farmer and breeder, was born in 1941 and was selected for the individual competition at the 1968 Olympic Games in Mexico City, riding the outstanding Hanoverian mare Simona.

A natural horseman whose whole life is wrapped up in his sport, Steenken won the Men's European Championship at Aachen in 1971 from Harvey Smith on Evan Jones, and a year later he helped the German team to win the gold medals at the Munich Olympic Games.

A badly fractured leg prevented him from defending his European title in 1973, but he was back in action later that season with Simona, who has proved herself to be one of the greats of the show-jumping world, and never more so than when she won for Steenken the men's world title in 1974.

Steenken's main opponent in the world championship was Ireland's Eddie Macken with Pele, and these two, after all the four finalists had swapped horses in the closing round, had to jump off for the title, which Steenken won by four faults to eight. A modest and unassuming man, he paid tribute to his horse after his victory and declared that the two Hanoverians, Simona and Hugo Simon's Lavendel, were the easiest to ride in the final.

Thiedemann, Fritz West Germany

The first of the West German riders to reach great heights after the war, Fritz Thiedemann was born in 1918 and all his victories were gained on Holstein horses, of which the best he ever rode was the bay gelding Meteor. On him he won the individual bronze medal at the Olympic Games in Helsinki in 1952, and at Stockholm four years later helped to win the first of three consecutive team gold medals for West Germany.

Thiedemann and Meteor were still in the team which won in the Rome Olympic Games in 1960, and for nearly a decade they were a basic point of the West German team, in much the same way as Wilf White and Nizefela were the corner-stones of the British international effort.

Individually, many Grands Prix came their way, and they won the King George V Gold Cup at the White City in 1954 and the European Championship in 1958, when it was held in Aachen, beating Piero d'Inzeo on The Rock and Hans Gunter Winkler on Halla.

Aachen was one of their happiest hunting-grounds, and they won the Grand Prix here on no fewer than three occasions. Their greatest consistency, however, was exemplified in the gruelling Hamburg Jumping Derby, in which they achieved a record number of five victories.

A man of sterling character, respected by all his opponents as well as his fellow members of the West German team, Thiedemann is also an instructor of considerable repute. At Elmshorn, the home of the Holstein stud, he was the stable jockey and later encouraged several of the young entry to publicise the Holstein horse, in particular Kurt Jarasinski, who succeeded him as first horseman at the stud.

But the Holsteins lacked sufficient quality for top-class international jumping in later years and more recently the German team has tended to emphasize a lighter, breedier type of horse.

Fritz Thiedemann, on Meteor.

Wiltfang, Gerd West Germany

Wiltfang was a baker of bread before he started show jumping, and although he describes himself, with some humour, as a 'part-time car park attendant', most of his time seems to be spent riding horses.

A member of the West German Team since 1968, though he did not go to the Mexico City Olympic Games, Wiltfang first came into his own in 1971, when he started riding for the Ruhr industrialist Josef Kun, who attracted considerable attention by purchasing a number of very expensive horses.

The most expensive, and the best of them all, was Askan, a grey Hanoverian who was bought for £56,000 from Paul Schockemöhle. He and Wiltfang were a formidable combination, and among their victories in 1971 was the King George V Gold Cup.

Gerd Wiltfang.

opposite: Hartwig Steenken riding Simona in the final of the 1974 Men's World Championship, which he eventually won.

A natural choice for the West German Olympic team in 1972, they helped to win the team gold medals in Munich but were under a cloud at Rotterdam the following week, when they jumped a fence backwards in the practising arena. Wiltfang was disciplined by being sent home before the end of the show, and in 1973 he was grounded for part of the year when his patron's horses were impounded by the Federal authorities during the bankruptcy proceedings.

He is now back in the team again.

Winkler, Hans Günter West Germany

Hans Günter Winkler.

Born in 1926, the son of a horse dealer from Westphalia, Hans Winkler, whose original ambition had been to become a cavalry officer, opted for civilian sport instead and competed in his first international show in Spain in 1952. Two years later, on his great chestnut mare Halla, he won the World Championship in Madrid from Pierre d'Oriola of France and the holder, 'Paco' Goyoaga of Spain.

In 1955, Winkler took the world title again in Aachen, after jumping off with Raimondo d'Inzeo, and the following year he won the Olympic individual gold medal in Stockholm. Having pulled a riding muscle in the Olympic arena, he was unable to defend his world title, but he won the first-ever Men's European Championship in 1957.

Having won almost every big competition in the world, Halla was retired in 1960 at the age of sixteen, but she bowed her way out by helping the Germans in the successful defence of their team gold medals before she went to stud.

Winkler's two King George V Gold Cup victories have been gained on Fortun and Enigk, and on the latter he was in the four-sided jump-off for the Olympic individual bronze, winning a team bronze medal as well. In 1971 he had the misfortune to lose what he hoped would be his Olympic horse, the brown thoroughbred Jägermeister, after an accident to a knee in Dublin, but a year later he still, for the fourth time, helped his team to win a fourth set of gold medals in the Munich Olympics, riding Torphy.

A brilliant individual with a highly idiosyncratic style, Hans Winkler is also a gifted instructor and has brought on many young riders to become an asset to the team.

Horses

Gran Geste   Brazil

The Derby specialist of Europe, having won three Hamburg Jumping Derbies and two British ones, Nelson Pessoa's grey gelding Gran Geste was foaled in 1952 and bred by Senor Raoul Gutierrez of Parana, Brazil, by an English thoroughbred stallion out of a native Criola mare. He was first produced by Major Alcindo Goncalves and upgraded in 1958. Pessoa brought him to Europe in 1961, when he won the Lonsdale Puissance in London and the Grand Prix in Brussels and St Gall.

The following year he won the Grand Prix de l'Europe and the Ruban de l'Atlantique, and scored his first Derby victory in Hamburg, in addition to Grand Prix victories in Royan, Biarritz and Vienna. In 1963 he brought off the double of the Hamburg and Hickstead Derbies, an achievement he repeated in 1965. He also won the Atlantic ribbon for the second time and staked a second claim to the Grand Prix in Biarritz.

In 1964 Gran Geste's victories included the Grand Prix of Europe, Dortmund and Aachen, to which he added a year later Frankfurt, Anwers, Hickstead's British Jumping Derby and four classes in Geneva.

Nelson Pessoa, a land agent from Rio de Janeiro, elected in 1961 to spend his summers touring Europe, based first in Geneva and then in France. He first came to Europe with the Brazilian team before the 1956 Olympic Games, and when he was nineteen rode the flea-bitten grey, Relincho, at the Royal International in London. He is now an integral part of the European jumping scene, and in 1974 became the first non-British international rider to turn professional, being sponsored by the French firm of Pernod.

Ali Baba   France

Ali Baba won the individual gold medal at the 1952 Olympic Games in Helsinki, ridden by the French ace, Pierre Jonquères d'Oriola. A French-bred Anglo-Arab (a distinct breed, with its own stud book), he was a chestnut gelding, 15.3 hands high, by the French National Stud stallion Frango, who stood in the south-west of France and was a son of the good jumping sire, Velox. Ali Baba's dam, Anita, was bred in Gers, where she foaled Ali Baba in 1941. The Olympic champion was Frango's most famous son, for the stallion died young and had few progeny.

At the end of World War II Ali Baba was discovered by the French *chef d'équipe*, Colonel Pierre Cavaillé, in a cavalry regiment where he had run in several army races and was also used as a polo pony. As he showed great aptitude for jumping, he was transferred to the National Centre at Fontainebleau. Capt. de Maupeou brought him out in international competitions and d'Oriola rode him for the first time at the Rome C.S.I.O. in 1952. Colonel Cavaillé advised d'Oriola not to ride Ali Baba in competitions again until the Olympic Games, and two months later they won the Olympic gold medal in Helsinki.

That autumn they won the championship at Harrisburg on the North American fall circuit, and in 1953 they won in Rome, London and Dublin. He was subsequently ridden by Captain Guy Lefrant with considerable success, and later returned to d'Oriola for the rest of his career.

opposite: Paddy McMahon of Great Britain riding Penwood Forgemill at Lucerne.

Lutteur B   France

It is given to few to win two individual gold medals at the Olympic Games, but Pierre Jonquères d'Oriola brought off this magnificent double at Tokyo in 1964, twelve years after he had won his first gold medal in Helsinki.

This time he was riding Lutteur B, a bay-brown gelding, foaled in Normandy in 1955, by that extraordinarily successful sire of jumpers Furioso, himself a thoroughbred by the English sire Precipitation out of a mare called Maureen.

Bred near Falaise, Lutteur was bought for the French cavalry school as a three-year-old and for some time worked with the famous Cadre Noir at Saumur. He was remarkably short of international experience when he went to Tokyo for the Olympics, having made his first international appearance in the same year in Madrid, where he won the Grand Prix. Only a few weeks later he confirmed that this was no fluke when he won the French Jumping Derby in La Baule.

In Tokyo in 1968, he and d'Oriola jumped a brilliant clear second round to win their Olympic gold medal and ensure for the French team the silver medals of second place behind the all-conquering West Germans. Unfortunately he died in 1969, when still in his prime.

Marquis III   France

Pierre Jonquères d'Oriola and Marquis III, a versatile little brown French-bred Anglo-Arab, were the sensation of the first post-war International Horse Show at London's White City Stadium in 1947, where they won the King George V Gold Cup and were in the winning French team for the Prince of Wales (Nations') Cup.

Foaled in 1935 and standing only some 15.2½ hands, he was bought by the captain of the French team, Colonel Cavaillé, from the Centre National des Sports Equestres at Fontainebleau, and it was believed that he first competed in the ring in 1939.

In 1947 he helped the French team to win Nations' Cups at Nice, Lucerne, London and Ostend, and individually won the Grand Prix in Nice and the pre-Olympic trial in Paris. He was on the reserve for the French Olympic team in 1948, as the second horse of Colonel Max Fresson, who, a tall man, eventually rode the bigger Decametre. That autumn he was ridden by Col. Cavaillé to win the officers' team jumping in Toronto. In 1949 he won the championship in Rome, ridden by d'Oriola, and ridden again by the *chef d'équipe* he won two competitions in Dublin, the second after jumping-off four times with Colonel Harry Llewellyn on Monty.

French Anglo-Arabs have gone out of vogue in the last quarter-century, chiefly because of their size, for the fences are now considerably higher than they were in the late 1940s. But Marquis III, whose volatile temperament was well attuned to that of his most successful rider, had, in d'Oriola's own words: 'Beaucoup de sang et beaucoup de coeur.'

Moet et Chandon   France

Moet et Chandon is one of the few horses with which the versatile d'Oriola was never able to establish a rapport. He started his career in Ireland with the top lady rider Iris Kellett, and in 1969 they won together the Ladies' European Championship in Dublin. During the following winter the horse, who was then called Morning Light, was sold to France for a sum reputed to be in the region of £35,000.

Moet et Chandon, ridden by Hubert Parot.

He was sent to Pierre d'Oriola, who farms in the Pyrenees, to be produced, and though this new combination won several competitions, it was never a happy partnership. 'The horse resents a dominant rider,' Iris Kellett told me sadly. 'He has a lot of character and you have to be very tactful with him and let him think he is the boss.' Iris, who is so slim and slight that she has to carry a lot of dead weight in her weight-cloth, must be supremely tactful, for she would have no chance of exerting her strength over this strong horse by dint of mere physical effort.

After a couple of disappointing seasons, Moet et Chandon was sent to Hubert Parot's stable, near Fontainebleau, and to some extent Parot succeeded where d'Oriola had failed. The horse has since won several competitions and gone well in Nations' Cup teams. However, he has never really regained the form he showed with Iris Kellett.

Pomone B   France

Pomone, a half-bred brown mare, was not up to the standard of most of d'Oriola's earlier horses, but she was a member of the French team which won the Olympic silver medals in Mexico City in 1968, and the Men's World Championship in Buenos Aires two years earlier also came her way.

A half-sister to d'Oriola's Olympic gold medal horse, Lutteur B, Pomone was good enough to beat Alvarez de Bohorques of Spain on Quizas, Raimondo d'Inzeo on Bowjack and Nelson Pessoa on Huipil.

In 1969 she won the second leg of the Men's European Championship at Hickstead, over the Nations' Cup course, tying with Alwin Schockemöhle on Donald Rex and Hans Gunter Winkler on Enigk; but she never produced this form again, and the following spring she was retired to stud.

Pomone B, ridden by Pierre Jonquères d'Oriola.

Rocket
France

Rocket.

Janou Lefebvre won an Olympic team silver medal, in Mexico City in 1968, and two Women's World Championships on her bay gelding Rocket, a thoroughbred horse who came to show jumping from the race course.

Rocket, who jumped a difficult course in two rounds for only 29¾ faults—1968 was a year in which astronomical totals were commonplace—put up the best performance of the French team and ensured it the silver medals of second place, a considerable achievement. But it was not until a year later that he really showed his worth, winning both the Grand Prix and the Championship at Nice in their home country, the Grand Prix in London and the coveted Meisterspringen in Aachen.

In Copenhagen a year later, Rocket and Janou Lefebvre justified their position as favourites for the women's world title and duly took it from the holder, Marion Mould with Stroller, and from Britain's other representative, Anneli Drummond-Hay with Merely-a-Monarch. But then their troubles began.

Rocket was laid low with impacted vertebrae, and though he was sent to Switzerland to be operated on by Dr Stihl, one of the best back-surgeons for horses in Europe, which kept him out of the women's European title fight in St Gall, he was still a shadow of his former self in the Olympic Games in Munich the following year, and many people had him written off.

Not so his owner, however. She took him to La Baule in July, 1974, and her confidence was amply justified when on Rocket she retained her world title, beating Michele McEvoy of the United States on Mr. Muskie and Caroline Bradley of Britain on True Lass. In that year also Janou and Rocket won the President's Cup in Washington.

Sucre de Pomme
France

Another 15.3 hands high French Anglo-Arab, the bay Sucre de Pomme won the individual bronze medal at the 1948 Olympic Games in London—the only horse to come within striking distance of the world-beating Mexicans. He was ridden by Jean d'Orgeix, now the Marquis, one of the exceptional horsemen of the post-war period and now trainer to the French team.

A bay gelding, Sucre de Pomme was foaled in May 1940 by Farandole IV out of Gousjun, and was bred at Verberie (Oise) by M Robert Peters, who owned him throughout his career.

Until April 1946 he was kept solely for hunting, but when Jean d'Orgeix had the opportunity of jumping a few fences on him he suggested trying him in the ring. Two months later he won the puissance in Paris, in August the Geneva Grand Prix and the Grand Prix in Ostend, and he also won at Berne in his first international season.

In 1947 he was even more successful, winning among many other prizes the puissance at Ostend and competitions in Paris, Geneva and Bordeaux, which he followed in 1948 with the Grand Prix and the championship in Rome and the Grand Prix in Paris. Although the French Olympic team was eliminated when Nankin fell and retired, lame, he tied on eight faults for the individual medal and finished third in the jump-off. In London shortly afterwards he finished second for the King George V Gold Cup and won the *Daily Mail* Cup for the championship of the show.

After a successful season in 1949, his career ended when his rider married the French lady rider, Michele Cancre, and went to Cambodia to school their jumping team.

Askan

Great Britain

Askan, a grey Hanoverian, was sold by Paul Schockemöhle in 1971 to the Ruhr industrialist Josef Kun for Gerd Wiltfang to ride. In a few weeks he had repaid at least some of his purchase price, when he won the Wills Grand Prix at Hickstead and the King George V Gold Cup in London.

A year later he was in the winning German team in the Munich Olympic Games, but by mid-1973 he was under a cloud, as his owner had declared bankruptcy and all his horses were impounded for some months. Eventually Askan was purchased by the brother of his original owner, but Alwin Schockemöhle did not find him suited to his style.

In 1974 Askan was bought from Alwin Shockemöhle by Trevor Banks for Harvey Smith to ride, and they made a good start in Rotterdam, where Smith was still getting to know the horse. Askan is related on his Dam's side to Salvador, the chestnut who was responsible for Harvey's third victory in the British Jumping Derby at Hickstead earlier in the year.

Askan.

Craven A

Great Britain

Craven A, a brown mare foaled in 1942, was bred in Sussex by the Robeson family and is the horse on which Peter Robeson made his name while he was still in his teens. She was by a small thoroughbred stallion called Victory, who was owned and hunted by the Master of the Surrey Union, Mr R. Sewill, out of a shire mare, and she first jumped in 1947. Two years later she competed internationally at Ostend and Le Zoute, jumping 6 ft 3 in in the puissance at Ostend to win from such horses as Marquis III, and at the end of the season she was runner-up for the Grand Prix de l'Europe in Paris.

From then on she was a regular member of the team and helped to win innumerable Nations' Cups in addition to winning many individual events—in Harrisburg she beat the Olympic individual gold medallist, Col. Humberto Mariles with Arete, after four barrages in 1950, and she blazed a successful trail across Europe before being selected as reserve for the Olympic team in 1952. She won the puissance at Harringay after a final barrage with Wilf White's

Craven A, ridden by Peter Robeson.

Nizefela, over a 6 ft 9 in wall, and also took the Victor Ludorum. In 1954 she won the puissance at the Royal International in London, and ended the week with the championship for the *Daily Mail* Cup.

She emerged from her retirement a few years ago to take part in a sponsored walk for charity, and she is still alive and well at the Robesons' home near Newport Pagnell at the remarkable age of thirty-three. During her career it was said of her: 'No more courageous animal ever existed. She touches her best form when the fences are impressive, in the region of 6 ft.'

Flanagan   Great Britain

Of all the good horses that Pat Smythe rode during her long and successful career, the best and most consistent was surely Flanagan, a chestnut Irish-bred horse who was first brought out as a five-year-old in three-day events, and was ridden round Badminton by Brigadier Lyndon Bolton.

He was subsequently bought by the late Bob Hanson and sent to Pat to produce as a show jumper. She brought him out in 1956 and, after winning eleven of the first twelve competitions in which they started in Britain, they went on to win three events in Paris. Shortly afterwards, Pat Smythe was selected for Britain's Olympic team for Stockholm, and became not only the first woman to ride in the Olympic Games but the first to win a medal—a team bronze.

The following year at the Belgian show at Spa she won with Flanagan the first-ever Ladies' European Championship. In 1960 they finished eleventh in the individual event at the Olympic Games in Rome, and in 1961 they initiated their hat-trick of European Championship successes at Deauville, Madrid and Hickstead. In 1962 they won the Wills British Jumping Derby at Hickstead—Pat Smythe was the first woman to do so—and it was the crowning achievement for a horse who had won all over Europe. He was no oil painting, but a real workman and utterly genuine.

He went into retirement after Pat's marriage to Swiss businessman Sam Koechlin in 1963, having kept her at the top of the international tree on the distaff side for eight seasons.

Foxhunter   Great Britain

Colonel Harry Llewellyn's Foxhunter, one of the greatest show jumpers of all time, was the horse who put Britain on the international show jumping map and also aroused public interest in the sport in Britain. He was bred by Ken Millard in Norfolk and foaled in 1941 by the premium stallion Erehwemos out of Catcall, a brilliant hunter who was by Step Forward out of a Clydesdale mare. As a foal he learned to jump in and out of his barn over a small rail, and later, turned out in a field surrounded by twelve-foot dykes, he jumped them for fun. Sold unbroken to Norman Holmes of Thrussington, he was hunted with the Quorn as a four- and five-year-old, brought out as a novice in 1946 and sold to Harry Llewellyn in July 1947.

He seldom competed other than internationally, after making the trip to Ostend and Le Zoute shortly after his purchase, and in 1948 he was one of the bronze-medal-winning British Olympic team at Wembley Stadium in London. A week later he won the King George V Gold Cup. In 1949 he took the Grand Prix in Paris and Nice and the Grand Prix de France. A back strain at the White City laid him off until Harringay, where he won two competitions before going on to win in Paris, Brussels and Geneva.

Flanagan, ridden by Pat Smythe.

In Lucerne the following year he took the individual prize in the Nations' Cup and two competitions, including the Grand Prix. He won the puissance in Vichy, the King George V Gold Cup for the second time as well as the puissance in London at 6 ft 6½ in three events including the Victor Ludorum and the puissance at the Horse of the Year Show, followed by four classes in North America; he ended the year with a tally of nineteen victories.

In 1951 he won in Nice and Rome; his score of eighteen wins included three in London (among them the *Daily Mail* Cup), Dublin and Zurich, with the highlights the Grands Prix in Ostend and Rotterdam and the Harringay puissance.

1952 was his greatest year, for he was in the only winning British team ever for the Olympic Prix des Nations in Helsinki, and his clear second round was vital to this achievement. He won three classes in Dublin and three in Lucerne—where he won the Grand Prix outright for the first time in its history—and two in London, where he helped to win the Prince of Wales Cup for the fourth time.

In 1953 he became the only horse ever to win the King George V Gold Cup three times and was unbeaten at the White City in London until the last day, when he was second to Merano for the *Daily Mail* Cup, having won the *Horse and Hound* Cup and divided the puissance with Uruguay and Galway Boy. He went on to win in New York, and in Toronto he helped the British team to win the Nations' Cup there for the first time ever.

He lost his confidence, the result of falls in America, and did not jump much in 1954, though he won the Olympic Trial, and he retired in 1955 to his owner's home near Abergavenny; he is now buried on the Welsh hills nearby. He was a horse in a million.

Foxhunter.

Merely-a-Monarch   Great Britain

Anneli Drummond-Hay's (as she was formerly known) superlative brown gelding Merely-a-Monarch, by Happy Monarch out of a mare by Merely-a-Minor, was a quite exceptional horse in that, before he started show jumping at top international level, he had reached the top of the tree in England as a three-day event horse, winning the inaugural competition at Burghley in 1961 and following up by winning the Badminton Horse Trials the following spring.

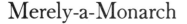

Merely-a-Monarch, ridden by Anneli Drummond-Hay.

Then he was switched to show jumping, and he soon began to make his mark in this new and entirely different sport, winning the Imperial Cup at the Royal International in London before finishing third in the Ladies' European Championship at Hickstead in 1963—a title he won in Rome five years later.

In 1964 he lost his place in the British Olympic team for Tokyo due to the fact that all was not well with him. Robert Hanson, who had bought him very reasonably with the proviso that Miss Drummond-Hay should continue to ride him until after the Olympic Games, decided to try a change of jockey and asked David Broome to ride him at the Royal International, but an injunction was obtained and the horse was removed from the show. Veterinary evidence was later produced to show that the horse was unwell, and eventually he returned to his original ownership, in partnership with Colonel Tom Greenhalgh.

In 1967 he won the Grand Prix in Geneva and the following year he won the European Championship in Rome. In 1970 he took the Queen Elizabeth II Cup at London's Royal International after trying to win it on many occasions, and he tied for second in the world title in Copenhagen.

Mister Softee   Great Britain

Mister Softee, ridden by David Broome.

Of all the good horses that the Massarella family have owned and produced from their place near Doncaster, where the late Andrew Massarella Senior founded an ice cream dynasty, the best was the chestnut Irish horse, Mister Softee, who won the Men's European championship three times—in 1962 with David Barker, and in 1967 and 1969 with David Broome.

A chestnut gelding with four white legs, he was bought by Mr Massarella at the Dublin Horse Show as a young horse after he had seen him jumping a pole on the lunge. The horse was pursued over it by a bevy of would-be helpers flapping their mackintoshes, and, not unnaturally unnerved, he landed so awkwardly that the helpers were moved to declare that the horse was wrong of his back. Fortunately undeterred, Andrew Massarella saw fit to disregard the advice to leave him alone, and acquired the best horse he ever owned.

After his European championship win he was an obvious choice for the Olympic short-list in 1964, but he did not stay sound that season. He was given to David Broome at the end of 1965, and the following season he won the King George V Gold Cup, the British Jumping Derby and the Victor Ludorum at Wembley. The next year he took the European title in Rotterdam—retaining it in 1969 at Hickstead—and in 1968 he won an Olympic individual bronze medal in Mexico City.

He was retired at the end of 1969, and after Softee had won his third European title Broome said: 'I wonder if people realise how lucky they are to see a horse like this?' He was so sensitive that he never needed schooling—just to hit a fence was enough of a reminder for him.

Nizefela   Great Britain

The full back of Britain's Nations' Cup team for many years in the 1950s, and an Olympic team gold medallist at Helsinki in 1952, Wilf White's Nizefela, who was characterised by his famous 'kick-back' over his fences, was described thus during his career by Colonel Harry Llewellyn: 'He is as steady as a rock, jumps big and clean with (to the foreigners) nerve-shattering regularity. There is no better Nations' Cup horse in the world.'

A brown gelding, bred in Lincolnshire in 1942, his working life started in the plough. Wilf bought him from a Mr Harrison of Bridgnorth, in Shropshire, and he made his first international appearance in 1949, when he went to Nice and Rome with the British team. In 1950 he was the hero of the British team's North American tour, winning five classes, dividing two, and placing fifteen times.

The highlight of his performances in 1952 came in the Olympic Games in Helsinki, where he was extremely unlucky not to add an individual gold medal to his team gold. He was a frequent winner in Rome and Nice, as well as in Dublin, and also campaigned extensively on the home front, finishing second on the list of national winners in 1953. He topped the list in 1954, when one of his most impressive performances was to win the puissance at Harringay after three barrages, ending at 6 ft 6 in; thus he avenged himself on Craven A, his vanquisher two years earlier. He won many big competitions in 1955, and lived to a ripe old age in retirement on his owner's farm in Cheshire. Wilf White rode the most successful horse of his day before the war, W.V. Grange's grey Desire, who won all over Britain.

O'Malley   Great Britain

O'Malley.

The first 'class' horse to be ridden by Harvey Smith, the Canadian-bred O'Malley won the international championship in Toronto as a six-year-old in 1961, ridden by Jim Elder. He was then bought by the late Robert Hanson, who sent him first to Richard Stillwell to iron out a few difficulties which, temperamental in basis, were never entirely resolved.

A 16.1 hand chestnut gelding, by Peepshow out of the half-bred hunter mare, Willow, O'Malley was bred by Miss Shaw of Quebec. His sire was an American thoroughbred, and O'Malley was successfully shown in breeding classes until he was three years old. At four he was bought by Canadian Olympic team rider Jim Elder, who rode him to many victories with the team. Less than a month after joining Harvey Smith's string, he won the John Player Trophy, the British Grand Prix, at the Royal International, and in 1964 he won the Grand Prix in Rome. Exactly ten years earlier his owner's son, the late Bill Hanson, had won this classic competition on The Monarch and Bob Hanson counted himself lucky to have won it twice.

In 1965, following a disagreement between Harvey Smith and the horse's owner, O'Malley was given over to David Barker, but they were not compatible and in 1966 the horse was ridden by Alison Westwood. This was barely more successful than the original change of jockeys, and the horse went back to Harvey, who had headed the list of National winners on him in 1963 and again in 1964 (a feat he repeated in 1965 and 1967 on Harvester and in 1968 on Doncella—later re-named Mattie Brown).

Pennwood Forgemill   Great Britain

Pennwood Forgemill, bought as a young horse in Ireland, was bred in Eire and sold to a Northern Irish dealer at a foal fair when he was just weaned. The dealer bought three foals and drove them back to the North in an open lorry. When he reached the border he declared them and was told: 'But you've only got two!' Forgemill was found seven miles back along the road, on his way home, and he still has a scar on his shoulder from falling on the road.

Fred Hartill bought him near Belfast on his way home from Kilrush Fair. He was three years old, unrideable, and awaiting his turn to go to the knacker's yard to be slaughtered. He was difficult and spoiled and impossible to back, but at £130 he was not dear and though it took weeks of driving in long reins to get him going, he eventually mended his ways. First brought out by Johnny

Wrathall, he really hit top form with Paddy McMahon.

Overlooked for the British Olympic team in 1972, he proceeded to fight back at the Horse of the Year Show at Wembley, where he won the Victor Ludorum in tremendous style and the volume of applause nearly raised the roof. He was an obvious choice for the Men's European Championship at Hickstead the following year, and he duly won it from Alwin Schockemöhle's Rex the Robber, going on to win the King George V Gold Cup shortly afterwards.

One of Britain's pair of horses involved in defending the Men's World Championship the following year, having finished 1973 as the leading horse in Britain, he was unfortunately defeated by the treble which ended the Nations' Cup-type course and failed to qualify for the final. But he is still only nine years old and has plenty of time to win another. As his owner says: 'A man finds a horse like Forgemill by accident, and then spends the rest of his life trying to find another.'

Psalm   Great Britain

Psalm.

Ann Moore's Psalm, a bay thoroughbred horse by Sermon, brought her to the top of the show-jumping tree and when he developed tendon trouble in 1974, having won her an Olympic individual silver medal and three European titles, she elected to retire from show jumping as a competitor, although she was only twenty-three years old.

It was in 1968, after a successful career in the junior classes, that she really made her mark, winning the Junior European Championship at the Midlands International Show at Stoneleigh, the Young Rider of the Year title at the Horse of the Year Show in London and the Young Riders' Championship of Great Britain at Hickstead—a triple crown that had never before been achieved.

Two years later she went to the World Championships in Copenhagen as a reserve in Britain's pair, and in 1971 Psalm won his first European Championship at St Gall in Switzerland. In Munich the following year he won his Olympic silver medal in the individual competition, but in the team event he was unable to negotiate the big combination fence and stopped in each round. Combinations were never easy for him.

He won the Queen Elizabeth II Cup in 1972 and the following year he finished equal first with Mr Banbury, ridden by Alison Dawes. In 1973 he retained his European title in Vienna.

In 1974 Psalm won the Ladies' National Championship at Royal Windsor— one of the few titles that had so far eluded him and his rider—but he jarred himself on the hard going and was not his usual self at the Devon County show the following week. He was taken home for veterinary attention on the second day, and at his final show at Arena North in June the decision was made to withdraw him from the World Championship in La Baule and to retire him from the show ring.

Stroller   Great Britain

Stroller, whom Marion Mould (then Marion Coakes) brought with her from the junior classes when she graduated to adult competitions, was one of those remarkable animals who perform better over big fences than they do over small ones.

An Irish-bred pony standing only 14.2 hand high, the only jumper of his size to achieve world-wide recognition, he was bought in Ireland by Tommy Grantham, the Sussex dealer, and sold to Sally Cripps, whose father is a butcher in Billingshurst. Marion took him over in 1960, and when her father proposed selling him, she begged him to give the pony a try in open classes. In his first season he took Seamus Hayes and Goodbye to a barrage before conceding victory in the 1964 British Jumping Derby.

The following year, when Marion was just eighteen, he won the Women's World Championship at Hickstead, where he won the Wills Hickstead medal for consistency in the open classes for no fewer than five consecutive seasons (1966 to 1970)—a record that must stand unsurpassed. He won the Dublin Championship in 1964 and 1965, helped to win innumerable Nations' Cups for Britain, and in 1965 became the youngest-ever winner of the Queen Elizabeth II Cup, and the smallest horse.

In 1968 Stroller was selected for the Olympic team, and in the individual competition jumped one of the only two clear rounds. In the barrage he had eight faults to the four of the U.S. team captain, Bill Steinkraus on Snowbound, but this was still good enough to give him the individual silver medal. And though, due to an abscess on a tooth, he stopped in the treble and was eliminated in the team event, his name was already written for all time in the annals of show jumping history. In 1967 he won the British Jumping Derby and in 1970 he was runner-up for the women's world title in Copenhagen, which he was defending, to Janou Lefebvre on the French horse, Rocket.

Stroller, ridden by Marion Mould.

Sunsalve   Great Britain

David Broome won many international competitions on horses like Wildfire and Ballan Silver Knight, but it was on the chestnut gelding Sunsalve, owned and bred by Oliver Anderson in Norfolk, by his own stallion Skoiter, that he first hit world-class form.

Sunsalve, who jumped in a highly individual way with his back as flat as a board, was first produced by Mr Anderson's daughter, Elizabeth, who rode him to victory in the Queen Elizabeth II Cup in 1957. When she married he was sent to David Broome to ride, in 1960, and within two weeks of taking him over, David won on him the King George V Gold Cup.

He was a natural choice for the British Olympic team, and he won the individual bronze medal in Rome before the season was out. (He could, indeed have won the gold medal, but for an unfortunate and controversial water fault.)

The following year, in Aachen, David Broome and Sunsalve won the Men's European Championship from a world-class field, defeating both the d'Inzeo brothers and enabling the next title fight to be held in London. Sadly, he was not invited to defend it, as Sunsalve had died and Broome was deemed not to have a horse good enough.

Uncle Max   Great Britain

Though this grey, American-bred ex-rodeo horse only joined the United States Equestrian Team in 1968, owner-rider Neal Shapiro had used him at home as a 'fun' horse for seven seasons. As ebullient as he was durable, Uncle Max was A.H.S.A. High-Score Green Jumper Champion in 1961 and P.H.A. High-Score Champion in 1963. However, so unorthodox was his style and personality that it took some time for Shapiro to consider him seriously as an international prospect.

Neal finally brought him to Europe with the team in 1968, and before going home sold him to Ted Edgar, whose extrovert temperament in many ways matched Max's own. Only a few weeks after changing stables and jockeys, Uncle

Max won the puissance at the Horse of the Year Show at Wembley.

In 1969 things did not go so well to start with, and—unbelievably—Ted received an official reprimand from the British Show Jumping Association when the television microphone relayed his voice to millions of viewers as, in the middle of a round, he cast aspersions on Uncle Max's parentage and called him both big and idle to boot. Selected for the British team in Aachen, they did not perform well, but at the Royal International in London soon afterwards Uncle Max won the King George V Gold Cup, and at the end of the season he took the Leading Show Jumper of the Year title.

These two bombastic characters later graced the hunting field in North Warwickshire, but Uncle Max failed to win any more big competitions and eventually he was retired.

Uncle Max, ridden by Ted Edgar.

Dundrum.

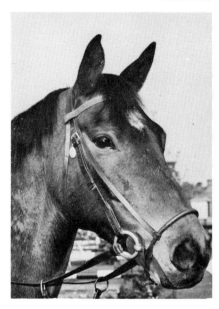

Dundrum   Ireland

This *multum in parvo* was a remarkable little horse, on whom Tommy Wade, the Tipperary rider, won many puissance competitions even though Dundrum stood only 15 hands 1½ inches high. He was by the thoroughbred sire, Blue Heaven, who was used a great deal to upgrade the native Irish ponies, out of a Connemara mare.

Foaled in 1952, he started life pulling a milk float around the streets of the town not far from Dublin whose name he bears. He was bred by Patrick Crowe of Monroe, Gooldscross, Co. Tipperary, and produced as a jumper by Tommy Wade, a farmer's son from the same village.

He won two international championships and nine national championships in Dublin, and three at the Royal Ulster show at Balmoral, Belfast, but his fame spread far beyond his native Ireland. When, in 1960, the Irish team was opened up to civilians, he was an automatic selection. In 1961 he won the Victor Ludorum at the Horse of the Year Show at Wembley, London, and the following year he won there the puissance and the Guinness Time Championship, in addition to the Vaux Gold Tankard at the Royal Highland, Edinburgh, and the Grands Prix in Ostend and Brussels. At Ostend that year he won every class in which he competed.

In 1963 he took the King George V Gold Cup at the Royal International at the White City, London, and the puissance at the Horse of the Year Show for the second time. In Dublin he jumped the only double clear to help Ireland win the Aga Khan Trophy.

In 1964 his rider was grounded through ill-health, but in 1967 they staged a comeback and again helped Ireland to win the Aga Khan Trophy.

Goodbye III   Ireland

Goodbye was surely the best of the many good horses ridden by Seamus Hayes throughout his long and distinguished career, which stretched over two decades. In 1960 he first rode the then-seven-year-old liver chestnut son of Renwood, bred in Co. Kerry, for Lord Harrington. The following year they won the inaugural Wills British Jumping Derby at Hickstead with the only clear round. Three years later, he won it again, after jumping off with Marion Coakes (now Mrs David Mould) on Stroller.

Bred by Mr Trent of Tralee, worked in a plough on the farm in his youth and, gelded relatively late, Goodbye also served four or five mares as a three-year-old. As a four-year-old he was bought by Lord Harrington for his daughter, Lady Jane Stanhope, and sent to be schooled and produced by Noel O'Dwyer, son of the pre-war Irish Army ace, Major Ged O'Dwyer.

Goodbye was a winner in Ostend, Rotterdam, Brussels, Antwerp, Amsterdam and Geneva, in addition to Dublin—where he won the puissance at the Spring Show in 1960, and London. In 1965 he won the puissance in Aachen, Dublin and Wembley and before he retired from the ring at the end of 1967 he jumped 7 ft 2 in on six occasions.

An extremely good-looking, typically Irish hunting horse, he was one of the few top performers who stayed in Ireland throughout his career, instead of being sold abroad in his youth. It is a little ironic that Ireland breeds some of the best horses in the world and sells so many of them to compete under foreign saddle-cloths.

Goodbye, ridden by Seamus Hayes.

Loch an Easpaig   Ireland

One of the best horses to have jumped for the Irish Army Jumping Team since the end of the World War II, Loch an Easpaig (Bishop's Loch) was a chestnut gelding foaled in 1951, by Knight's Crusader out of a mare by Marshal Ney; he was bred at Mullinavat, Co. Kilkenny, by John Delehunty. His mother was then twenty-five years old and he, her nineteenth foal, was so weak when he was born that for the first few days of his life he was unable to stand without assistance.

As a two-year-old he showed a fine disregard for boundary fences and at four he was broken simultaneously to saddle, plough and harrow. Then he was alternately hunted and worked on the farm until he was seven, when he was bought by the Wexford trainer Martin French; French sold him at the Enniscorthy show to Mrs B. Lawlor, who runs a well-known catering firm at Naas in Co. Kildare. She in turn sold him on to the army in August 1958. The following year he was the outstanding novice horse in Rotterdam, having already won a competition in Dublin a few weeks earlier.

He was ridden throughout his career by Billy (now Col. W.R.) Ringrose, who had joined the team in 1954. In 1960 they won together in Marseilles and took the puissance in Dublin. Their best season was 1961, when they won in Nice, took the coveted Rome Grand Prix, and won in London, Washington, New York, and Toronto. The following year they took the puissance in Barcelona, in 1963 the first leg of the European Championship in Rome and two competitions in Harrisburg.

In 1965 Loch an Easpaig won the Grand Prix in Nice and the Piazza di Siena prize in Rome, and the following year the *Daily Mail* Championship at the Royal International in London. A dependable Nations' Cup horse, he was clear in the first round at Ostend in 1967 but died in harness during the second.

Pele   Ireland

The chestnut gelding Pele, by the Co. Cork stallion Go Tabaan, foaled in 1966, was the top horse in Ireland in 1974 and proved himself to be one of the best young horses in the world at Hickstead, when having won the first two legs of the Men's World Championship he was runner-up for the title in the four-horse final, beaten only by Hartwig Steenken's Simona, from West Germany.

Pele started his working life as a show hunter, when owned by Miss Fiona Kinnear, and was champion hunter at the Royal Ulster Show as a four-year-old, after which he won the ladies' championship under a side-saddle in Dublin.

Jack Bamber, the noted and respected dealer from Ballymena, Co. Antrim, in Northern Ireland, who has found such great horses as Douglas Bunn's Beethoven (winner of the 1970 Men's World Championship in La Baule, ridden by David Broome), and Alison Dawes's The Maverick (now Mr Banbury), eventually succeeded in buying him, and sold him on to Iris Kellett for her jockey, Eddie Macken, to ride.

Brought on quietly in 1973, when he was seven years old, Pele went well at the Wills Easter meeting at Hickstead to win an international class, and Miss Kellett then predicted a brilliant future for him. Just how soon that future was to start even she could have had little idea, but he proved his class beyond all doubt at Hickstead, jumping massive courses coolly and confidently in the men's title fight, and eventually going under by only one fence to the best combination in the world.

Pele won the Wills Hickstead Gold Medal in 1974, a points championship for consistency in the international classes there throughout the season.

Pele, ridden by Eddie Macken.

Ambassador   Italy

A grey Irish horse by Nordlys, Ambassador was brought out by Tommy Brennan for dealer Frank Kernan, and was bought by Graziano Mancinelli with the Olympic Games specifically in view during the winter of 1971.

He duly obliged his new owner by winning for him the Olympic individual gold medal in Riem, near Munich, beating Ann Moore and Psalm. In 1973 he was ridden by Nelly Mancinelli without success. A hard-pulling horse who requires strong checking, he has a big jump but does not appear to be a horseman's *beau idéal*, though he was very successful in Ireland with Brennan.

There have certainly been more worthy Olympic champions—but luck plays its part in show jumping, and this was undoubtedly Ambassador's and Mancinelli's lucky day. It did not hold through to the team competition, in which they incurred twenty-eight faults, though the team finished in third place and won the bronze medals.

Ambassador, foaled in 1964, was bred by Thomas Clancey of Stradbally, Co. Waterford, and bought from Jimmy McEvoy, one of three farming, hunting and dealing brothers from Co. Down, and when owned by Frank Kernan jumped on many Irish teams. He first jumped for Italy in 1971, and before the Olympics won the Grands Prix in Rome, La Baule and Geneva and the Italian National Championship in Milan.

Ambassador, ridden by Graziano Mancinelli.

Bellevue   Italy

This remarkable black Irish-bred horse seemed to be better than ever when, at the Dublin Horse Show in 1974, he enabled Raimondo d'Inzeo to win the Guiness Gold Tankard for the leading rider of the week, having cleared 7 ft 1 in to share the spoils with Captain Ned Campion of Ireland on Inis Cara; he won the Player-Wills International and was only narrowly beaten in the Irish Distillers' Six Bars competition.

Bellevue has been Raimondo d'Inzeo's extremely successful Grand Prix and puissance specialist for more years than probably either cares to remember. Yet in 1973, his rider did not start him, or, for that matter, any other of his horses, in Rome. He maintained that Bellevue, at sixteen, was too old to start his season so early in the year, and that his other horses were too young. Bellevue, who has remained sound in his back and his limbs throughout a long and distinguished career in top-class competition, continues to belie his age.

His victories are too numerous to catalogue but although they have never included an Olympic medal or a world or European title, they are more impressive than the records of many horses who have won both.

Bellevue, already a legend in his lifetime, was bred in Ireland by Thomas McGrath of Dungarvan, Co. Waterford, and sold to Italy by Frank Kernan, who also sold the Olympic gold medal horse Ambassador to Italy from his yard at Crossmaglen in Co. Down, Northern Ireland. An unusually versatile horse who has also won speed competitions, in addition to power championships, he is by Whitsuntide, was bought off the farm as a two-year-old and sold to Raimondo when he was coming four.

Bellevue, ridden by Raimondo d'Inzeo.

Easter Light   Italy

A bay gelding who came from Iris Kellett in Ireland, Easter Light was Piero d'Inzeo's Olympic horse in the 1972 Olympic Games, but he went so badly that Piero retired him from both rounds of the competition. Later he said that the

Fiorello.

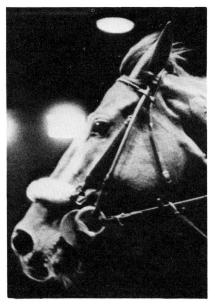

Gone Away.

horse had not been itself since arriving in Munich, and he suspected that it had been 'got at'. 'If I had not been obliged to jump, because it was the Olympic Games, I should not have taken him in the ring at all.'

The following spring, Easter Light proved his well-being by winning no fewer than four competitions in Rome, including the Grand Prix and the championship, and a year later he triumphed in the championship again. But when he went through the final testing treble in the Nations' Cup phase of the 1974 Men's World Championship at Hickstead some ten weeks later, he was withdrawn from the fray.

Fidux   Italy

A bay German horse who was a wild, strong and erratic ride, Fidux was bought as a team horse for Piero d'Inzeo to ride, but despite a number of successes, he was not Piero's type of horse at all and eventually he was taken over by Graziano Mancinelli.

His finest hour came in the Men's World Championship in La Baule in 1970. He qualified for the final; and thereafter it was largely because, of the other riders, only David Broome could ride him when the time came for swapping horses, that Broome emerged victorious from this stiff title fight.

Fiorello   Italy

An Italian-bred chestnut, Fiorello was Raimondo d'Inzeo's main hope for the 1972 Olympics in Munich. He helped to win a team bronze medal and won several good competitions in Europe beforehand—including a divided first in the puissance at the Horse of the Year Show at Wembley in London a year earlier shared with the former show hack, Lucky Strike, ridden by Malcolm Pyrah; however, his rider now prefers to ride the stronger Irish horses, like Bellevue and Gone Away, and sold him to his fellow rider on the Italian team, Dr Vittorio Orlandi, in the winter of 1972/73.

Gone Away   Italy

A chestnut gelding by Nordlys, foaled in 1963, Gone Away started his working life in Ireland with Mrs Tom Morgan, joint-Master and huntsman of the West Waterford Hounds. She showed him with great success in Dublin, where he won the middleweight championship, and sold him to Raimondo d'Inzeo for a sum in the region of £27,000. She had already sold the lightweight show hunter, Red Fox, to Piero d'Inzeo.

Gone Away, a powerful horse with great scope, was brought on slowly in international competitions and after his initiation in 1969 soon made the grade. He won the puissance at the Royal International in London in 1972, clearing 7 ft 2 in, and has been successful at most of the major European meetings. In 1974 he won the Grand Prix and the Premio Martini Rossi in Rome.

Merano   Italy

Merano was the horse on whom Raimondo d'Inzeo achieved his first really impressive victories, and unlike most of his successors, he was bred in Italy. A bay gelding, 16 hands high, he was foaled in 1946 and bred at Pontecagana, near

Merano, ridden by Raimondo d'Inzeo.

Salerno, where show jumpers have been bred for many years, among them the pre-war Italian team horses Piccola Mia, and Lettera d'Amore, by Guiseppe Morese, who had forty-five mares before the war but reduced his stud to five after the war ended.

Merano, who was by Ugolino da Siena, a son of the 1935 Italian Derby winner Ortello, out of an Irish hunter mare called Dalila was bought by Raimondo for only £200. His breeder could have made a far better price of him, but having seen him jump a gate as a yearling he wanted him to have every opportunity, with a great rider. He was amply repaid. Merano came out in 1952 and a year later he had won £1,200—a large sum in those days—including two competitions in Rome, before he won the *Daily Mail* Champion Cup in London.

At the end of the season he was sold for £4,000 to Alessandro Perrone, editor of Italy's leading national daily newspaper. They won two classes, one in Geneva, but were not a happy combination, for the new owner could not hold the horse in a snaffle and Merano did not go kindly in any other bit. So he was sold to the Italian Federation for £3,000 and returned to Raimondo. In 1954 Merano and Raimondo d'Inzeo won twice and were second three times in Aachen, a record they exceeded all over Europe in 1955; and in 1956 they won the Men's World Championship and two Olympic silver medals, team and individual, in the Olympic Games in Stockholm. Merano continued to win Grands Prix all over Europe until the end of 1959—three in Rome, two in Nice, one in Paris, and one in Aachen.

Merano was Raimondo's favourite horse, and ended his days in retirement at his home.

Posillipo   Italy

opposite: Alwin Schockemöhle of West Germany riding Donald Rex at Hickstead.

Like his brilliant predecessor, Merano, Posillipo was bred by Nobile Morese by the same sire, Ugolino da Siena, out of an Irish mare called Veronica. A chestnut gelding of great quality, he too was owned by his rider, who brought him out in 1958, and the following season he won in Rome and Aachen and took the Grand Prix in Geneva.

In 1960 he won the Olympic individual gold medal in Rome, at the expense of his owner-rider's brother Piero on The Rock. As a team horse he helped to win numerous Nations' Cups for Italy and assisted in two consecutive campaigns, in 1960 and again in 1964, to win the team bronze medals for Italy at the Olympic Games.

Like Merano, in whose footsteps he followed, he won major competitions all over Europe for the best part of ten seasons, and after he retired from the ring his rider found him difficult to replace for several years.

Posillipo, ridden by Raimondo d'Inzeo.

The Rock, ridden by Piero d'Inzeo.

The Rock Italy

The Rock, who headed the list of Italian money winners for some years, was an enormous grey gelding bred by Mr T. O'Haurhan in Ireland in 1948, by Water Serpent out of a mare by Sandyman. His first full season came in 1957, when he won in Paris, took the puissance in London at 7 ft 1 in, and won at Dublin and two events in Geneva.

The personal property of Piero d'Inzeo, he was a regular winner in London, Dublin, Rome, Paris and Aachen, and in 1960 at the Rome Olympics he won a team bronze medal and an individual silver. In 1958 in Aachen he finished second for the men's European title and in 1962 in London he finished equal second for this championship with Hans Gunter Winkler on Romanus for West Germany.

After his rider fell out with his national federation, The Rock was taken over by Graziano Mancinelli, who was already riding his alleged half-sister, Rockette. But this was not an ideal arrangement and the horse was already past his best, having campaigned for some eight or nine seasons, winning puissance and Grand Prix competitions all over Europe, where he dominated the scene for several years.

Uruguay   Italy

Uruguay, a big chestnut gelding with an enormous jump, was the horse who first brought Piero d'Inzeo into the limelight. He was foaled in 1942, bred in France by M.P. Cherruau, by the thoroughbred sire Lord Magique out of the half-bred mare Praline. He was bought by Natalie Perrone for her husband, then editor of a leading Italian daily newspaper, to ride. Later the horse was sold to the Italian Federation and leased to the army.

With Piero d'Inzeo, Uruguay's best performance was in the 1956 Olympic Games in Stockholm, where he won the bronze individual medal, and a fourth place in the Men's World Championship in 1953 in Paris. In England he is best remembered for his performance in the Moss Bros. Puissance in the same year, when with the red wall at 6 ft 6 in in the third barrage divided the spoils with Colonel Harry Llewellyn's Foxhunter and Alan Oliver on Galway Boy. Two years later he won this competition at the fourth barrage, after a great struggle with Alan Oliver again, this time on Red Admiral; in 1957 he won the King George V Gold Cup. Two years later he won the Men's European championship in Aachen and two more events, including the puissance, where he cleared 7 ft 2 in to share honours with the Dutch horse, Hubertus.

He won puissance competitions all over Europe and was the only French-bred horse to star in the Italian team, which has recently been almost exclusively Irish.

Arete   Mexico

The first of the post-war individual Olympic gold-medallists, Arete and Colonel Humberto Mariles were the individual champions of the 1948 Olympic Games at London's Wembley Stadium.

A wiry little native-bred horse, Arete was as bold as a lion and as wiry as a polo pony, which he greatly resembled. He won his medal over a very testing course built by the late Phil Blackmore with a total of only 6¼ faults—a foot in the water, and 2¼ faults for exceeding the time allowed.

Arete was also a perennial star performer on the North American international circuit, winning the Individual Championship at New York in 1948 and again in 1951, among many other victories. His success was all the more remarkable for the fact that he was blind in one eye.

Democrat   U.S.A.

The most remarkable American show jumper in twenty years, his career spanning both the pre-war and the post-war eras, Democrat was described by Bill Steinkraus in the 1950s as the best horse he had ever ridden. Bred by the U.S. Army Remount Service, and foaled in 1933 at Fort Robinson, Nebraska, he was a 15.3 hands high brown thoroughbred gelding, by Gordon Russell out of Princess Bon. As a four-year-old he was sent to the Cavalry School at Fort Riley, Kansas, and in 1940 he competed at the National Horse Show at New York's Madison Square Garden. Ridden by the then Captain F.F. Wing, he won the international championship, and the following year he won two classes, including the Whitney Stone Trophy, named after the President of the U.S.E.T., on whose Morven Stud in Virginia he was eventually pensioned off.

During the war years he never saw a show ring, but in 1946 he came back to win in New York and Toronto. A repeat performance the following year earned him a place in the U.S. Olympic Team, and he was shipped to Europe in the

Democrat, ridden by C. D. Russell.

Idle Dice, ridden by Rodney Jenkins.

fall of 1947. He won as an individual in Lucerne, Aachen, London and Dublin and helped to win the Nations' Cups in Lucerne and Dublin, piloted by his old partner, Colonel Wing. Finally he was fourth in the Olympics with two fences down.

Later that year the U.S. Army was completely mechanised, the army team disbanded and Democrat returned to Fort Riley, his career ostensibly at an end. But early in 1952, when the civilian team was formed, he was brought out of retirement at the age of nineteen, and helped to win the Olympic bronze medals in Helsinki, ridden by Major John Russell. On his return home, he was ridden by Bill Steinkraus on the North American circuit and won every individual class in which he competed—one in Harrisburg, four in New York and three in Toronto, including the Championship. Thereafter he enjoyed an honourable retirement, wisely begun while he was still at the top of the tree.

Idle Dice U.S.A.

Idle Dice, a thoroughbred brown gelding, 17.1 hands high, by Hay Hook and foaled in 1963, is owned by Harry Gill of Collegeville, Pennsylvania. He crossed to Europe in 1974 as the most successful jumper of all time in the United States, where he has won virtually every important competition and amassed a record sum of over $125,000 in prize money.

Shown only lightly, mostly in hunter classes, as a four-year-old, he was brought along slowly as a jumper, and his record has been a model of consistency ever since. Twice a winner of the American Gold Cup at Philadelphia, he has also won Washington's President's Cup twice, the American Invitational at Tampa, and innumerable other stake and puissance competitions.

He and his rider, the top professional Rodney Jenkins, first joined the United States Equestrian Team in the autumn of 1973 and helped it to win two Nations' Cups in addition to notching up six individual wins, among them the Grand Prix of New York. On the U.S.E.T.'s summer tour in 1974 he was less fortunate, finishing only eighth in the qualifications for the Men's World Championship, and was eclipsed for much of the time by his younger stable companion, the chestnut nine-year-old Number One Spy. Idle Dice's best show of the tour was Dublin, where he took the Irish Distillers' Six Bars and enabled his rider, as second high-point rider of the week behind Raimondo d'Inzeo, to win the Guinness Silver Tankard.

Ksar d'Esprit U.S.A.

Ksar d'Esprit, a striking grey American thoroughbred standing 17.1½ hands high, was for some years the U.S.E.T.'s best and most reliable horse. Bred in Maryland by Hugh Wiley and foaled in 1946, he was sold as a youngster to a Canadian Mr V.G. Cardy, and was later bought by the Thomas family for their nineteen-year-old daughter Shirley, who rode him with the Canadian team under the name of Revlon's White Sable.

He first visited Europe with the Canadian team in 1954 and concluded the tour by winning the Irish Trophy in Dublin with the only clear round over a course which included both the double and the single banks. Two years later he returned to the land of his birth and was sold to Miss Eleonora Sears of Boston, an outstanding woman then in her seventies, who before the war had been the champion American lady squash-racquets player, and who had also played polo and won races.

Bill Steinkraus was Ksar d'Esprit's regular rider, and together they won puissance and Grand Prix competitions all over Europe and in the United States. Calm, bold and powerful, Ksar d'Esprit was worth every penny of the £10,000 he was said to have cost—a record sum for a show jumper in those days. In Rome in 1960 he helped the U.S. team to win the silver medals, and his classical style won him many admirers all over the world. Jumping big heights seemed to involve no particular effort for him, with his big natural jump, and oddly enough it was usually the little fences that gave him trouble.

Apart from a tendency to slip a stifle, which kept him off the active list from time to time, he fell victim to none of the ills to which these enormous horses are often prone and he was always an impressive performer.

Ksar d'Esprit.

Mainspring U.S.A.

Mainspring, who was donated to the U.S.E.T. by William D. Haggard III of Far Hills, New Jersey, was leading horse in the 1972 Olympic Prix des Nations, ridden by Bill Steinkraus to only one water fault in two rounds over a particularly testing course.

A chestnut gelding 16.1 hands high foaled in 1960, Mainspring is by a half-bred sire out of a mare thought to have a Clydesdale cross. He was purchased for the team in 1971 after winning five civilian classes at the National Horse Show in New York for owner Lee Barney and rider Rodney Jenkins.

Mainspring was bred in Canada by Clifford Sifton, M.F.H. of the Toronto and North York Hunt, who sold him as a three-year-old to Minnesota. As Mr Sandman he distinguished himself as a junior jumper and then as an open jumper in the mid-west, and was finally spotted as a team prospect by Charles Dennehy, who had ridden in the U.S. team in 1954, and who entrusted him to Rodney Jenkins in 1971.

He won eight international competitions during the 1972 U.S.E.T. season for Bill Steinkraus and when he returned to Europe in 1974 he continued to distinguish himself, ridden by Frank Chapot.

Mainspring's first triumph came in England at Hickstead, where he qualified for the final of the Men's World Championship in 1974 and finished equal third in the classification. In London the following week he won the King George V Cup for the U.S., to record America's sixth victory in this competition since World War II.

Nautical U.S.A.

The hero of the Walt Disney film *The Horse with the Flying Tail*, Nautical was a palomino gelding with china-blue eyes, a brand mark, and the 1959 King George V Gold Cup to his credit, which he won for his owner-rider, Hugh Wiley. In the same year he won the Grand Prix in London.

Foaled in 1944 in New Mexico by Muchacho de Oro he started his career there in Western classes, until he demonstrated his vast energy and jumping ability and was sold, as Peter de Oro, to a professional show-jumping stable in Virginia, and then to Pennsylvania.

Hugh Wiley bought him as Injun Joe from Pat Dixon with the reputation of being a great jumper who was difficult to ride and sometimes highly unpredictable. Dixon had achieved some outstanding successes with him, but had also taken several serious falls, and Nautical was regarded as a horse who could never go against the clock without coming completely unstuck. It took two years of patient re-making by Bert de Nemethy at the U.S.E.T.'s training centre at Gladstone, New Jersey, before he became the brilliant performer who won in Wiesbaden, Aachen, Paris and Ostend, as well as in London, Dublin and North America.

His first trip to Europe, in 1955, was not crowned with success, but in 1958 in Dublin he showed his unusual versatility by winning against the clock in a speed class, over a course of big fences in the puissance and finally over one big obstacle in the High Jump Over Poles—the last occasion, incidentally, on which this forerunner of the puissance was ever held at Ballsbridge.

In 1959 Nautical jumped two clear rounds in the American Nations' Cup victory in Rome, and at the Royal International in London he swept the board, winning the *Horse and Hound* Cup, the King George V Gold Cup and finally the *Daily Mail* Cup. He stood sixteen hands high and was endowed with endless stamina by his quarter-horse ancestors, though his strength and grace derived from his thoroughbred grandsire.

San Lucas U.S.A.

In a career which spanned eleven successful seasons, the enormous chestnut gelding San Lucas holds the world record for competing in Nations' Cups. He started in forty-three Nations' Cup competitions, of which the United States

Mainspring, ridden by Frank Chapot.

Nautical, ridden by Hugh Wiley.

team won twenty-six and finished second on twelve occasions. Colonel Harry Llewellyn's Foxhunter, with thirty-four starts, is his closest rival, and Hans Winkler's Halla's record stands at thirty.

Bred in Nevada in 1955, by Interpretation out of Gold Loma by Brig o'Doon, San Lucas (registered as Kwe-We) who stood 17.3 hands high, was not a successful racehorse. He started seven times in 1958, and was second once and third twice. The next year he was only fourth once in ten starts. That was the end of his attempts to win races, and Sir John Galvin bought him as a five-year-old and loaned him to the U.S.E.T. with the suggestion that he might be a 'useful hack'.

Surely no horse jumped over seven feet so many times, in so many places, for so long as San Lucas; he competed in seventy-two international competitions on four continents, in twenty-three different places in eleven countries. He won four Grands Prix, and thirty-one individual classes; he was placed 137 times. His regular ride was Frank Chapot; though during his last two seasons he was also ridden successfully on occasion by Bill Steinkraus, Neal Shapiro and Joe Fargis.

Among his most outstanding successes are the President's Cup in Washington, D.C., and the North American Championship in Toronto (both in 1965), the Wiesbaden Grand Prix in 1966, individual fourth place in the Mexico Olympic Games in 1968, and victory in the Rothmans North American Championships in Toronto again in 1971. Surely the national anthem of the United States was played more times for him than for any other horse, and he could easily hold the world record for participation in Nations' Cup competitions in perpetuity. At the end of the Munich Olympic Games he was retired and returned, with Snowbound, to his owner in Ireland.

San Lucas, ridden by Frank Chapot.

Sinjon   U.S.A.

During the 1960s, the bay thoroughbred gelding Sinjon, who was foaled in 1951 by Vino Puro out of Helen Abrigail, was Bill Steinkraus's best horse.

Sinjon, like most of his team-mates, started his working life on the racecourse. He was produced as a jumper by Harry De Leyer in 1957 and joined the United States Equestrian Team in 1958, loaned by Eileen Dineen and later by Walter Devereux. Two years later he was a member of the U.S. Olympic team in Rome. Ridden by George Morris Sinjon and the rest of the U.S.E.T. came on to win the team silver medals and finished in fourth place individually, behind Sunsalve.

Sinjon, ridden by Bill Steinkraus.

Ridden by Bill Steinkraus, the U.S.E.T. captain, he was the leading horse on the European tour of 1962, and he was equally successful on the team's next visit, two years later. Among his individual triumphs was the King George V Gold Cup in London, and he was a confident choice for the Olympic team in Tokyo. Unhappily, he was not sound on the great day, as a result of an injury sustained in training, and neither he nor his rider were able to start.

Although he recovered almost completely, and went on winning top-class international competitions for two more seasons, it was clear that the combination of his increasing age and the results of his injury were catching up with him, and he was formally retired in a ceremony at the National Horse Show in 1970, surrounded by all his riders. He is now a pensioner on Bill Steinkraus's Connecticut farm.

Sloopy U.S.A.

Sloopy.

A bay thoroughbred gelding and another former racehorse, Sloopy's reputation had already travelled ahead of him when he first arrived in Europe as a six-year-old in 1971 ridden by Neal Shapiro, and even at his first European C.S.I.O., at Fontainebleau, he was already rated the horse that was coveted most by all the top riders. The following year he won an Olympic individual bronze.

H.O. (for 'Hang On') Sloopy first attracted attention at the age of four when Rodney Jenkins won the Oak Brook Grand Prix with him for owner Tiffany Travrig. Subsequently he was sold to Patrick Butler, who had already loaned the U.S.E.T. such good horses as Untouchable and Fire One, and who considered him a prime prospect for Munich.

A violent dislike of air travel and a resolute refusal to be loaded aboard the plane meant that he had to cross the Atlantic by boat, while the other team horses flew in a chartered aircraft. But he soon made it clear that he was well worth the time and trouble. In Aachen he finished equal first in the Grand Prix with Marcel Rozier of France on Sans Souci—this was the championship in which Shapiro had enjoyed his first major victory in Europe, five years earlier.

Then, in London, Sloopy won the *Horse and Hound* Cup on the first night of the Royal International before the team returned home to compete in the Pan American Games.

His triumph in Munich was well deserved. Two months earlier he had been under a cloud, and his chances of getting to the Olympic Games at all were in some doubt. But he was cured of a virus infection in time, survived a serious cut sustained while schooling at Riem, and his only mistake in the first round of the individual Grand Prix was at the water tape. In the second round, he hit the penultimate fence, a big oxer, which left him level on eight faults with Ambassador and Psalm and meant a jump-off for all three medals. This time he made two errors—going into the treble and at the last, another big oxer—while his rivals had a clear and a stop respectively.

One of the very few to retain his form for the team event a week later, Sloopy jumped one of the three clear rounds, though in the opening sortie a knockdown, a stop caused by the slippery going, and 1.25 time penalties were a disappointment to the team, who finished second by that quarter-fault.

Snowbound U.S.A.

The horse with whom Bill Steinkraus won his Olympic individual gold medal in 1968, Snowbound was a brown gelding, 16.1 hands high, registered as Gay Vic, by Hail Victory out of Gay Alvena by Gay World. He was foaled on 11 March 1958 at the ranch owned by William A. Steffan in Sacramento, California.

A bowed tendon sustained when he was a two-year-old kept him off the racecourse and a succession of tendon injuries dogged him throughout his career. His first owners allegedly offered him for sale for $50.00 with no takers, but finally he was bought by Barbara Worth of California, who showed him lightly as a green working hunter and then sold him in 1962 to Sir John Galvin.

When Sir John moved from California to Ireland, he took Snowbound with him, but shortly afterwards, while Bert de Nemethy was visiting the Galvins in Dublin, Sir John offered to loan the horse to the team. In 1963 Snowbound was shipped to Gladstone for training. He was, de Nemethy says, 'the best-co-ordinated, bravest, most confident jumper I ever had—a witty, interesting personality with soundness problems from start to finish. Lack of soundness limited his training and competitive appearances, but his chance to get to the top was obvious.'

Snowbound's eight years on the team took him to nine countries on three continents, yet he participated in only thirty-seven international competitions. In addition to the dozen big classes he won, and his gold medal triumph, he will be best remembered for his Grand Prix win in New York in 1965 and his *Daily Mail* Cup in London three years later.

Snowbound, ridden by Bill Steinkraus.

Sympatico U.S.A.

A striking dark bay thoroughbred by The Hammer foaled in 1965, Alligator Farm's Sympatico has probably been the most admired of all the national open jumpers in the United States since 1972 when he climaxed a big year by winning four classes at Madison Square Garden. Originally shown by owner Sally Edelman as an Amateur-Owner Jumper, Sympatico, whose jumping style is as sympathetic as his name, blossomed when trainer Carl Knee suggested that Tony D'Ambrosio be given the ride on him in the 'big division'. A big horse at 17.1

Sympatico, ridden by Tony d'Ambrosio.

hands, Sympatico looks more a man's mount even though his temperament seems ideal. Something of a specialist in Grand Prix and puissance classes, he holds the American puissance record at 7 ft 4 in, set at the National Horse Show in 1973. In 1974 he jumped 7 ft even to win Washington's International puissance, but never laid a toe at any height.

Untouchable   U.S.A.

Untouchable, the horse on whom Kathy Kusner achieved her greatest successes, was foaled in 1952. A chestnut gelding by Bolero, he was first produced as a show jumper in the Mid-West. He achieved national prominence in 1963 after having been bought by the late Benny O'Meara, a former blacksmith who became the leading professional rider in the United States but died in a tragic accident, piloting his own aircraft, in 1966.

Ridden by Kathy Kusner, Untouchable won at shows all over the East in 1963, and rounded off a brilliant season by winning the championship at the National Horse Show in New York.

He made his first trip to Europe the following season, when he scored one of two consecutive victories in Dublin's Irish Grand Prix and won the big pre-Olympic championship in Rotterdam. He was then a natural selection for the U.S. Olympic team in Tokyo, and finished thirteenth individually.

In 1965, by now the property of Mr and Mrs Paul Butler from St Paul, Minnesota, Untouchable returned to Europe with his rider as an individual competitor in time for Dublin, where he won the Grand Prix again before going on to Hickstead for the first-ever running of the Women's World Championship. He started a hot favourite, but was beaten at the finish by Marion Coakes and Stroller, to whom he was runner-up.

Two years later Untouchable won the women's European title in Fontainebleau, and in 1968 he was a member of the Olympic team which lost the bronze medals to West Germany in Mexico City by a mere quarter of a fault. He also contributed to that year's American victory in the President's Cup of the world team championship.

Donald Rex   West Germany

A chestnut gelding of Hanoverian breeding who was the best-classified horse in the team event at the 1968 Olympic Games in Mexico City, ridden by Alwin Schockemöhle, Donald Rex helped the German team to win the bronze medals on that occasion.

Earlier that season, Donald Rex had divided the Aachen Grand Prix with Hendrik Snoek on Dorina, and the following year the horse was almost unbeatable in Europe. He won all the big competitions in Fontainebleau, took the international championship in Aachen, and, having finished third for the Men's European Championship in 1967, only went under in the final furlong in the title fight at Hickstead. It took David Broome on the legendary Mister Softee to beat him.

In 1970 in La Baule he got through to the final of the Men's World Championship, in which Alwin Schockemöhle eventually finished fourth, but he deteriorated later with back trouble, which a fall at Hickstead, when jumping-off with Harvey Smith on Mattie Brown for the British Jumping Derby, did nothing to assist.

He underwent an operation to relieve the pressure, but was never able to fight his way back to the top, and he sang his swan song after being hailed as the best horse in Europe for four seasons.

Halla   West Germany

Hans Gunter Winkler's Halla, who won him two World Championships and three Olympic gold medals, one individual (in 1956) and two team (1956 and 1960), was the most consistent mare in post-war show jumping history, though Simona may one day prove to be the second best.

Foaled in 1944, she was a brown mare by the trotting stallion Oberst out of a half-bred mare called Helene, nearly thoroughbred in appearance; she was bred at Domane Hofmeirei, near Darmstadt, by Gustav Vierling, who always owned her.

A failed racehorse, she was tried in three-day events by the Olympic committee, but she was too nervous for the dressage and was sent to Hans Winkler. She won her first competition in 1952, and for the next two years was the top horse in Germany. In 1953 she gave Winkler his first winning ride in Rome, took the puissance in Madrid, and won in Rotterdam, Paris and Pinerolo, as well as many classes in her native land.

In 1954 she won three classes in Dortmund in the spring, won the championship in Rome, and a class in Lucerne, and in Madrid she won the third leg of the second Men's World Championship, giving the title to her rider. Her other victories that year were in Aachen, Dublin and Pinerolo, where she achieved two firsts. Then she went on the North American circuit, giving Germany her first American win in over twenty years in the Harrisburg high jump and the individual championship. In New York she won four major competitions, and another in Toronto.

A year later Halla enabled Winkler to retain his world title, and in 1956 she won the individual gold medal at the Stockholm Olympics and helped West Germany to take the team gold medals. In 1958 she was only third in the European Championship, but she was still Winkler's choice for the 1960 Olympic Games in Rome and she helped to win a second team gold medal for West Germany before she retired to stud.

Meteor   West Germany

Meteor, a 16.3 hands bay Holstein gelding, is one of the old type of heavy German show jumpers with a large proportion of cold blood in their veins, who have now been replaced with horses of greater quality to cope with modern conditions. But he was a highly successful precision horse in the 1950s, and he and his rider, Fritz Thiedemann, won many top international competitions.

Donald Rex, ridden by Alwin Schockemöhle.

Halla.

Bred in 1942, by Diskus out of Konkurrentin on the farm near Elmshorn in the heart of the Holstein breeding country, by Otto Dreesen, his first notable win was the Grand Prix in Berlin in 1950, when ridden by Elke Brandt. He won the Hamburg Jumping Derby ridden by Thiedemann, who rode him for the rest of his career, and also in Rome and Aachen.

In 1952 he won an individual bronze medal at the Helsinki Olympic Games. The following year he won the puissance in Rome and a class in Madrid, and in 1954 he competed in London, winning the King George V Gold Cup and also the *Country Life* Cup. In New York he won the individual championship, and he nearly made it a double in Toronto. In 1955 he won the Aachen Grand Prix with the only double clear over a course including a six-foot wall, thus recording a hat-trick of victories in this classic.

In the 1956 Olympics Meteor helped Germany to win her first of three successive team gold medals, and finished fourth individually, and he remained in the team until after the 1960 Olympics, helping to win again in Rome, and finishing sixth individually. He also carried Thiedemann to victory in the European Championship of 1958.

Meteor, ridden by Fritz Thiedemann.

Rex the Robber   West Germany

Alwin Schockemöhle's successor to Donald Rex was the grey Hanoverian Rex the Robber, and though this horse lacks the consistency of his predecessor, and in 1974 was eliminated after three refusals in the first leg of the Men's World Championship at Hickstead, he is brilliant on his day and has won innumerable top-class competitions since 1972, among them many in London, at Wembley and Olympia.

His best season was in 1973, when he won many major competitions though the one he coveted most, the Men's European Championship, did not come his way. Rex the Robber gave Schockemöhle a heavy fall at the water in the second leg, and though he fought back gamely and won the third leg, he was too far behind on points to beat Paddy McMahon and Pennwood Forgemill in the final, to whom he finished as runner-up.

Selected quite early in the season as one of West Germany's pair to fight the men's world title in 1974, Rex the Robber stopped on several occasions at his last couple of shows, including La Baule, before going to Hickstead, and his elimination at the twin waters proved that he was not himself. After treatment, he was fit enough to win the Amateur title at the Benson and Hedges Pro-Am show at Cardiff Castle early in August.

Rex the Robber.

Simona   West Germany

Simona.

Simona, a chestnut Hanoverian mare, was sixteen years old when she won the Men's World Championship at Hickstead for Hartwig Steenken in 1974; she had been in the top German team since 1968, when she was Steenken's mount in the individual competition at the Olympic Games.

She first shone individually in Aachen in 1971, when she enabled her rider to win the European title, and the following year she was a member of the winning West German Olympic team in Munich. She also finished equal fourth in the individual competition, dividing on 8¾ faults with Steelmaster, ridden by Jim Day of Canada, and Lavendel, ridden by Hugo Simon of Austria.

That ¾, for exceeding the time allowed, was all-important to the issue, for without it Simona, Steelmaster and Lavendel would have been eligible for the medal jump-off with Mancinelli's Ambassador, Ann Moore's Psalm and Neal Shapiro's Sloopy.

In 1973 Simona did very little, for Hartwig broke his leg in two different places at two different times, and was only able to ride again from late August onwards. But in 1974 he was Germany's first choice for the Men's World Championship, and Simona carried him gallantly to victory, thus compensating him for his inability to defend his European title a year earlier. She alone jumped a double clear round over a really tough Nations' Cup course which was big enough to put paid to both d'Inzeo brothers, the defending champion David Broome, Harvey Smith, Rodney Jenkins with Idle Dice and many more of the world's top riders, both amateur and professional.

Simona, who was valued at the world record price of £100,000, and was probably even worth it, is a strong mare who needs determined checking, but the nearest thing to a precision jumping-machine in existence. She finished 1974 with tendon trouble; she was retired early in 1975.

Competition Results

compiled by Findlay Davidson

The raising of the F.E.I. standard.

Olympic Games

Show jumping was first held during the 1912 Olympic Games in Stockholm when each country was allowed to enter six competitors in the individual event, and four with three counting in the team event. After 1924 teams were reduced to three riders with all to count and it was only in Munich, in 1972, that the team competition was run in the same way as Nations' Cups, with four riders participating in the team event, and the best three scores in each round counting towards the total.

Stockholm 1912

Team

Gold	Sweden	Lt. Graf Gustav Lewenhaupt/ Medusa
		Lt. Gustaf Kielman/Gatan
		Lt. Graf Hans von Rosen/Lord Iron
		Lt. Frederick Rosencrantz/Drabant
Silver	France	Lt. d'Astafort/Amazone
		Capt. Jean Cariou/Mignon
		Capt. Meyer/Allons-y
		Lt. Seigneur/Cocotte
Bronze	Germany	Oblt. S. Freyer/Ultimus
		Lt. Graf von Hohenau/Pretty Girl
		Lt. Deloch/Hubertus
		Lt. Prince Karl von Preussen/ Gibson Boy

Individual

Gold	Capt. Jean Cariou (*France*)/Mignon
Silver	Lt. von Krocher (*Germany*)/Dohna
Bronze	Baron Emmanuel de Blomaert de Soye (*Belgium*)/Clonmore

Antwerp 1920

Team

Gold	Sweden	Lt. C. von Koenig/Trésor
		Lt. Graf Hans von Rosen/ Poor Boy
		Lt. Daniel Norling/Eros II
		Lt. Martin/Kohort
Silver	Belgium	Lt. Coumans/Lisette
		Lt. de Gaiffier/Miss
		Comdt. Comte d'Oultremont/ Lord Kitchener
		Lt. Laame/Biscuit
Bronze	Italy	Major Ettore Caffaratti/Traditore
		Capt. Asinari S. Marzano/Varone
		Capt. Giulio Cacciandra/Fortunello
		Capt. Alessandro Alvisi/Raggio di Sole

Individual

Gold	Lt. Tommaso Lequio (*Italy*)/Trebecco
Silver	Major Alessandro Valerio (*Italy*)/Cento
Bronze	Capt. Carl Gustaf Lewenhaupt (*Sweden*)/Mon Coeur

Paris 1924

Team

Gold	Sweden	Lt. Ake Thelning/Loke
		Lt. Axel Stahle/Cecil
		Lt. Age Lundström/Anvers
		Capt. von Braun/Diana
Silver	Switzerland	Lt. Alphons Gemuseus/Lucette
		Lt. Werner Stuber/Girandole
		Hptm. Hans Bühler/Sailor Boy
		Hptm. von der Weid/Admiral
Bronze	Portugal	Borges d'Almeida/Reginald
		Lt. de Sousa Martin/Avro
		Capt. Martinez de Albuquerque/ Hetrugo
		Cardozo de Menezes Margaride/ Profond

Individual

Gold	Lt. Alphonse Gemuseus (*Switzerland*)/Lucette
Silver	Lt. Tommaso Lequio (*Italy*)/Trebecco
Bronze	Lt. Adam Krolikiewicz (*Poland*)/Picador

Amsterdam 1928

Team

Gold	Spain	Capt. J. Navarro Morenes/Zapataso
		Capt. J.A. Marquis de los Truijillos/Zalamero
		Capt. J. Garcia Fernandez/Revistada
Silver	Poland	Lt. K. Gzowski/Mylord
		Lt. K. Szosland/Ali
		Capt. M. Antoniewicz/Readgleadt
Bronze	Sweden	Lt. C. Hansen/Gerold
		Comdt. C. Björnstjerna/Kornett
		Lt. F. Hallberg/Loke

Individual

Gold	Capt. Frantisek Ventura (*Czechoslovakia*)/Eliot
Silver	Capt. Bertran de Balanda (*France*)/Papillon
Bronze	Major Charles Kuhn (*Switzerland*)/Pepita

Los Angeles 1932

Team

No awards made as no team finished.

Individual

Gold	Lt. Baron Takeichi Nishi (*Japan*)/Granus
Silver	Major Harry Chamberlin (*U.S.A.*)/Show Girl
Bronze	Lt. Clarence von Rosen (*Sweden*)/Empire

Berlin 1936

Team

Gold	Germany	Hptm. Marten von Barnekow/Nordland
		Oblt. Kurt Hasse/Tora
		Hptm. Heinze Brandt/Alchimist
Silver	Holland	Lt. Henri van Schaik/Santa Bell
		Lt. Jan de Bruine/Trixie
		Lt. Johan Greter/Ernica
Bronze	Portugal	Lt. Mena Silva/Fossette II
		Marquis de Funchal/Merle Blanc
		Lt. José Beltrano/Biscuit

Individual

Gold	Lt. Kurt Hasse (*Germany*)/Tora
Silver	Lt. Henri Rang (*Rumania*)/Delphis
Bronze	Capt. Joszef von Platthy (*Hungary*)/Selloe

London 1948

Team

Gold	Mexico	Col. Humberto Mariles/Arete
		Lt. Alberto Valdes/Chihucho
		Lt. Ruben Uriza/Hatuey
Silver	Spain	Col. Navarro Morenes/Quorum
		Jaime Garcia Cruz/Bizarro
		M. Gavilan y Ponce de Leon/Farajido
Bronze	G.B.	Lt.-Col. Henry Nicoll/Kilgeddin
		Major Arthur Carr/Monty
		Lt.-Col. Harry Llewellyn/Foxhunter

Individual

Gold	Colonel Humberto Mariles (*Mexico*)/Arete
Silver	Lt. Ruben Uriza (*Mexico*)/Hatuey
Bronze	Jean d'Orgeix (*France*)/Sucre de Pomme

Helsinki 1952

Team

Gold	G.B.	Lt.-Col. Douglas Stewart/Aherlow
		Wilf White/Nizefela
		Harry Llewellyn/Foxhunter
Silver	Chile	Ricardo Echeverria/Lindo Peal
		Oscar Cristi/Bambi
		Cesar Mendoza/Pillan
Bronze	U.S.A.	Arthur McCashin/Miss Budweiser
		John Russel/Democrat
		William Steinkraus/Hollandia

Individual

Gold	Pierre J. d'Oriola (*France*)/Ali Baba
Silver	Oscar Christi (*Chile*)/Bambi
Bronze	Fritz Thiedemann (*Germany*)/Meteor

Stockholm 1956

Team

Gold	W.Germany	Alfons Lütke-Westhues/Ala
		Fritz Thiedemann/Meteor
		Hans Günter Winkler/Halla
Silver	Italy	Lt. Piero d'Inzeo/Uruguay
		Capt. Salvatore Oppes/Pagoro
		Lt. Raimondo d'Inzeo/Merano
Bronze	G.B.	Wilf White/Nizefela
		Pat Smythe/Flanagan
		Peter Robeson/Scorchin

Individual

Gold	Hans Günter Winkler (*W.Germany*)/Halla
Silver	Lt. Raimondo d'Inzeo (*Italy*)/Merano
Bronze	Lt. Piero d'Inzeo (*Italy*)/Uruguay

Rome 1960

Team

Gold	W.Germany	Alwin Schockemöhle/Ferdl
		Fritz Thiedemann/Meteor
		Hans Günter Winkler/Halla
Silver	U.S.A.	George Morris/Sinjon
		Frank Chapot/Trail Guide
		William Steinkraus/Ksar d'Esprit
Bronze	Italy	Antonio Oppes/The Scholar
		Capt. Piero d'Inzeo/The Rock
		Capt. Raimondo d'Inzeo/Posillipo

Individual

Gold	Capt. Raimondo d'Inzeo (*Italy*)/Posillipo
Silver	Capt. Piero d'Inzeo (*Italy*)/The Rock
Bronze	David Broome (*G.B.*)/Sunsalve

Tokyo 1964

Team

Gold	W.Germany	Hermann Schridde/Dozent II
		Kurt Jarasinski/Torro
		Hans Günter Winkler/Fidelitas
Silver	France	Cmdt. Guy Lefrant/Monsieur de Litry
		Janou Lefebvre/Kenavo
Bronze	Italy	Graziano Mancinelli/Rockette
		Capt. Piero d'Inzeo/Sunbeam
		Capt. Raimondo d'Inzeo/Posillipo

Individual

Gold	Pierre J. d'Oriola (*France*)/Lutteur B
Silver	Hermann Schridde (*W. Germany*)/Dozent II
Bronze	Peter Robeson (*G.B.*)/Firecrest

Mexico 1968

Team

Gold	Canada	Tom Gayford/Big Dee
		Jim Day/Canadian Club
		James Elder/The Immigrant
Silver	France	Marcel Rozier/Quo Vadis
		Janou Lefebvre/Rocket
		Pierre J. d'Oriola/Nagir
Bronze	W.Germany	Hermann Schridde/Dozent II
		Alwin Schockemöhle/Donald Rex
		Hans Günter Winkler/Enigk

Individual

Gold	William Steinkraus (*U.S.A.*)/Snowbound
Silver	Marion Coakes (*G.B.*)/Stroller
Bronze	David Broome (*G.B.*)/Mister Softee

Munich 1972

Team

Gold	W.Germany	Fritz Ligges/Robin
		Gerd Wiltfang/Askan
		Hartwig Steenken/Simona
		Hans Günter Winkler/Torphy
Silver	U.S.A.	Neal Shapiro/Sloopy
		Kathy Kusner/Fleet Apple
		Frank Chapot/White Lightning
		William Steinkraus/Mainspring
Bronze	Italy	Vittorio Orlandi/Fulmer Feather Duster
		Graziano Mancinelli/Ambassador
		Capt. Raimondo d'Inzeo/Fiorello
		Major Piero d'Inzeo/Easter Light

Individual

Gold	Graziano Mancinelli (*Italy*)/Ambassador
Silver	Ann Moore (*G.B.*)/Psalm
Bronze	Neal Shapiro (*U.S.A.*)/Sloopy

Men's World Championships

The Men's World Championships, initially held annually and later during the even-numbered years between Olympic Games, are run under a unique and controversial formula. Points are given for placings in each of speed, puissance and Nations' Cup-type competitions, the four riders with the highest number of points going forward to the final.

In this each in turn rides his own horse and then each of the other three horses. In the event of equality of faults after the four rounds of the final there is a jump-off with time deciding.

The tables below are designed to show the leading horse as well as the winning rider.

1953 Paris

	Quorum	Ali Baba	Diamant	Uruguay	Total
1. Francisco Goyoaga (Spain)	0	0	4	4	8
2. Fritz Thiedemann (W.Germany)	4¼	0	0	4	8¼
3. Pierre J. d'Oriola (France)	0	0	4	12	16
4. Piero d'Inzeo (Italy)	0	8	4	12	24

1954 Madrid

	Pagoro	Arlequin D	Halla	Quoniam	Total
1. Hans Günter Winkler (W.Germany)	4	0	0	0	4
2. Pierre J. d'Oriola (France)	4	0	4	0	8
3. Francisco Goyoaga (Spain)*	0	8	0	4*	12
4. Salvatore Oppes (Italy)	0	4	4	8	16
5. J. Garcia Cruz (Spain)	0	4	26	0	30

*The reigning champion, who at that time automatically qualified for the final, rode his own horse, Baden, instead of Quoniam

1955 Aachen

	Merano	Voulette	Orient	Bones	Total
1. Hans Günter Winkler (W.Germany)	0	0	4	4	8
2. Raimondo d'Inzeo (Italy)	0	4	0	4	8
3. Ronnie Dallas (G.B.)	4	8	20	8	40
4. Pierre J. d'Oriola (France)	0	4	4	R	48

After a jump-off on both Halla and Nadir, Winkler had 4 faults and d'Inzeo 8 faults.

1956 Aachen

	Meteor	Merano	Discutido	Fahnenkönig	Total
1. Raimondo d'Inzeo (Italy)	0	½	0	1¼	1¾
2. Francisco Goyoaga (Spain)	0	3	0	0	3
3. Fritz Thiedemann (W.Germany)	0	0	0	4	4
4. Carlos Delia (Argentine)	4	4	9	8	25

1960 Venice

	Huipil	Ksar d'Esprit	Gowran Girl	Sunsalve	Total
1. Raimondo d'Inzeo (Italy)	0	0	0	4	4
2. Carlos Delia (Argentine)	0	8	12	4	24
3. David Broome (G.B.)	4	4	16	4	28
4. William Steinkraus (U.S.A.)	0	4	16	R	56

1966 Buenos Aires

	Huipil	Bowjack	Pomone B	Quizas	Total
1. Pierre J. d'Oriola (France)	4	8	0	4	16
2. José A. de Bohorques (Spain)	0	0	4	15	19
3. Raimondo d'Inzeo (Italy)	4	10	8	8	30
4. Nelson Pessoa (Brazil)	10	0	10½	14¾	35¼

1970 La Baule

	Donald Rex	Fidux	Beethoven	Mattie Brown	Total
1. David Broome (G.B.)	4	0	0	0	4
2. Graziano Mancinelli (Italy)	0	0	4	4	8
3. Harvey Smith (G.B.)	¾	4	4	5	13¾
4. Alwin Schockemöhle (W.Germany)	0	4	4	8	16

note: where the rider retires (R) 20 faults are added onto the worst round overall to make up the total.

1974 Hickstead

	Simona	Pele	Mainspring	Lavendel	Total
1. Hartwig Steenken (W.Germany)	0	0	4	0	4*
2. Eddie Macken (Ireland)	0	0	4	0	4*
3. Frank Chapot (U.S.A.)	0	4	0	4	8
3. Hugo Simon (Austria)	4	4	0	0	8

*As a result of equality for first place, the leading two riders jumped off on their own horses. Maken on Pele going first had 8 faults in 45.6 seconds. Steenken had just four faults in the much slower time of 65.6 seconds.

Ladies' World Championships

The Ladies' World Championship was run on a points formula over three competitions. Each rider could participate with two horses in the initial rounds, but had to nominate one for the last round. The European Championships are run using the same formula. After the 1974 season the Men's and Ladies' World Championships (and European Championships) were amalgamated.

1965 Hickstead
1. Marion Coakes (*G.B.*)/Stroller
2. Kathy Kusner (*U.S.A.*)/Untouchable
3. Alison Westwood (*G.B.*)/The Maverick

1970 Copenhagen
1. Janou Lefebvre (*France*)/Rocket
2. Marion Mould (*G.B.*)/Stroller
3. Anneli Drummond-Hay (*G.B.*)/
   Mereley-a-Monarch

1974 La Baule
1. Janou Tissot (*France*)/Rocket
2. Michele McEvoy (*U.S.A.*)/Mr. Muskie
3. Barbara Kerr (*Canada*)/Magnor

Men's European Championships

1957 Rotterdam
1. Hans Günter Winkler (*W.Germany*)/Sonnenglanz
2. Bernard de Fombelle (*France*)/Bucephale
3. Salvatore Oppes (*Italy*)/Pagoro

1958 Aachen
1. Fritz Thiedemann (*W.Germany*)/Meteor
2. Piero d'Inzeo (*Italy*)/The Rock
3. Hans Günter Winkler (*W.Germany*)/Halla

1959 Paris
1. Piero d'Inzeo (*Italy*)/Uruguay
2. Pierre d'Oriola (*France*)/Virtuoso
3. Fritz Thiedemann (*W.Germany*)/Godewind

1961 Aachen
1. David Broome (*G.B.*)/Sunsalve
2. Piero d'Inzeo (*Italy*)/Pioneer
3. Hans Günter Winkler (*W.Germany*)/Romanus

1962 London
1. C. David Barker (*G.B.*)/Mister Softee
2. Hans Günter Winkler (*W.Germany*)/Romanus
2. Piero d'Inzeo (*Italy*)/The Rock

1963 Rome
1. Graziano Mancinelli (*Italy*)/Rockette
2. Alwin Schockemöhle (*W.Germany*)/Freiherr
3. Harvey Smith (*G.B.*)/O'Malley

1965 Aachen
1. Hermann Schridde (*W.Germany*)/Dozent
2. Nelson Pessoa (*Brazil*)/Gran Geste
3. Alwin Schockemöhle (*W.Germany*)/Exakt

1966 Lucerne
1. Nelson Pessoa (*Brazil*)/Gran Geste
2. Frank Chapot (*U.S.A.*)/San Lucas
3. Hugo Arrambide (*Argentine*)/Chimbote

1967 Rotterdam
1. David Broome (*G.B.*)/Mister Softee
2. Harvey Smith (*G.B.*)/Harvester
3. Alwin Schockemöhle (*W.Germany*)/Donald Rex

1969 Hickstead
1. David Broome (*G.B.*)/Mister Softee
2. Alwin Schockemöhle (*W.Germany*)/Donald Rex
3. Hans Günter Winkler (*W.Germany*)/Enigk

1971 Aachen
1. Hartwig Steenken (*W.Germany*)/Simona
2. Harvey Smith (*G.B.*)/Evan Jones
3. Paul Weier (*Switzerland*)/Wulf

1973 Hickstead
1. Paddy McMahon (*G.B.*)/Pennwood Forgemill
2. Alwin Schockemöhle (*W.Germany*)/Rex the Robber
3. Hubert Parot (*France*)/Tic

Ladies' European Championships

1957 Spa
1. Pat Smythe (*G.B.*)/Flanagan
2. Giulia Serventi (*Italy*)/Doly
3. Michèle d'Orgeix (*France*)/ Oceane

1958 Palermo
1. Giulia Serventi (*Italy*)/Doly
2. Anna Clement (*W.Germany*)/Nico
3. Irène Jansen (*Holland*)/Adelbloom

1959 Rotterdam
1. Ann Townsend (*G.B.*)/Bandit IV
2. Pat Smythe (*G.B.*)/Flanagan
3. Anna Clement (*W.Germany*)/Nico
3. Giulia Serventi (*Italy*)/Doly

1960 Copenhagen
1. Sue Cohen (*G.B.*)/Clare Castle
2. Dawn Wofford (*G.B.*)/Hollandia
3. Anna Clement (*W.Germany*)/Nico

1961 Deauville
1. Pat Smythe (*G.B.*)/Flanagan
2. Irène Jansen (*Holland*)/Icare II
3. Michèle Cancre (*France*)/Oceane

1962 Madrid
1. Pat Smythe (*G.B.*)/Flanagan
2. Helga Köhler (*W.Germany*)/Cremona
3. Elizalde de Goyoaga (*Spain*)/Kif Kif

1963 Hickstead
1. Pat Smythe (*G.B.*)/Flanagan
2. Arline Givaudan (*Brazil*)/Huipil
3. Anneli Drummond-Hay (*G.B.*)/Merely-a-Monarch

1966 Gijon
1. Janou Lefebvre (*France*)/Kenavo
2. Monica Bachmann (*Switzerland*)/Sandra
3. Lalla Novo (*Italy*)/Oxo Bob

1967 Fontainebleau
1. Kathy Kusner (*U.S.A.*)/Untouchable
2. Lalla Novo (*Italy*)/Predestine
3. Monica Bachmann (*Switzerland*)/Erbach

1968 Rome
1. Anneli Drummond-Hay (*G.B.*)/Merely-a-Monarch
2. Giulia Serventi (*Italy*)/Gay Monarch
3. Marion Coakes (*G.B.*)/Stroller
3. Janou Lefebvre (*France*)/Rocket

1969 Dublin
1. Iris Kellett (*Ireland*)/Morning Light
2. Anneli Drummond-Hay (*G.B.*)/Xanthos
3. Alison Westwood (*G.B.*)/The Maverick

1971 St. Gallen
1. Ann Moore (*G.B.*)/Psalm
2. Alison Dawes (*G.B.*)/The Maverick
3. Monica Leitenberger (*Austria*)/Limbarra de Porto Conte

1973 Vienna
1. Ann Moore (*G.B.*)/Psalm
2. Caroline Bradley (*G.B.*)/True Lass
3. Monica Weier (*Switzerland*)/Erbach

After the 1974 season, the Men's and Ladies' Championships were amalgamated. All championships thereafter will be open to both sexes.

Pan American Games

Buenos Aires 1951

Team

Gold | Chile | A. Larraguibel/Julepe
| | J. Larrain/Pillan
| | R. Echevarria/Bambi
| | C. Mendoza/Van Dick

Silver | Argentine
Bronze | Mexico

Individual

Gold | A. Larraguibel (*Chile*)/Julepe
Silver | C. Delia (*Argentine*)/El Linyera
Bronze | J. Larrain (*Chile*)/Pillan

Mexico 1955

Team

Gold | Mexico | R. Vinals/Acapulco
| | J. de la Garzia/14 de Agosto
| | d'Harcourt/Petrolero
| | H. Mariles/Chinucho

Silver | Argentine
Bronze | Chile

Individual

Gold | R. Vinals (*Mexico*)/Acapulco
Silver | J. Lucardi (*Argentine*)/Baturro
Bronze | J. de la Garza (*Mexico*)/14 de Agosto (sic)

Chicago 1959

Team

Gold | U.S.A. | F. Chapot/Diamant
| | H. Wiley/Nautical
| | W. Steinkraus/Riviera Wonder
| | G. Morris/Night Owl

Silver | Brazil
Bronze | Chile

There was no individual classification in Chicago.

Sao Paolo 1963

Team

Gold | U.S.A. | Miss M. Mairs/Tomboy
| | F. Chapot/San Lucas
| | Miss K. Kusner/Unusual
| | W. Steinkraus/Sinjon

Silver | Argentine
Bronze | Chile

Individual

Gold | Mary Mairs (*U.S.A.*)/Tomboy
Silver | C. Delia (*Argentine*)/Popin
Bronze | A. Simonetti (*Chile*)/El Gitano

Winnipeg 1967

Team

Gold | Brazil | N. Pessoa/Gran Geste
| | A. Alegria-Simoes/Samurai
| | J. Fernandez/Cantal
| | R.P. Guimares Ferreira/Shannon
| | Shamrock

Silver | United States
Bronze | Canada

Individual

Gold | J. Day (*Canada*)/Canadian Club
Silver | N. Pessoa (*Brazil*)/Gran Geste
Bronze | M.M. Yocupicio (*Mexico*)/Veracruz

Cali 1971

Team

Gold | Canada | T. Gayford/Big Dee
| | T. Miller/Le Dauphin
| | J. Elder/Shoeman
| | Miss B. Simpson/Magnor

Silver | Mexico
Bronze | Chile

Individual

Gold | Elisa Perez de las Heras (*Mexico*)/Eleonora
Silver | J. Llambi (*Argentine*)/Always
Bronze | T. Miller (*Canada*)/Le Dauphin

The President's Cup

In 1965, the President's Cup was instituted by the F.E.I. as the International Team Jumping Championship. It is open to any country represented in Nations' Cups by a minimum of six riders during the year 1 December to 30 November.

Classification is decided on a points system based on the results of not more than six Nations' Cups, which can have taken place anywhere. For those nations taking part in more than six, only their best six scores are considered.

If five or fewer than five teams start in a Nations' Cup, the winning team receives 5 points, the second 4 points and so on. But when six or seven teams compete, the winning team receives 6 or 7 points and so on down the line. When more than seven teams start, the winning team receives only 7 points, and those placed 7th and lower receive just one point. A country that retires its team after starting will receive one point. Points are shared for places shared.

In the event of there being an equal number of points gained by two countries at the end of a year, the winner will be the country with the greater number of first places. If still equal, then second places determine the champion country and so on.

Listed are the first six countries in the President's Cup since 1965.

1965
1. Great Britain 34 points
2. Italy 30 points
3. West Germany 28 points
4. Spain 15 points
5. Ireland 19½ points
6. France 15 points

1966
1. United States 26 points
2. Spain 26 points
3. France 20 points
4. Italy 18 points
5. West Germany 12 points
6. Great Britain 10 points

1967
1. Great Britain 37 points
2. West Germany 26 points
3. Italy 20½ points
4. Ireland 17½ points
5. France 17½ points
6. United States 15 points

1968
1. United States 33 points
2. Great Britain 25 points
3. Italy 24 points
4. West Germany 24 points
5. France 21 points
6. Switzerland 17 points

1969
1. West Germany 39 points
2. Great Britain 35 points
3. Italy 29 points
4. France 23½ points
5. Switzerland 17 points
6. Poland 16 points

1970
1. Great Britain 36 points
2. West Germany 35 points
3. United States 26½ points
4. France 21½ points
5. Canada 21 points
6. Italy 21 points

1971
1. West Germany 37 points
2. Great Britain 33 points
3. United States 28 points
4. Italy 24½ points
5. France 19½ points
6. Switzerland 14 points

1972
1. Great Britain 33 points
2. West Germany 32 points
(-) United States 23 points*
3. Italy 18 points
4. France 18 points
5. Switzerland 15 points
6. Canada 12 points

1973
1. Great Britain 34 points
2. West Germany 33 points
3. Switzerland 22 points
4. Italy 19 points
5. Holland 16 points
6. France 15 points

1974
1. Great Britain 37 points
2. West Germany 33½ points
3. France 31 points
4. United States 29 points
5. Italy 18½ points
6. Spain 15 points

*In 1972 the United States team only started five riders, and so were unplaced.

Grands Prix

The Grand Prix of a show is the major individual class, normally carrying the greatest amount of prize money and prestige. It is usual for it to be the last class of a show. The rules for the class vary slightly from country to country, but if run on the same lines as an Olympic Grand Prix there are two rounds, with the faults added together. In the event of equality of faults there is then a jump off over a shortened course.

The results of the Grand Prix at Official Internationals are given here for the major shows of the President's Cup circuit since 1960. Faults are not given because of variations in the rules.

Belgium (Ostend)

1960	William Steinkraus (*U.S.A.*)/Ksar d'Esprit
1961	Hans Günter Winkler (*W.Germany*)/Romanus
1962	Tommy Wade (*Ireland*)/Dundrum
	Max Hauri (*Switzerland*)/Preslaw
1963	C. David Barker (*G.B.*)/Mister Softee
1964	Seamus Hayes (*Ireland*)/Goodbye
1965	Gerd Wiltfang (*Germany*)/Ferdl
1966	Nelson Pessoa (*Brazil*)/Caribe
1967	Fritz Ligges (*W.Germany*)/Alk
1968	William Steinkraus (*U.S.A.*)/Blue Plum
1969	Thierry Storme (*Belgium*)/Roi de Cretteville
1970	Lutz Merkel (*W.Germany*)/Sir
1971	Paddy McMahon (*G.B.*)/Pennwood Forgemill
1972	Philippe Jouy (*Belgium*)/Prince B
1973	Ann Moore (*G.B.*)/Psalm
1974	Lionel Dunning (*G.B.*)/Fanny Hill

Holland (Rotterdam)

1960	Anna Clement (*W.Germany*)/Nico
1961	Valerie Clark (*G.B.*)/Atalanta
1962	Harvey Smith (*G.B.*)/O'Malley
1963	C. David Barker (*G.B.*)/Mister Softee
1964	Seamus Hayes (*Ireland*)/Goodbye
1965	William Barker (*G.B.*)/North Flight
1966	Nelson Pessoa (*Brazil*)/Caribe
1967	David Broome (*G.B.*)/Mister Softee
1968	Carol Hofmann (*U.S.A.*)/Out Late
1969	Harry Wouters van den Oudenweijer (*Holland*)/Abadan
1970	Hauke Schmidt (*W.Germany*)/Causa
1971	Alison Dawes (*G.B.*)/The Maverick
1972	Hendrik Snoek (*W.Germany*)/Faustus
1973	Alwin Schockemöhle (*W.Germany*)/Rex the Robber
1974	Piero d'Inzeo (*Italy*)/Easter Light
	Harvey Smith (*G.B.*)/Salvador

West Germany (Aachen)

1960	George Morris (*U.S.A.*)/Night Owl
1961	Piero d'Inzeo (*Italy*)/The Rock
1962	Alwin Schockemöhle (*W.Germany*)/Freiherr
1963	Raimondo d'Inzeo (*Italy*)/Posillipo
1964	Nelson Pessoa (*Brazil*)/Gran Geste
1965	Hugo Arrambide (*Argentine*)/Chimbote
	Piero d'Inzeo (*Italy*/Ballyblack
1966	Neal Shapiro (*U.S.A.*)/Jacks or Better
1967	Andrew Fielder (*G.B.*)/Vibart
1968	Alwin Schockemöhle (*W.Germany*)/Donald Rex
	Hendrik Snoek (*W.Germany*)/Dorina
1969	Alwin Schockemöhle (*W.Germany*)/Wimpel
1970	Herman Schridde (*W.Germany*)/Heureka
1971	Marcel Rozier (*France*)/Sans Souci
	Neal Shapiro (*U.S.A.*)/Sloopy
1972	Nelson Pessoa (*Brazil*)/Nagir
1973	Paul Weier (*Switzerland*)/Fink
1974	Paul Schockemöhle (*W.Germany*)/Talisman

Ireland (Dublin)

1960	David Broome (*G.B.*)/Sunsalve
1961	Tommy Wade (*Ireland*)/Dundrum
1962	Piero d'Inzeo (*Italy*)/The Rock
1963	Tommy Wade (*Ireland*)/Dundrum
1964	Kathy Kusner (*U.S.A.*)/Untouchable
1965	Kathy Kusner (*U.S.A.*)/Untouchable
1966	Diana Conolly-Carew (*Ireland*)/Barrymore
1967	David Broome (*G.B.*)/Mister Softee
1968	David Broome (*G.B.*)/Mister Softee
1969	Raimondo d'Inzeo (*Italy*)/Bellevue
1970	Harvey Smith (*G.B.*)/Mattie Brown
1971	Graham Fletcher (*G.B.*)/Buttevant Boy
1972	Alwin Schockemöhle (*W. Germany*)/The Robber
1973	Johan Heins (*Holland*)/Antrieb
1974	Buddy Brown (*U.S.A.*)/Sandsablaze

Italy (Rome)

1961	William Ringrose (*Ireland*)/Loch an Easpaig
1962	Piero d'Inzeo (*Italy*)/Sunbeam
1963	Harvey Smith (*G.B.*)/O'Malley
1964	Alfonso Queipo de Llano (*Spain*)/Infernal
1965	Hugo Arrambide (*Argentine*)/Chimbote
1966	Paul Weier (*Switzerland*)/Junker
1967	Piero d'Inzeo (*Italy*)/Navarette
1968	Piero d'Inzeo (*Italy*)/Fidux
1969	Salvatore Danno (*Italy*)/Kimando
1970	Piero d'Inzeo (*Italy*)/Red Fox
1971	Raimondo d'Inzeo (*Italy*)/Fiorello
1972	Graziano Mancinelli (*Italy*)/Ambassador
1973	Piero d'Inzeo (*Italy*)/Easter Light
1974	Raimondo d'Inzeo (*Italy*)/Gone Away

Great Britain (London)

Year		
1960	Pat Smythe (*G.B.*)/Scorchin	
1961	Graciano Mancinelli (*Italy*)/Rockette	
1962	Pat Smythe (*G.B.*)/Scorchin	
1963	Anne Townsend (*G.B.*)/Dunboyne	
1964	Peter Robeson (*G.B.*)/Firecrest	
1965	Seamus Hayes (*Ireland*)/Goodbye	
1966	William Ringrose (*Ireland*)/Loch an Easpaig	
1967	Graziano Mancinelli (*Italy*)/Petter Patter	
1968	William Steinkraus (*U.S.A.*)/Snowbound	
1970	Marion Mould (*G.B.*)/Stroller	
1971	William Steinkraus (*U.S.A.*)/Fleet Apple	
1972	Harvey Smith (*G.B.*)/Summertime	
1973	Harvey Smith (*G.B.*)/Salvador	
1974	Rodney Jenkins (*U.S.A.*)/Number One Spy	

Switzerland Lucerne (L) or Geneva (G)

1960(L) Pat Smythe (*G.B.*)/Flanagan
1961(G) Raimondo d'Inzeo (*Spain*)/Posillipo
1962(L) Hans Günter Winkler (*W.Germany*)/Romanus
         Piero d'Inzeo (*Italy*)/The Rock
1963(G) Werner Weber (*Switzerland*)/Lansquenet
1964(L) Hans Möhr (*Switzerland*)/Trall
1965(G) Andrew Fielder (*G.B.*)/Vibart
1966(L) Kathy Kusner (*U.S.A.*)/Untouchable
1967(G) Anneli Drummond Hay (*G.B.*)/Merely-a-Monarch
1968(L) Hubert Parot (*France*)/Garant
1969(G) Raimondo d'Inzeo (*Italy*)/Bellevue
1970(L) Paul Weier (*Switzerland*)/Wildfeuer
1971(G) Raimondo d'Inzeo (*Italy*)/Fiorello
1972(L) Hugo Arrambide (*Argentine*)/Camalote
1973(G) Hendrik Snoek (*W.Germany*)/Rasputin
1974(L) Robert Ridland (*U.S.A.*)/Almost Persuaded

France
(normally Nice, but Paris in 1966, La Baule in 1970
and 1974 and in Fontainbleau in 1971)

1960   Pierre J. d'Oriola (*France*)/Gerboise
1961   Jose de Bohorques (*Spain*)/Descosido
1962   Piero d'Inzeo (*Italy*)/Sunbeam
1963   Graziano Mancinelli (*Italy*)/Rockette
1964   Graziano Mancinelli (*Italy*)/Turvey
1965   William Ringrose (*Ireland*)/Loch an Easpaig
1966   Guy Lefrant (*France*)/Labrador C
1967   Harvey Smith (*G.B.*)/O'Malley
1968   Ferson Monteiro (*Brazil*)/Arachan
1969   Janou Lefebvre (*France*)/Rocket
1970   Michael Saywell (*G.B.*)/Hideaway
1971   Alwin Schockemöhle (*W.Germany*)/Donald Rex
1972   Marc Deuquet (*France*)/Ulpienne
1973   Johan Heins (*Holland*)/Antrieb
1974   Hartwig Steenken (*W.Germany*)/Simona

United States (New York)

1962   C. David Barker (*G.B.*)/Mister Softee
1963   Gail Ross (*Canada*)/Thunderbird
1964   Tom Gayford (*Canada*)/Blue Beau
1965   William Steinkraus (*U.S.A.*)/Snowbound
1966   Mary Chapot (*U.S.A.*)/Tomboy
1967   Harvey Smith (*G.B.*)/O'Malley
1968   Mary Chapot (*U.S.A.*)/White Lightning
1969   Hugo Arrambide (*Argentine*)/Adagio
1970   Hans Günter Winkler (*W.Germany*)/Terminus
1971   Robert Ridland (*U.S.A.*)/Almost Persuaded
1972   Frank Chapot (*U.S.A.*)/Good Twist
1973   Rodney Jenkins (*U.S.A.*)/Idle Dice
1974   Juan Rieckenhoff (*Puerto Rico*)/Don Juan

King George V Gold Cup and Queen Elizabeth II Cup

Generally these are considered to be the two most prestigious competitions confined to male and female riders respectively. Both are held at the Royal International Horse Show in London. The King George V Gold Cup was won outright by Jack Talbot-Ponsonby in 1934 and then re-presented by him for perpetual competition. Before Her Majesty's accession her cup was known as the Princess Elizabeth Cup.

King George V Gold Cup

1911	Dimitri d'Exe (*Russia*)/Piccollo
1912	Lt. Delvoie (*Belgium*)/Murat
1913	Lt. Baron de Meslon (*France*)/Amazone
1914	Lt. Baron de Meslon (*France*)/Amazone
1920	Auguste de Lassardiere (*France*)/Dignité
1921	Geoffrey Brooke (*G.B.*)/Combined Training
1922	Count Antonelli (*Italy*)/Bluff
1923	Auguste de Laissardiere (*France*)/Grey Fox
1924	Count Borsarelli (*Italy*)/Don Chisciotte
1925	Malise Graham (*G.B.*)/Broncho
1926	Fred Bontecou (*U.S.A.*)/Ballymacshane
1927	Xavier Bizard (*France*)/Quinine
1928	A.G. Martyr (*G.B.*)/Forty Six
1929	Lt. Gibault (*France*)/Mandarin
1930	Jack Talbot-Ponsonby (*G.B.*)/Chelsea
1931	Jacques Misonne (*Belgium*)/The Parson
1932	Jack Talbot-Ponsonby (*G.B.*)/Chelsea
1934	Jack Talbot-Ponsonby (*G.B.*)/Best Girl
1935	John Lewis (*Ireland*)/Tramore Bay
1936	Ged O'Dwyer (*Ireland*)/Limerick Lace
1937	Xavier Bizard (*France*)/Honduras
1938	Jack Friedberger (*G.B.*)/Derek
1939	Alessandro Bettoni (*Italy*)/Adigrat
1947	Pierre d'Oriola (*France*)/Marquis III
1948	Harry Llewellyn (*G.B.*)/Foxhunter
1949	Brian Butler (*G.B.*)/Tankard
1950	Harry Llewellyn (*G.B.*)/Foxhunter
1951	Kevin Barry (*Ireland*)/Ballyneety
1952	Carlos Figueroa (*Spain*)/Gracieux
1953	Harry Llewellyn (*G.B.*)/Foxhunter
1954	Fritz Thiedemann (*Germany*)/Meteor
1955	Luigi Cartasegna (*Italy*)/Brando
1956	William Steinkraus (*U.S.A.*)/First Boy
1957	Piero d'Inzeo (*Italy*)/Uruguay
1958	Hugh Wiley (*U.S.A.*)/Master William
1959	Hugh Wiley (*U.S.A.*)/Nautical
1960	David Broome (*G.B.*)/Sunsalve
1961	Piero d'Inzeo (*Italy*)/The Rock
1962	Piero d'Inzeo (*Italy*)/The Rock
1963	Tommy Wade (*Ireland*)/Dundrum
1964	William Steinkraus (*U.S.A.*)/Sinjon
1965	Hans Günter Winkler (*W.Germany*)/Fortun
1966	David Broome (*G.B.*)/Mister Softee
1967	Peter Robeson (*G.B.*)/Firecrest
1968	Hans Günter Winkler (*W.Germany*)/Enigk
1969	Ted Edgar (*G.B.*)/Uncle Max
1970	Harvey Smith (*G.B.*)/Mattie Brown
1971	Gerd Wiltfang (*W.Germany*)/Askan
1972	David Broome (*G.B.*)/Sportsman
1973	Paddy MacMahon (*G.B.*)/Pennwood Forgemill
1974	Frank Chapot (*U.S.A.*)/Mainspring

Queen Elizabeth II Cup

1949	Iris Kellett (*Ireland*)/Rusty
1950	Jill Palethorpe (*G.B.*)/Silver Cloud
1951	Iris Kellett (*Ireland*)/Rusty
1952	Audrey Rich (*G.B.*)/Quicksilver
1953	Marie Delfosse (*G.B.*)/Fanny Rosa
1954	Jose Bonnaud (*France*)/Charleston
1955	Dawn Palethorpe (*G.B.*)/Earlsrath Rambler
1956	Dawn Palethorpe (*G.B.*)/Earlsrath Rambler
1957	Elizabeth Anderson (*G.B.*)/Sunsalve
1958	Pat Smythe (*G.B.*)/Mr Pollard
1959	Anna Clement (*W.Germany*)/Nico
1960	Sue Cohen (*G.B.*)/Clare Castle
1961	Lady Sarah FitzAlan-Howard (*G.B.*)/Oorskiet
1962	Judy Crago (*G.B.*)/Spring Fever
1963	Julie Nash (*G.B.*)/Trigger Hill
1964	Gillian Makin (*G.B.*)/Jubilant
1965	Marion Coakes (*G.B.*)/Stroller
1966	Althea Roger Smith (*G.B.*)/Havana Royal
1967	Betty Jennaway (*G.B.*)/Grey Leg
1968	Mary Chapot (*U.S.A.*)/White Lightning
1969	Alison Dawes (*G.B.*)/The Maverick
1970	Anneli Drummond-Hay (*G.B.*)/Mereley-a-Monarch
1971	Marion Mould (*G.B.*)/Stroller
1972	Ann Moore (*G.B.*)/Psalm
1973	Ann Moore (*G.B.*)/Psalm
	Alison Dawes (*G.B.*)/Mr Banbury
1974	Jean Davenport (*G.B.*)/All Trumps

Nations' Cups

These are held at every official international show (C.S.I.O.) where there are three or more teams participating. Normally four riders from each country take part, but a country represented by just three riders must still form a team. The best three scores in each round count, and in the event of equality of faults after both rounds there is a barrage, or jump-off, in which the overall time for the best three riders of the team will determine first place in the event of further equality. The figure in brackets after the venue gives the number of teams that started.

The winning team in all Nations Cups since the start of the President's Cup in 1965 are given here with their scores in the two (or three) rounds. A rider retiring is indicated by R, and one eliminated by E. A rider who does not have to start in the second round by virtue of his or her team having already won is indicated by NS.

1965

Nice (6) Italy 8 faults

Piero d'Inzeo/Ballyblack	4	+	0
Lalla Novo/Rahin	4	+	0
Graziano Mancinelli/The Rock	0	+	0
Stefano Angioni/Canio	4	+	4¼

Rome (6) Italy 16 faults

Piero d'Inzeo/Ballyblack	4	+	0
Lalla Novo/Rahin	8	+	8
Graziano Mancinelli/The Rock	0	+	0
Stefano Angioni/Canio	12	+	4

Madrid (5) Great Britain 24 faults

Harvey Smith/Harvester	4	+	0
Fred Welch/Brule Tout	8	+	8
Andrew Fielder/Vibart	4	+	4
Peter Robeson/Firecrest	4	+	NS

Lisbon (3) Portugal 20 faults

Antonio Pimenta da Gama/Mazarino	1½	+	½
Manuel Malta da Costa/Palpite	9¼	+	8
Arthur Brito da Cruz/Foxglove	4	+	5
Jorge Mathias/Joc de l'Ile	8	+	8

Laurenco Marques (3) South Africa (0 faults in barrage)

Ernest Hayward/Flash
Peter Levor/Shaza
George Myburg/Moby Dick
William Angus/Foxfire

Olsztyn (8) Great Britain 28 faults

Marion Coakes/Stroller	8	+	4
David B. Barker/North Riding	4	+	8
George Hobbs/Brandy Soda	4	+	4
Douglas Bunn/Beethoven	4	+	R

Aachen (6) Italy 28¼ faults

Piero d'Inzeo/Ballyblack	¼	+	8
Graziano Mancinelli/The Rock	4	+	4
Stefano Angioni/Canio	8	+	4
Lalla Novo/Sunbeam	12	+	NS

London (5) Italy 24 faults

Piero d'Inzeo/Ballyblack	4	+	8
Stefano Angioni/Canio	4	+	4
Graziano Mancinelli/The Rock	0	+	4
Lalla Novo/Rahin	8	+	NS

Dublin (5) Great Britain 20 faults

C. David Barker/O'Malley	8	+	4
Marion Coakes/Stroller	0	+	4
Valerie Barker/Atalanta	4	+	4
Harvey Smith/Harvester	4	+	8½

Copenhagen (7) Great Britain 3½ faults

Ted Williams/Carnaval	0	+	8
Alison Westwood/The Maverick	3½	+	0
Marion Coakes/Stroller	0	+	0
Andrew Fielder/Vibart	E	+	0

Ostend (5) Great Britain 24 faults

Althea Roger Smith/Havana Royal	8	+	4
Andrew Fielder/Vibart	12	+	4
John Kidd/Bali Hai II	8	+	0
Douglas Bunn/Beethoven	0	+	R

Rotterdam (5) Great Britain 20 faults

Harvey Smith/Harvester	0	+	0
Judy Crago/Spring Fever	4	+	8
William Barker/North Flight	4	+	8
Alison Westwood/The Maverick	0	+	NS

Harrisburg (4) U.S.A. 4 faults

Mary Chapot/Tomboy	4	+	0
Kathy Kusner/Untouchable	0	+	0
Frank Chapot/San Lucas	4	+	4
William Steinkraus/Sinjon	0	+	0

New York (5) U.S.A. 0 faults

Mary Chapot/Tomboy	0	+	0
Kathy Kusner/Fire One	0	+	0
Frank Chapot/San Lucas	0	+	0
William Steinkraus/Snowbound	7¾	+	NS

Toronto (4) U.S.A. 8 faults

Carol Hofmann/San Pedro	0	+	0
Kathy Kusner/Untouchable	4	+	0
Mary Chapot/Tomboy	4	+	0
Frank Chapot/San Lucas	4	+	NS

Geneva (7) Spain 15¾ faults
José de Bohorques/Quinzas	1¼	+	½
Alfonso Queipo de Llano/Infernal	14½	+	10½
Francisco Goyoaga/Kif-Kif	0	+	0
Enrique Martinez de Vallejo/Opium	12¾	+	1¼

1966

Paris (6) Great Britain 17 faults
Harvey Smith/Warpaint	0	+	4½
Ted Williams/Carnaval	1½	+	2½
Alison Westwood/O'Malley	9	+	4
George Hobbs/Brandy Soda	4¾	+	NS

Rome (5) Italy 16 faults
Graziano Mancinelli/The Rock	0	+	0
Lalla Novo/Rahin	4	+	4
Adriano Capuzzo/Rubicon	8	+	8
Stefano Angioni/Canio	4	+	4

Lisbon (3) Portugal 31 faults
Jennifer Holroyd/Zawenda	8	+	4
Antonio Pimenta da Gama/Mistral	8	+	12
Arthur Brito da Cruz/Foxglove	4	+	11
Eduardo Netto de Almeida/Joc de l'Ile	4	+	0

Barcelona (4) Spain 16 faults
Enrique Martinez de Vallejo/Opium	8	+	4
José de Bohorques/Quizas	8	+	12
Alfonso Queipo de Llano/Infernal	4	+	0
Francisco Goyoago/Kif-Kif	0	+	0

Olsztyn (5) East Germany 16 faults
Reinhold Schierle/Kasbek	8	+	8
Rudolf Beerbohm/Domos	11¾	+	0
Helmut Gille/Sandor	0	+	8
Werner Hakus/Koran	0	+	0

Lucerne (8) U.S.A. 24 faults
Mary Chapot/Tomboy	8	+	23¾
Kathy Kusner/Untouchable	4	+	0
Frank Chapot/San Lucas	4	+	4
William Steinkraus/Sinjon	R	+	4

Laurenco Marques (3) South Africa 16 faults
William Angus/Foxfire	4	+	4
Peter Levor/Shaza	8	+	4
Yvonne Johnson/Gay Lord	0	+	4
George Myburg/Moby Dick	0	+	4

Leipzig (4) Poland 12¼ faults
F. Ciebielski/Hrabia	31	+	12
Jan Kowalczyk/Ronceval	4	+	0
Marian Kozicki/Tyras	4	+	0
Antoni Pacynski/Chrenowska	4	+	¼

Aachen (6) Italy 20 faults
Graziano Mancinelli/Turvey	0	+	0
Adriano Capuzzo/Rubicon	4	+	16
Stefano Angioni/Canio	28	+	4
Raimondo d'Inzeo/Posillipo	4	+	8

Ostend (4) Brazil 7 faults
Antonio Alegria-Simoes/Samurai	0	+	3
José Reynoso-Fernandez/Cantal	4	+	0
Nelson Pessoa/Caribe	0	+	0

Rotterdam (7) Spain 17½ faults
Alfredo Goyeneche/Jasseur	8	+	20
Duque de Aveiro/Pascha du Bourg	13½	+	1½
Manuel Ordovas/Naughty Girl	8	+	0
Eduardo Amoros/Rabanito	0	+	0

Harrisburg (4) U.S.A. 0 faults
Mary Chapot/Tomboy	0	+	0
Chrystine Jones/Fru	0	+	0
Frank Chapot/San Lucas	0	+	0
William Steinkraus/Snowbound	0	+	NS

New York (4) U.S.A. 4 faults
Mary Chapot/Tomboy	0	+	0
William Steinkraus/Bold Minstrel	0	+	4
Frank Chapot/San Lucas	0	+	8
Kathy Kusner/Untouchable	R	+	0

Toronto (4) Canada
Moffat Dunlap/Grand Nouvel			
Tom Gayford/Canadiana			
Gail Ross/The Hood			
Jim Day/Canadian Club			

1967

Nice (5) Great Britain 0 faults
Harvey Smith/O'Malley	4	+	0
Anneli Drummond-Hay/Merely-a-Monarch	0	+	0
Douglas Bunn/Beethoven	0	+	0
Peter Robeson/Firecrest	0	+	0

Rome (6) Switzerland 16¾ faults
Arthur Blickenstorfer/Marianka	12	+	0
Frank Lombard/Page	0	+	24
Monica Bachmann/Erbach	13¼	+	¾
Paul Weier/Satan III	4	+	0

Olsztyn (8) Great Britain 16 faults
John Kidd/Mill Street	8	+	0
Simon Rodgerson/Nearberry	4	+	8
Caroline Bradley/Franco	0	+	4
John Baillie/Dominic IV	8	+	0

Laurenco Marques (3) South Africa 8 faults

André Ferreira/Knight's Gambit	4	+	8	
George Myburg/The Laird	4	+	0	
Peter Levor/Shaza	4	+	0	
William Angus/Foxfire	0	+	0	

Leipzig (6) Great Britain 15 faults

John Kidd/Mill Street	4	+	0	
Robin Leyland/Ebony	16	+	4	
Caroline Bradley/Franco	0	+	0	
John Baillie/Dominic IV	7	+	NS	

Aachen (10) Great Britain 4¼ faults

Andrew Fielder/Vibart	¼	+	9	
Althea Roger Smith/Havana Royal	0	+	0	
John Baillie/Dominic IV	0	+	4	
Ted Williams/Carnaval	8	+	0	

London (4) Great Britain 8 faults

Harvey Smith/O'Malley	0	+	4	
Althea Roger Smith/Havana Royal	0	+	0	
Andrew Fielder/Vibart	4	+	4	
David Broome/Mister Softee	0	+	NS	

Dublin (3) Ireland 20¼ faults

Seamus Hayes/Goodbye	8	+	0	
Edward Campion/Liathdruim	¼	+	8	
Tommy Wade/Dundrum	22	+	0	
William Ringrose/Loch an Easpaig	4	+	NS	

Ostend (6) West Germany 8 faults

Herbert Meyer/Deichgraf	8	+	0	
Michael Gockel/Enzi	0	+	0	
Fritz Ligges/Alk	4	+	0	
Kurt Jarasinski/Revale	4	+	NS	

Rotterdam (9) Great Britain 12 faults

Harvey Smith/Harvester	4¼	+	4	
Marion Coakes/Stroller	0	+	0	
Peter Robeson/Firecrest	4	+	0	
David Broome/Mister Softee	4	+	0	

Budapest (6) U.S.S.R. 41¾ faults

Victor Durkot/Dissacharia	6¾	+	14	
Victor Nenachov/Saur	0	+	12	
Victor Matveev/Krochotnom	5	+	4	
Vladimir Konjkov/Gerach	9¼	+	16½	

Geneva (5) Brazil 13¾ faults

Antonio Alegria-Simoes/Nechochea	5	+	0	
José Reynoso-Fernandez/Cantal	4½	+	4	
Nelson Pessoa/Gran Geste	0	+	¼	

New York (3) U.S.A. 0 faults (4 in barrage)

Neal Shapiro/Night Spree	0	+	0	+	0
Carol Hofmann/Salem	0	+	0	+	4
Kathy Kusner/Untouchable	0	+	4	+	0
William Steinkraus/Snowbound	0	+	0	+	NS

Toronto (3) U.S.A. 12 faults

Neal Shapiro/Night Spree	8	+	4	
Chrystine Jones/Trick Track	0	+	4	
Mary Chapot/Anakonda	4	+	4	
Kathy Kusner/Untouchable	0	+	0	

1968

Nice (9) Italy 20½ faults

Piero d'Inzeo/Fidux	0	+	0	
Gualtiero Castellini/King's Coin	4	+	4¼	
Ugo d'Amelio/Sensation	R	+	NS	
Vittorio Orlandi/Fulmer Feather Duster	12¼	+	0	

Rome (6) Italy 12 faults

Piero d'Inzeo/Fidux	8	+	4	
Vittorio Orlandi/Fulmer Feather Duster	4	+	0	
Giulia Serventi/Gay Monarch	0	+	8	
Graziano Mancinelli/Petter Patter	4	+	0	

Madrid (3) Portugal 32 faults

Antonio Pimenta da Gama/Castico	12	+	4	
Vasco Ramirez/Namur du Payre	4	+	4	
Arthur Brito da Cruz/Marau	44	+	7	
Henrique Callado/Joc de l'Ile	4	+	4	

Lucerne (6) Switzerland 29¾ faults

Arthur Blickenstorfer/Marianka	12	+	12	
Monica Bachmann/Erbach	8¾	+	1	
Max Hauri/Telstar	4	+	4	
Paul Weier/Satan III	8	+	4	

Lisbon (3) Portugal 32½ faults

Antonio Pimenta da Gama/Castico	E	+	E	
Vasco Ramirez/Namur du Payre	8	+	4	
Arthur Brito da Cruz/Marau	0	+	11¾	
Henrique Callado/Joc de l'Ile	0	+	8¾	

Olsztyn (6) Poland 15 faults

Jan Kowalczyk/Drobnica	0	+	0	
Stefan Grodzicki/Biszka	8	+	12	
Piotr Wawryniuk/Poprad	4	+	0	
Marian Kozicki/Berr	4	+	7	

Leipzig (4) U.S.S.R. 13 faults

Genady Samosiedenko/Aeron	4½	+	4
Evgeny Kuzin/Figlar	8	+	4
Victor Nenachov/Saur	4	+	½
Vjatzscheslav Kartavski/Vaterpass	0	+	0

Laurenco Marques (3) South Africa 4 faults

George Myburg/Moby Dick	0	+	0
Micky Louw/Esprit	4	+	¼
Janie Myburg/Maltrap	0	+	0
Peter Levor/Shaza	4	+	0

Aachen (10) Italy 0 faults

Graziano Mancinelli/Doneraile	0	+	0
Raimondo d'Inzeo/Bellevue	0	+	0
Gualtiero Gastellini/King's Coin	4	+	0
Piero d'Inzeo/Fidux	0	+	NS

London (5) U.S.A. 12 faults

Mary Chapot/White Lightning	4	+	0
Kathy Kusner/Untouchable	4	+	4
Frank Chapot/San Lucas	4	+	4
William Steinkraus/Snowbound	0	+	0

Dublin (6) U.S.A. 4¼ faults

Mary Chapot/White Lightning	0	+	4
Kathy Kusner/Fru	0	+	4
Frank Chapot/San Lucas	4¾	+	¼
William Steinkraus/Snowbound	0	+	0

Copenhagen (4) West Germany 17¾ faults

Kurt Jarasinski/Pirat	0	+	5½
Manfred Kloess/Antea	0	+	12
Lutz Merkel/Sir IV	4	+	0
Fritz Ligges/Zuckerpuppe	¼	+	NS

Ostend (5) U.S.A. 20 faults

Mary Chapot/White Lightning	4	+	0
Carol Hofmann/Out Late	0	+	0
Kathy Kusner/Untouchable	4	+	8
Frank Chapot/San Lucas	0	+	NS

Rotterdam (10) U.S.A. 4 faults

Mary Chapot/White Lightning	4	+	0
Carol Hofmann/Out Late	0	+	0
Kathy Kusner/Untouchable	4	+	0
Frank Chapot/San Lucas	0	+	NS

New York (5) U.S.A. 12 faults

Mary Chapot/White Lightning	4	+	0
Frank Chapot/San Lucas	12	+	4
Carol Hofmann/Salem	0	+	4
William Steinkraus/Bold Minstrel	0	+	NS

Toronto (5) U.S.A. 16½ faults

Mary Chapot/White Lightning			
Neal Shapiro/Trick Track			
Carol Hofmann/Salem			
Frank Chapot/San Lucas			

1969

Nice (6) France 6 faults

Marcel Rozier/Quo Vadis	8	+	4
Janou Lefèbvre/Rocket	0	+	4
Gilles Bertran de Balanda/Sigurd	0	+	0
Phillippe Jouy/Prélude de Paulstra	8	+	5½

Rome (4) West Germany 16½ faults

Gerd Wiltfang/Domjunge	4½	+	0
Manfred Kloess/Der Lord	4	+	8
Fritz Ligges/Zuckerpuppe	8¾	+	20¾
Hartwig Steenken/Simona	0	+	0

Barcelona (5) Great Britain 0 faults

Alan Oliver/Sweep III	¾	+	0
Paddy McMahon/Hideaway	0	+	4
George Hobbs/War Lord	0	+	0
David Broome/Top of the Morning	0	+	0

Laurenco Marques (3) South Africa 0 faults

Micky Louw/Clowhorse	0	+	0
Gonda Butters/Ratification	0	+	0
Peter Levor/Esprit	0	+	0
George Myburg/The Laird	0	+	0

Olsztyn (5) Poland 4 faults

Marian Kozicki/Bronc	0	+	0
Henryk Hucz/Deptak	4	+	4
Jan Kowalczyk/Brezscot	8	+	4
Piotr Wawryniuk/Poprad	0	+	0

Leipzig (4) U.S.S.R. 35¾ faults

Victor Nenachov/Saur	9¼	+	3¾
Vjatzscheslav Kartavski/Epigraf	4	+	8
S. Chodirev/Arsenal	8	+	4
Victor Durkot/Disacharid	8	+	8

Aachen (8) West Germany 24 faults

Gerd Wiltfang/Extra	4	+	0
Hartwig Steenken/Simona	0	+	12
Hans Günter Winkler/Torphy	8	+	4
Alwin Schockemöhle/Donald Rex	4	+	NS

London (7) West Germany 0 faults

Lutz Merkel/Anmut	0	+	8
Hartwig Steenken/Simona	4	+	0
Hans Günter Winkler/Torphy	0	+	0
Alwin Schockemöhle/Donald Rex	0	+	0

Dublin (7) West Germany 4 faults (0 in barrage)

Lutz Merkel/Sir IV	4	+ 0	+	0
Hartwig Steenken/Simona	4	+ 0	+	4
Hans Günter Winkler/Torphy	0	+ 0	+	0
Alwin Schockemöhle/Donald Rex	0	+ NS	+	0

Ostend (6) West Germany 4 faults

Hendrik Snoek/Feiner Kerl	0	+ 0
Manfred Kloess/Der Lord	4	+ 4
Fritz Ligges/Zuckerpuppe	0	+ 4½
Lutz Merkel/Sir IV	0	+ 0

Rotterdam (8) Great Britain 12¼ faults

Anne Backhouse/Cardinal	19	+ 4
Stephen Pritchard/Telstar	0	+ 0
Aileen Ross/Trevarrion	4	+ ¼
George Hobbs/Battling Pedulas	4	+ NS

Lisbon (6) Switzerland 12 faults

Monica Bachmann/Erbach	0	+ 4
Ernst Eglin/Carver Doone	4	+ 0
Mario Baumgartner/Waldersee	4	+ 8
Paul Weier/Wildfeuer	0	+ 4

Geneva (8) West Germany 8½ faults

Lutz Merkel/Sir IV	0	+ 4
Hartwig Steenken/Simona	4	+ 0
Hermann Schridde/Heureka	½	+ 4
Alwin Schockemöhle/Donald Rex	4	+ 0

Harrisburg (4) U.S.A. ¼ fault

Neal Shapiro/Trick Track	0	+ 0
Jared Brinsmade/Triple Crown	7	+ 0
Frank Chapot/San Lucas	0	+ ¼
William Steinkraus/Bold Minstrel	0	+ NS

New York (4) U.S.A. 16 faults

Jared Brinsmade/Triple Crown	0	+ 0
Kathy Kusner/Wicked City	8	+ 4
Frank Chapot/San Lucas	12	+ 4
William Steinkraus/Bold Minstrel	0	+ NS

Toronto (4) Canada 8 faults

Moffat Dunlap/Grand Nouvel	4	+ 0
Tom Gayford/Big Dee	8	+ 16
Jim Day/Canadian Club	0	+ 4
Jim Elder/The Emmigrant	0	+ 0

1970

Rome (5) Great Britain 20½ faults

Anneli Drummond-Hay/Mereley-a-Monarch	8	+ 0
Harvey Smith/Ten to Twelve	4	+ ½
David Broome/Top of the Morning	4	+ 8
George Hobbs/Battling Pedulas	13¼	+ 4

Madrid (4) West Germany 12¼ faults

Hauke Schmidt/Wolfdieter	12	+ 4
Bernd Kuwertz/Sieno	0	+ 4
Sönke Sönksen/Palisander	4	+ 4
Hans Günter Winkler/Torphy	0	+ ¼

Lucerne (5) U.S.A. 8 faults

Neal Shapiro/San Lucas	0	+ 4
Joe Fargis/Bonte II	0	+ 4
Kathy Kusner/Silver Scot	8	+ 12
William Steinkraus/Snowbound	0	+ 0

Olsztyn (7) U.S.S.R. 23¾ faults

Victor Durkot/Abzak	48	+ 8
W. Pohanowski/Gejzer	8	+ 8
Victor Lisitsin/Penteli	3¾	+ 0
Yuri Ziabrew/Grim	4	+ 0

Laurenco Marques (3) South Africa 3 faults

Peter Levor/Format	0	+ 0
Theo Laros/Goya	3	+ 0
Wendy Grayston/King Canute	4	+ 0
Micky Louw/Torch Sign	0	+ 4

Aachen (7) West Germany 4 faults

Hendrik Snoek/Dorina	4	+ 4
Gerd Wiltfang/Goldika	0	+ 0
Lutz Merkel/Sir IV	0	+ 4
Hartwig Steenken/Simona	0	+ 0

La Baule (10) Canada 12 faults (0 in barrage)

Tom Gayford/Big Dee	0	+ 0	+	4
Jim Day/Canadian Club	4	+ 4	+	0
Moffat Dunlap/Argyll	12	+ 4	+	0
Jim Elder/The Shoeman	4	+ 0	+	0

London (6) Great Britain 12 faults

Michael Saywell/Hideaway	4	+ 4
Marion Mould/Stroller	0	+ 0
Harvey Smith/Mattie Brown	0	+ 4
David Broome/Beethoven	7¾	+ NS

Dublin (7) Great Britain 8 faults

Harvey Smith/Mattie Brown	0	+ 0
Michael Saywell/Hideaway	4	+ 0
George Hobbs/Battling Pedulas	11¼	+ 8¼
David Broome/Manhattan	0	+ 4

Ostend (6) Great Britain 18½ faults

Raymond Howe/Balmain	2	+ 8
Ann Moore/Psalm	0	+ 0
Stephen Hadley/Prospero	8	+ 4½
Anneli Drummond-Hay/Xanthos	4	+ NS

Rotterdam (9) West Germany 12¼ faults

Bernd Kuwertz/Sieno	12½ +	8
Willibert Mehlkopf/Fidelus	8 +	4¼
Hartwig Steenken/Tasso	0 +	0
Gerd Wiltfang/Goldika	0 +	0

Budapest (5) East Germany 40½ faults

Fredo Kasten/Orkus	12 +	0
Manfred Nietzschmann/Fermor	4 +	8
Siegfried Hohloch/Freiherr	5 +	17¾
Heinz Schulenburg/Fakir	8¼ +	8¼

Lisbon (4) Switzerland 4 faults

Monica Bachmann/Erbach	0 +	0
Mario Baumgartner/Waldersee	7½ +	4
Ernst Eglin/Carver Doone	0 +	0
Paul Weier/Wildfeuer	0 +	NS

Harrisburg (5) West Germany 0 faults

Lutz Merkel/Sir IV	0 +	0
Gerd Wiltfang/Goldika	4 +	0
Hartwig Steenken/Simona	0 +	0
Hans Günter Winkler/Torphy	0 +	NS

New York (5) West Germany 0 faults

Lutz Merkel/Sir IV	0 +	0
Gerd Wiltfang/Goldika	0 +	0
Hartwig Steenken/Simona	0 +	0
Hans Günter Winkler/Torphy	4 +	NS

Toronto (5) West Germany 4½ faults

Gerd Wiltfang/Goldika	4 +	0
Hartwig Steenken/Simona	½ +	0
Hans Günter Winkler/Torphy	0 +	0
Lutz Merkel/Sir IV	4 +	4

1971

Rome (4) West Germany 16 faults

Lutz Merkel/Gonzales	4 +	12
Paul Schockemöhle/Askan	4 +	4
Hartwig Steenken/Simona	0 +	4
Hans Günter Winkler/Torphy	4 +	0

Barcelona (4) Spain 8 faults

Duque de Aveiro/Sunday Beau	4 +	0
Alfonso Segovia/Sableuse	0 +	0
Luis Alvarez Cervera/Acorne	4 +	0
Enrique Martinez de Vallejo/Romantico	0 +	4

Fontainebleau (7) West Germany 5¼ faults

Paul Schockemöhle/Askan	4 +	4
Hartwig Steenken/Simona	¼ +	0
Alwin Schockemöhle/Donald Rex	4 +	0
Hans Günter Winkler/Torphy	½ +	½

Laurenco Marques (3) South Africa 24 faults

Anthony Lewis/Take a Chance	4 +	8
Gonda Butters/BP Superblend	4 +	0
Peter Levor/Format	4 +	16
Wendy Grayston/King Canute	0 +	8

Olsztyn (5) Poland 40 faults

Marian Kozicki/Bronc	0 +	8
Jan Kowalczyk/Via Vitae	16 +	16
Norbert Wieja/Aral	8 +	16
Piotr Wawryniuk/Poprad	4 +	4

Aachen (12) U.S.A. 16 faults (0 in barrage)

Joe Fargis/Bonte II	4 +	4 +	0
Conrad Homfeld/Triple Crown	4 +	4 +	0
Neal Shapiro/Sloopy	0 +	0 +	0
William Steinkraus/Fleet Apple	4 +	NS +	0

Dublin (9) West Germany 33¼ faults

Hendrik Snoek/Faustus	13 +	4¼
Gerd Wiltfang/Askan	8 +	7¼
Hans Günter Winkler/Torphy	18 +	4
Hartwig Steenken/Simona	0 +	4

Ostend (4) Ireland 8¼ faults

Edward Campion/Garrai Eoin	0 +	0
Eddie Macken/Oatfield Hills	¼ +	0
Lawrence Kiely/Inis Cara	0 +	4

Rotterdam (6) West Germany 0 faults

Hendrik Snoek/Faustus	0 +	0
Hugo Simon/Fair Lady	0 +	0
Fritz Ligges/Robin	0 +	0
Hans Günter Winkler/Torphy	0 +	NS

Budapest (8) West Germany 28 faults (13½ in barrage)

Lutz Gössing/Frappant	4 +	12 +	8
Bernd Kuwertz/Wartburg	4 +	0 +	4
Sönke Sönksen/Palisander	12 +	8 +	1½
Kurt Jarasinski/Revale	4 +	8 +	NS

Lisbon (7) Great Britain 16 faults

Peter Robeson/Grebe	4 +	0
Faith Panton/Alcatraz	8 +	12
Caroline Bradley/Wood Nymph	4 +	4
Alison Dawes/The Maverick	0 +	4

Geneva (5) West Germany 8¼ faults

Fritz Ligges/Robin	¾ +	¼
Lutz Merkel/Sir IV	7 +	4
Gerd Wiltfang/Dorian Grey	8 +	0
Hans Günter Winkler/Torphy	0 +	0

Harrisburg (3) U.S.A. 4¼ faults
Joe Fargis/Bonte II		0	+	0
Neal Shapiro/Sloopy		½	+	0
Frank Chapot/San Lucas		¼	+	4
William Steinkraus/Fleet Apple		0	+	NS

New York (3) Canada 7 faults
Eleanor MacCowan/Hombre		8	+	8
Barbara Simpson/Catbird		4	+	0
Terrance Millar/Le Dauphin		0	+	0
Jim Day/Sundancer		3	+	0

Toronto (3) Canada 4 faults (4 in barrage)
Moffat Dunlap/Intrepid	0	+	8	+	4
Barbara Simpson/Magnor	0	+	0	+	0
Terrance Millar/Le Dauphin	8	+	0	+	4
Jim Day/Sundancer	4	+	0	+	0

1972

Nice (6) Great Britain 10 faults
Lionel Dunning/Arun Blaze		12	+	0
Simon Rodgerson/Savannah III		0	+	4
Stephen Hadley/Freeman IV		¼	+	5¾
Peter Robeson/Grebe		0	+	NS

Rome (7) Italy 12 faults
Graziano Mancinelli/Ambassador		4	+	0
Vittorio Orlandi/Valetta		8	+	8
Raimondo d'Inzeo/Fiorello		0	+	0
Piero d'Inzeo/Red Fox		4	+	4

Madrid (5) Great Britain 0 faults (9 in barrage)
Peter Robeson/Grebe	0	+	0	+	1¾
Anne Backhouse/Cardinal	0	+	0	+	1¼
Lionel Dunning/Arun Blaze	0	+	0	+	6
Alison Dawes/The Maverick	0	+	0	+	NS

Lucerne (5) West Germany 33 faults
Lutz Merkel/Gonzales		7	+	1½
Michael Gockel/Bonanza		14½	+	22
Hauke Schmidt/Trumpf		1¼	+	1¼
Sönke Sönksen/Kwept		0	+	NS

Olstyn (7) Great Britain 36 faults (4 in barrage)
John Greenwood/Mr Punch II	8	+	8	+	0
Stephen Pritchard/Telstar	12	+	4	+	0
Derek Ricketts/Dakota	0	+	4	+	4

Ostend (4) West Germany 24 faults
Achaz von Buchwaldt/Askari	8¼	+	0
Peter Schmitz/Panama	4	+	0
Manfred Kloess/Nadir	8	+	4
Lutz Merkel/Sir IV	8	+	NS

Aachen (11) West Germany 20 faults
Fritz Ligges/Robin		0	+	0
Hermann Schridde/Kadett		4	+	4
Gerd Wiltfang/Dorian Grey		8	+	4
Hartwig Steenken/Kosmos		8	+	NS

London (3) Great Britain 4 faults
Alan Oliver/Sweep III		0	+	4
Paddy McMahon/Forgemill		4	+	0
Harvey Smith/Mattie Brown		0	+	0
David Broome/Sportsman		0	+	NS

Dublin (4) West Germany 8 faults
Hendrik Snoek/Faustus		0	+	4
Karl-Heinz Giebmanns/The Saint		16	+	4
Lutz Merkel/Gonzales		0	+	0
Alwin Schockemöhle/The Robber		0	+	NS

Rotterdam (4) West Germany 8 faults
Fritz Ligges/Robin		0	+	0
Gerd Wiltfang/Askan		7¾	+	22¾
Alwin Schockemöhle/The Robber		0	+	4
Hartwig Steenken/Simona		0	+	4

Lisbon (3) Switzerland 16 faults
Monica Weier/Vasall II		0	+	4
Mario Baumgartner/Frustra		16	+	12
Kurt Maeder/Abraxon		12	+	0
Paul Weier/Fink		0	+	0

Harrisburg (3) U.S.A. 5 faults
Neal Shapiro/Duke's Honor		¾	+	0
Kathy Kusner/Triple Crown		4¾	+	0
Frank Chapot/Good Twist		0	+	¼
William Steinkraus/Mainspring		4	+	NS

New York (3) U.S.A. 8 faults (0 in 97.7 secs in barrage)
Neal Shapiro/Duke's Honor	8	+	0	+	0
Kathy Kusner/Triple Crown	0	+	4	+	4
Frank Chapot/Good Twist	0	+	4	+	0
William Steinkraus/Mainspring	0	+	4	+	0

Toronto (3) U.S.A. 0 faults
Neal Shapiro/Trick Track		0	+	0
Kathy Kusner/Triple Crown		0	+	0
William Steinkraus/Mainspring		0	+	0
Frank Chapot/Good Twist		R	+	NS

1973

Nice (7) Great Britain 20¾ faults
John Greenwood/Mr Punch II		8	+	0
Caroline Bradley/True Lass		7¼	+	5¼
Lionel Dunning/Arun Blaze		4	+	7
Ted Edgar/Everest Peak		0	+	4¼

Rome (5) Great Britain 16 faults

Harvey Smith/Summertime	4 +	0
Ann Moore/April Love	0 +	17
Lionel Dunning/Arun Blaze	4 +	8
Peter Robeson/Grebe	8 +	0

Madrid (3) Great Britain 20 faults

Raymond Howe/Fanta	4 +	0
Malcolm Pyrah/Trevarrion	4 +	4
Anne Backhouse/Cardinal	4 +	4
Paddy McMahon/Pennwood Forgemill	8 +	NS

Laurenco Marques (3) South Africa 8 faults

Gonda Betrix/Esprit	0 +	0
Anthony Lewis/Red Gambit	0 +	4
Wendy Grayston/King Cole	4 +	8
Micky Louw/Torch Sign	4 +	0

Olsztyn (5) West Germany 20 faults

Peter Schmitz/Panama	0 +	0
Bernd Kuwertz/Girl	0 +	0
Hartmut Roeder/Rebell	8 +	12
Manfred Kloess/Nadir	8 +	NS

Aachen (6) West Wermany 8 faults

Gerd Wiltfang/Askan	0 +	8
Hartwig Steenken/Kosmos	12 +	0
Hans Günter Winkler/Torphy	4 +	0
Alwin Schockemöhle/Rex the Robber	4 +	NS

London (3) West Germany 0 faults

Alwin Schockemöhle/Rex the Robber	0 +	0
Paul Schockemöhle/Abadir	0 +	0
Fritz Ligges/Genius	4 +	4
Hans Günter Winkler/Torphy	0 +	0

Dublin (5) Great Britain 0 faults

Ann Moore/Psalm	0 +	0
Paddy McMahon/Pennwood Forgemill	0 +	0
David Broome/Manhattan	0 +	0
Peter Robeson/Grebe	0 +	NS

Rotterdam (9) West Germany 9 faults

Hermann Schridde/Kadett	13¾ +	8
Fritz Ligges/Genius	4 +	4
Hartwig Steenken/Kosmos	½ +	½
Alwin Schockemöhle/Rex the Robber	0 +	0

Ostend (6) Great Britain 12 faults

Derek Ricketts/Beau Supreme	8 +	0
Tony Newbery/Warwick III	8 +	0
Rowland Fernyhough/Autumatic	4 +	9¼
Ann Moore/Psalm	0 +	0

Lisbon (5) Switzerland 31½ faults

Monica Weier/Vasall II	4 +	7¼
Peter Reid/Casanova	4 +	8¼
Jürg Friedli/Rocket	4 +	12
Paul Weier/Fink	0 +	NS

Washington (4) U.S.A. 12 faults (0 in barrage)

Michael Matz/Snow Flurry		+	0
Mac Cone/Triple Crown		+	0
Rodney Jenkins/Idle Dice	0 +	0 +	0
Frank Chapot/Mainspring			

New York (4) Great Britain 8 faults

Harvey Smith/Salvador	4 +	0
Graham Fletcher/Buttevant Boy	0 +	4
Derek Ricketts/Beau Supreme	0 +	8
David Broome/Sportsman	8 +	0

Toronto (4) U.S.A. 8¼ faults

Mac Cone/Triple Crown	9½ +	4
Michael Matz/Mighty Ruler	0 +	0
Rodney Jenkins/Idle Dice	4 +	0
Frank Chapot/Mainspring	4½ +	0

Geneva (6) West Germany 16 faults

Gerd Wiltfang/Frederikus Rex	0 +	4
Hendrik Snoek/Rasputin	4 +	12
Lutz Merkel/Humphrey	4½ +	8
Hartwig Steenken/Simona	0 +	0

Sao Paulo (3) Chile 15 faults

Rene Varas/Quintral	0 +	4
Victor Contador/Bony	3 +	0
Americo Simonetti/Atulfo	0 +	8

Buenos Aires (4) Argentine
Carlos Delia/Cardon
Hugo Arrambide/Camalote
Jorge Llambi/O.K. Amigo
Carlos Marcelli/Chopin

1974

Rome (5) Italy 12 faults (8 in barrage)

Adriano Capuzzo/Beau Regard	4 +	0 +	4
Vittorio Orlandi/Fulmer Feather Duster	0 +	8 +	4
Graziano Mancinelli/Bel Oiseau	0 +	8 +	4
Piero d'Inzeo/Easter Light	0 +	4 +	0

Barcelona (4) Italy 4 faults (0 in barrage)

Stefano Angioni/Puckoon	4 +	0 +	0
Stefano Lupis/Drummage	0 +	4 +	4
Graziano Mancinelli/Ambassador	8 +	0 +	0
Piero d'Inzeo/Easter Light	0 +	0 +	0

Lucerne (8) Great Britain 20 faults			
Malcolm Pyrah/Law Court	4	+	4
Rowland Fernyhough/Autumatic	4	+	12¼
Judy Crago/Brevitt Bouncer	12½	+	4
Paddy McMahon/Pennwood Forgemill	4	+	0

Olsztyn (8) Poland 28 faults			
Stefan Migdalski/Balsam	4	+	8
Rudolf Mrugala/Farsa	4	+	12
Henryk Hucz/Bertyn	8	+	0
Jan Kowalczyk/Blekot	8	+	4

Trinwillershagen (4) Poland 20 faults			
Wojciech Dabrewski/Babinicz	8	+	0
Stefan Migdalski/Balsam	4	+	4
Zbigniew Ciesielski/Tenor	4	+	49
Henryk Hucz/Bertyn	0	+	8

La Baule (9) West Germany 12½ faults			
Paul Schockemöhle/Agent	0	+	4
Hans Günter Winkler/Torphy	0	+	4¼
Alwin Schockemöhle/Rex the Robber	4	+	5¾
Hartwig Steenken/Simona	4	+	¼

London (7) Great Britain 0 faults			
Harvey Smith/Salvador	4	+	0
Graham Fletcher/Buttevant Boy	0	+	0
Malcolm Pyrah/Trevarrion	0	+	0
David Broome/Sportsman	0	+	0

Washington (4) U.S.A. 12 faults			
Buddy Brown/Sandsablaze	0	+	4
Thom Hardy/Coming Attraction	0	+	0
Dennis Murphy/Do Right	4	+	8
Rodney Jenkins/Number One Spy	4½	+	4

New York (4) U.S.A. 0 faults			
Buddy Brown/Sandsablaze	0	+	0
Thom Hardy/Coming Attraction	0	+	0
Dennis Murphy/Do Right	0	+	0
Frank Chapot/Mainspring	11¾	+	NS

Toronto (4) France 12 faults (0 in barrage)					
Hubert Parot/Rivage				+	0
Michel Roche/Un Espoir	0	+	0	+	0
Pierre Durand/Varin				+	0
Janou Tissot/Rocket	0	+	0	+	NS

Dublin (4) Great Britain ¾ fault			
Harvey Smith/Salvador	0	+	0
Tony Newbery/Warwick III	½	+	0
David Broome/Sportsman	0	+	4
Peter Robeson/Grebe	12	+	¼

Rotterdam (8) Great Britain 4 faults			
Harvey Smith/Salvador	4	+	0
Derek Ricketts/Beau Supreme	4	+	0
David Broome/Manhattan	0	+	0
Peter Robeson/Grebe	0	+	NS

Ostend (4) France 8¾ faults			
Pierre Durand/Varin	0	+	0
Laurent Pesyn/Boulzicourt	12	+	4
Daniel Constant/Vicomte Aubinier	4½	+	¼
Michel Roche/Un Espoir	0	+	NS

Aachen (6) West Germany 12 faults			
Gerd Wiltfang/Firlefanz	4	+	4
Paul Schockemöhle/Talisman	4	+	0
Hartwig Steenken/Erle	4	+	0
Alwin Schockemöhle/Rex the Robber	0	+	NS

Lisbon (7) France 8 faults			
Hubert Parot/Rivage	0	+	0
Philippe Henry/Bamby	4	+	4
Daniel Constant/Vicomte Aubinier	4	+	0
Pierre Durand/Varin	0	+	NS

Laxenburg (5) West Germany 8 faults			
Gerd Wiltfang/Firlefanz	4	+	0
Fritz Ligges/Thronfolger	0	+	0
Herman Schridde/Kadett	4	+	4
Hans Günter Winkler/Torphy	4	+	0

World Records

Unlike other sports it is impossible to compare say two Grands Prix to establish which was performed in a faster time, due to the fences and distances invariably being different. There are therefore only two records officially recognised by the F.E.I., the High Jump and Long Jump records.

F.E.I. rules require any fresh records to be set in public at a show officially recognised by the Federation of the country in which it is being held. They must be set in the presence of a delegate of the National Federation concerned and if possible a delegate of the F.E.I. It is this latter ruling that causes certain Australian performances not to be recognised.

In order to beat a record a horse and rider must clear the previous height by a minimum of 2 cm, or a spread by 10 cm beyond the earlier record distance.

The record performances in order of their achievement are:

High Jump

1906 Capitaine Crousse (France) on Conspirateur cleared 2.35 m (7 ft 8.8 in) at the Grand Palais in Paris.

1912 August 17. F. de Juge Montespieu (France) on Biskra, and René Ricard (France) on Montjoie III both cleared 2.36 m (7 ft 9.2 in) at Vittel in France.

1933 April 10. Lt. Christian de Castries (France) on Vol-au-Vent cleared 2.38 m (7 ft 10 in) at the Grand Palais in Paris.

1938 October 27. Captain Antonio Gutierrez (Italy) on Osoppo cleared 2.44 m (8 ft 0.4 in) during the Italian National Championship meeting in Rome.

1949 February 5. Captain Alberto Larraguibel Morales (Chile) on Huaso cleared 2.47 m (8 ft 1.6 in) during the C.H.I. at Viña del Mar, near Santiago in Chile. This record still stands.

Long Jump

1912 Monsieur J. Delesalle (France) on Pick Me Up cleared a distance of 7.50 m (24 ft 8.3 in) in Le Touquet.

1935 July 18. Lt. Christian de Castries (France)on Tenace cleared a distance of 7.60 m (25 ft 0.2 in) at the Spa C.H.I.O. in Belgium. At this time he thus held both world records.

1946 December 1. Jorge Fraga Patrao (Argentine) on his own Guarana cleared a distance of 7.7 m (25 ft 4.2 in) during the C.S.I.O. in Buenes Aires.

1948 September 12. Commandant Nogueras Marquez (Spain) on Balcamo, and Captain Maestre Salinas (Spain) on Faun both cleared 7.80 m (25 ft 7 in) during the C.S.I.O. in Bilbao. Commandant Nogueras Marquez and Balcamo went on to clear a distance of 8 metres (26 ft 3.6 in).

1949 August 14. B.van der Voort (Holland) on Coeur Joli cleared a distance of 8.10 m (26 ft 8 in) during the show at La Haye, Holland.

1950 September 2. Lt.-Col. Nogueras Marquez (Spain) regained his record on Balcamo by clearing a distance of 8.20 m (27 ft) during the C.S.I.O. in Bilbao.

1951 Colonel Fernando Lopez del Hierro (Spain) on Amado Mio cleared a distance of 8.30 m (27 ft 3.9 in) at Barcelona. This record still stands.

Further Reading

Historical and biographical

l'Année Hippique (published annually, 1943 to date).
Ansell, Col. Sir Michael. *Riding High.* 1974.
Baranowski, Zdislaw. *International Horseman's Dictionary.* 1959.
Broome, David. *Jump-off.* 1971.
Clayton, Michael, and Tracey, Dick. *Hickstead: the First Twelve Years.* 1972.
Chenevix Trench, Charles. *A History of Horsemanship.* 1970.
ffrench-Blake, Neil. *The World of Show Jumping.* 1967.
Horse and Hound Year Book (published annually).
Horseman's Year, The (published annually, 1946 to date. The first twelve
    volumes edited by W.E. Lyon).
d'Inzeo, Piero. *More Than Victory Alone.* 1970.
Macgregor-Morris, Pamela. *The World's Show Jumpers.* 1955.
Martin, Ann. *The Trainers.* 1972.
Moore, Ann. *Clear to Win.* 1973.
Murphy, Genevieve. *The Show Jumping Book.* 1969.
Nicoll, Jane Vere. *Take Off* (John Kidd's story). 1972.
Sack, Kristine, W. *North American Show Stoppers.* 1973.
Savitt, Sam. *The Equestrian Olympic Sketchbook.* 1969.
Smith, Alan, and Macgregor-Morris, Pamela. *Horse and Rider Year Book.*
    (published annually, 1973 *et seq.*)
Smith, Harvey. *Harvesting Success.* 1968.
    V is for Victory. 1972.
Smyly, P. *The Anatomy of a Show Jumper* (Anneli Drummond-Hay). 1970.
Smythe, Pat. *Jump for Joy.* 1954.
    Show Jumping. 1967.
Spector, David. *Grand Prix Jumping.* 1974.
Stratton, Charles. *Encyclopaedia of Show Jumping and Combined Training.*
    1973.
Webber, Capt. G.H.S. *Show Jumping International.* 1969.
Williams, Dorian. *Show Jumping.* 1968.
    The Great Ones. 1970
    Show Jumping—Great Moments in Sport. 1973.

Technique

Ansell, Col. Sir. Michael. *Show Jumping Obstacles and Courses.* 1951.
Benoist-Gironière, Yves. *The Conquest of the Horse.* 1952.
Chamberlin, Brig. Gen. Harry D. *Training Hunters, Jumpers and Hacks.* 1970.
Froissard, Jean. *Jumping: Learning and Teaching.* 1972.
Froud, Lt. Col. 'Bill'. *Teach Your Horse to Jump.* 1971.
Know the Game: Show Jumping. (B.S.J.A.). 1963.
Jackson, G.N. *Effective Horsemanship.* 1967.
Rodzianko, Paul. *Modern Horsemanship.* 1950.
Smythe, Pat. *Bred to Jump.* 1965.
Steinkraus, William C. *Riding and Jumping.* 1971.
Talbot-Ponsonby, Lt. Col. J. *Harmony in Horsemanship.* 1972.
Toptani, Count. *Modern Show Jumping.* 1972.
Williams, Moyra. *A Breed of Horses.* 1971.

Glossary

Affiliated show A show affiliated to and held under the regulations of the national governing federation.

A.H.S.A. American Horse Shows Association. This was founded in 1917 and became the governing body of American show jumping and the national federation in 1937.

Bank A form of permanent obstacle.

Bareme (Fr.) The Table of rules governing the judging of a competition under international rules. Under Bareme (Table) A, to jumping penalties are added penalties for exceeding the time allowed. Under Bareme B 10 seconds are added to the time taken for each obstacle knocked down. B may only be used when the course is more than 700 m long. Under Bareme C the number of seconds added, for each obstacle knocked down, to the time taken is determined according to the length of the course.

B.S.J.A. British Show Jumping Association. The Association was formed in 1925 and is concerned only with show jumping.

Cavalletti A small wooden jump used in schooling.

Cavesson A kind of nose-band used to curb a horse and render him manageable.

Collecting ring A ring next to the main jumping ring from which the competitors make their entrance. It may contain practice jumps.

Combination A series of jumps placed at related distances apart, and thus requiring the horse to take a certain number of strides between each one.

Conformation The anatomical characteristics of a horse.

C.S.I. Concours Saute International. A competition open to riders from abroad, who must be invited by the host nation and authorised by their own federation to compete. Organisation of a C.S.I. requires the permission of both the F.E.I. and the appropriate national federation.

C.S.I.O. Concours Saute International Officiel. An official international horse show at which a Nations' Cup competition is held. Every country is restricted to holding one C.S.I.O. per year except for the U.S.A., which is allowed to hold two because of its size.

Dressage Training of a horse in obedience and deportment.

Fault Penalty point.

F.E.I. Federation Equestre Internationale. The international governing body of equestrian sport, founded in 1921. The equestrian competitions in the Olympic Games are conducted under F.E.I. rules, as are all international competitions run by national federations affiliated to the F.E.I. The headquarters is at Avenue Hamoir 38, Brussels 18, Belgium.

Frog The elastic, horny substance in the middle of the sole of a horse's foot.

Grand Prix The major individual class at an international show, normally carrying the greatest amount of prize money and prestige. It is usually the last class of a show.

High jump A competition held over one single fence increasing in height.

Impulsion The controlled power of a horse when coming into a jump.

Jumping Derby A show jumping competition over a long course involving natural obstacles.

Jump-off. Also known sometimes as a 'barrage', a jump-off is a round held to decide a competition in which competitors have tied for first place.

Lane A series of fences with a rail down each side, which allows a horse to be jumped loose without being able to escape.

Nations' Cup An international team competition held at every official show (C.S.I.O.) where there are three or more teams participating. Normally four riders from each country take part, but a country represented by just three riders must still form a team.

Neck strap A strap put round the horse's neck to allow the rider to stay in position without having to hang onto the reins.

Overface To ask a horse to do more than it is capable of achieving.

Oxer An oxer was originally constructed of parallel poles with a hedge in between; it was so called because poles were sometimes used in English country districts to protect natural hedges from oxen. The terms 'oxer' and 'parallel' are now often used more or less interchangeably.

Parallel A spread jump consisting of two parallel obstacles.

Permanent fence A permanent fixture in a show jumping course, such as a water-jump, ditch, or bank. These were originally more common in continental Europe than in Britain or America, but are now commonly found also in those countries.

Placing pole A pole placed on the ground in front of a fence to ensure that the horse meets the fence on the correct stride.

Puissance A competition in which the emphasis is on the height of a decreasing number of obstacles. It is also sometimes known as the 'test'.

Rapping A method of trying to make a horse jump more cleanly. As the horse jumps a pole is raised to rap his legs.

Rustic poles Poles used in the construction of jumps which are unpainted and in their natural colour.

Six Bar competition A test of power and skill involving six obstacles in a straight line, all of the same construction, of the same or progressive heights, with about two strides between them.

Snaffle The simplest form of bit.

Spread A jump consisting of more than one element—e.g. an oxer or a staircase.

Staircase See triple bar.

Test See puissance.

Thoroughbred A horse of pure breeding.

Three-day event A combined training competition consisting of three parts: dressage; speed, endurance and cross-country; and show jumping.

Touch class A class in which faults are given for touching an obstacle as well as for knocking it down.

Triple bar A jump consisting of three poles set one after the other in ascending order of height, to form a spread obstacle.

Upright A jump consisting of a single vertical obstacle (as opposed to an oxer or a triple bar, for example).

Vertical See upright.

U.S.E.T. United States Equestrian Team.

Water jump One of the most common permanent obstacles.

Contributors

Michael Clayton (Editor)

Michael Clayton became Editor of *Horse and Hound,* the world's most authoritative weekly equestrian publication, in 1973. Before that he was a news journalist, having worked in London's Fleet Street as a reporter and news executive, and then for the B.B.C. as a staff television and radio correspondent, specialising in trouble-spot reporting in different parts of the world. Vietnam, the Middle East and Northern Ireland were frequent assignments. Clayton is a lifelong horseman, most of his active riding being in the hunting field. He has hunted extensively in Britain and in the Irish Republic, visiting as many as thirty hunting countries in one season—and riding strange horses in each—in writing *Horse and Hound's* weekly hunting diary, by 'Foxford'. In addition he keeps his own hunters in Dorset.

Keenly concerned with all equestrian sports, Clayton has had ten books published in the field, including the only full-length history of the All England Show Jumping Course at Hickstead, and four wide-ranging show-jumping books published in partnership with former Ladies' World Champion Marion Mould. Clayton broadcasts frequently, and has joined the B.B.C. Television commentating teams at Hickstead, and at the famous Badminton Three Day Event. He is married to Fleet Street writer Mary Watson; they have two children, and live in the English county of Buckinghamshire.

William C. Steinkraus (Associate Editor in America)

Bill Steinkraus was the captain and senior member of the United States Equestrian Team for many triumphant years; he was the first, and at the time of writing the only, American rider to win an Olympic gold medal for show jumping. He has been a member of six Olympic teams, the last occasion being 1972.

He started riding when he was ten, and was a successful show jumping rider even before World War II. He served in the war, and afterwards graduated from Yale University, first joining the U.S.E.T. in 1951. A New Englander from Connecticut, he worked for some years on Wall Street, but has spent the past ten years in the publishing business. Two of his other favourite activities are book-collecting and music. He is a keen amateur violinist.

He is married with three young sons; although he has retired from international sport to spend more time with his wife and family, he still rides daily.

Dorian Williams (Show Jumping in Europe)

Dorian Williams, who was educated at Harrow School, is married with two children. In 1951 he became equestrian commentator for the B.B.C., and that was also the year in which he first became a Master of Hounds. Since 1954 he has been Master of the Whaddon Chase. In 1964 he was awarded the British Horse Society Medal of Honour, and three years later he became Honorary Director of the British Horse Society (of which he is now Chairman) and the National Equestrian Centre at Stoneleigh.

His interests are not only equestrian—in 1945 he founded Pendley Manor, Tring, his family home, as a Centre of Adult Education; and over 100 courses, half of which are connected with industry, are held annually for 4,000 people. In 1949 the Pendley Open Air Shakespeare Festival was founded, and is directed by Dorian Williams every year.

He is the author of over twenty-five books.

Ann Martin (Show Jumping in North America)

Ann Martin has broadcast on equestrian events for fifteen years and written regularly for *Horse and Hound, The Field,* and the *Birmingham Post.* She has been Public Relations Officer for the British Horse Society at the National Equestrian Centre.

In 1972 and 1973, her first two books were published—on the world's leading equestrian trainers and the Olympic silver-medal-winning show jumper Ann Moore. She lives in the English county of Warwickshire on the side of Edgehill where she has established a small hunter stud. In her spare time she has had many successes in the show ring.

Judy Crago (Selection, Training and Care)

Judy Crago's first big win in the show jumping world came in 1960 when, as Judy Shepherd, she won Britain's National Ladies' Championship on Thou Swell. In the spring of that year she bought a young mare which she called Spring Fever, and on which she was to gain most of her successes in the 1960s. These included the coveted Queen Elizabeth II Cup in 1962. In 1961 Judy married Brian Crago, a member of the Australian Olympic three-day event team which won the gold medal in Rome the previous year.

For the next six years Judy and her two horses were regular members of the British team, with husband Brian travelling with her as 'trainer'.

Following the retirement of Spring Fever and Thou Swell, and the birth of her two children, Judy was restricted to small local shows with novice horses. However she and Brian acquired a very promising youngster which, in the name of Brevitt Bouncer, was to bring Judy back to the international scene. In 1974, his first international year, Brevitt Bouncer was in the British team at Lucerne, La Baule and Ostend C.S.I.O.s, jumping in the Nations' Cup teams at all three shows, and contributing to Great Britain's winning the President's Cup for the third year running.

Raymond Brooks-Ward (Show Organisation)

Raymond Brooks-Ward is one of the best known radio and television commentators on show jumping. He started commentating professionally in 1954, and from 1955 to 1960 worked occasionally for the B.B.C. He then spent a period with the rival Independent Television network from 1960 to 1971, returning to the B.B.C. in that year. His work has involved him in a good deal of travelling—he has covered the last three Olympic Games for radio, and has acted as a guest commentator in places as diverse as Johannesburg, New York and Washington. From 1955 to 1967 Brooks-Ward was engaged in farming; at the present time he is managing director of an equestrian public relations organisation, which acts for the British Field Sports Society, the British Show Jumping Association, and the British Horse Society.

His interests include hunting—he was Master of the West Lodge from 1958 to 1971, and is at the time of writing the Joint Master of the Enfield Chase. He is married, and has three sons.

Pamela Carruthers (Course Building)

Pamela Carruthers has always been interested in horses—in fact at the age of fifteen she was sent away to Paris to forget about them! But while she was there, she managed to take part in some ladies' show jumping competitions, riding the horses of many top French riders. Thence sprang her interest in course designing—the courses on the Continent at that time were much more interesting to ride than those then common in Britain. After World War II, she jumped with the British team on a horse called Galway Bay, whom she sold in due course, whereupon she herself started designing courses at small shows, progressing in due course to top events. Since she first went to the U.S. to design courses at the International Show at Washington D.C. in the mid-1960s, she has worked at many top American shows, including the National at Madison Square Garden; she has worked all over the U.S.A., Canada, Mexico, France, Holland, and South Africa. She has designed the courses for one Men's and one Ladies' World Championship, two Men's European, one Ladies' European, and two Junior European Championships. She won the major course designer's award in the U.S.A. in 1971, and in Britain in 1974. She has also recently been awarded the President of the United States and People to People Committee's award as Sports Ambassador of the U.S.A.

Pamela Macgregor-Morris (Famous Riders and Horses)

Besides being an equestrian journalist, Pamela Macgregor-Morris owns, rides and breeds horses. She has been a regular contributor to *Horse and Hound* for over thirty years; she has written for *The Times* of London for over twenty years, and as that newspaper's equestrian correspondent has covered all the major international events in Europe. With her husband Rudolf Jurkschat, and their three small children, she lives on the edge of Dartmoor in the south-west of England, where she runs a small stud and breeds Irish wolfhounds. She is the author of twenty-three books, and a contributor to numerous publications on both sides of the Atlantic, including *Riding, Light Horse, Irish Horseman*, and *The Chronicle of the Horse*.

Picture Acknowledgements

The page numbers of the colour photographs are printed in italics.

F. Bescoby, Bespix, 119. J. Bridel, 222 (bottom). Budd Studio, New York, 32-33, *36* (both), 38, 39 (bottom), 105, 137, *179*, 226. Rex Coleman, 6, 27, *35*, *53* (both), *54*, 81, 84, 88, *108*, 130, 152 (bottom), 157, 160, *161*, *162* (top), 175 (both), 182, 190, 193 (centre), 195 (top), 205 (bottom), 208, 218 (both), 227 (bottom). Findlay Davidson, *17*, *18*, 39 (top), 46 (top), *72* (both), 86, *89*, *90*, 98, 102, *107*, 121, *126* (bottom), *143*, *144*, 146, 147, 148 (top), 149 (both), 152 (top), 154 (bottom), 158, *162* (bottom), 164, 165 (both), 166, 167, 171, 172 (both), *180*, 181 (both), 183 (both), 185 (bottom), 186, 187 (both), 188, 189 (bottom), 191, 192 (both), 196, *197*, *198*, 201 (both), 210 (top), 213 (bottom), 214 (bottom), *215*, *216*, 222 (top), 225, 229 (top). Werner Ernst, 133, 202, 213 (top). Leigh Francis, 44, 79 (bottom), 93. Charles C. Fennell, 210 (bottom). David A. Guiver, 184, 188 (bottom). C. Hiles, 76, 82. Tim Hinder, 73, 79 (top), 91, 97. *Irish Times*, 87. Theodor Janssen, 221. Keystone Press Agency, London, 178. E.D. Lacey, 80, 150, 151, 154 (top), 155, 156, 159 (both), 168, 170, 185 (top), 193 (bottom), 194, 206, 207, 209, 214 (top), 220 (bottom), 223 (top), 229 (bottom). Leslie Lane, 141, 203 (top), 224, 227, 258. F. Meads, 24 (bottom), 193 (top). Monty, 75 (bottom), 83 (bottom), 148 (bottom). Pressebild Guido, Essen, 223 (bottom). Radio Times Hulton Picture Library, London, 14, 19, 23, 24 (top), 37, 101, 205 (top). Royal Dublin Society, 140, 169 (bottom), 212, 230. Sport and General Press Agency, London, 8, 163, 169 (top), 173, 174, 177, 189 (top), 195 (bottom), 203 (bottom), 204, 210 (bottom), 211, 217, 228, 256. Foto Tiedemann, Hanover, 220 (top). H-H Voigtländer, 117 (bottom), *125* (both), 126 (top). W.D. & H.O. Wills, photograph by R.M. Knutsen, 76 (bottom).

The following photographs were specially taken for this book by Rex Coleman: 45, 49, 51, 52, 55 (both), 56 (both), 57 (both), 58, 59, 60 (both), 61, 62 (both), 64 (both), 65, 66, 67 (both), 68 (both), 71, 83, 91 (top), 94, 95, 96 (both), 110, 112 (both), 113 (both), 115 (all), 116 (all), 117 (top and centre). The Editors would like to thank Stephen Dee, Hugh Thomas and Brian Crago, who appear in many of the special photographs, for their collaboration.

Jacket photographs by Findlay Davidson.

Endpapers drawn by Stephen Chapman L.S.I.A. from a photograph by Findlay Davidson.

Title page illustration from a photograph by E.D. Lacey.
Line drawings by Amaryllis May.

opposite: Hartwig Steenken, riding Fairness.

Index

Page numbers which appear in *italics* indicate either a whole entry in Great Riders and Horses, or a reference in the caption to a colour illustration. The index does not include individual references in Competition Results, or, with a few exceptions, the names of individual shows, which occur throughout the book.